★

STRANGE
BEDFELLOWS

★

STRANGE
BEDFELLOWS

How Television

and the Presidential Candidates

Changed American Politics,

1992

By

Tom Rosenstiel

HYPERION

Library of Congress Cataloging-in-Publication Data

Rosenstiel, Tom.
Strange bedfellows : how television and the presidential candidates changed American politics, 1992 / by Tom Rosenstiel. — 1st ed.
p. cm.
Includes index.
ISBN 1-56282-859-2
1. Television in politics—United States. 2. Presidents—United States—Election—1992. 3. Mass media—Political aspects.
I. Title.
HE800.76.U6R67 1993
324.7′3′097309049—dc20   93-18786
                                                      CIP

Design by ROBERT BULL DESIGN

First Edition

10 9 8 7 6 5 4 3 2 1

For my parents and Rima

★

ACKNOWLEDGMENTS

MANY PEOPLE MADE this book possible. Count-
less thanks go to Judith Riven, my editor at Hyperion, who devoted more time to this project than I could have reasonably
expected, and whose counsel and care made the book immeasurably better. Dominick Abel, my wise agent, was always right and
always right there when I needed him. Bob Miller earned my
gratitude for his support, as did others at Hyperion. Ken Davidoff
did research all summer long, painstakingly reading the *New York
Times* and Washington *Post* and cataloguing every political story.
At the Los Angeles *Times*, three friends and readers offered more
help than they realize: John Balzar for teaching me about politics
and encouraging my work even when it was bad; Roger Smith and
Don Frederick, for words that helped get me on the right track at
a key time. Thanks to my friends John Gomperts and Katherine
Klein, who helped me by reading the beginning at the end and who
suffered me through the year. My thanks, too, to Mike Miller and
Shelby Coffey of the Los Angeles *Times* for granting me the time
to finish the book. And thank you to my wife, Rima Sirota, who
suffered my absences during her pregnancy and the first seven
months of our daughter, Leah's, life. I am grateful to many colleagues in the press, at the Los Angeles *Times* and elsewhere, for
their help, wisdom, and advice. Finally, I am indebted to the staff

of ABC News, NBC News, and CBS News who made this book possible, including Peter Jennings, Arnot Walker, Paul Friedman, Bill Wheatley, and many others, perhaps most of whom would prefer not to be named. I wonder whether my brethren in the print press would ever invite such scrutiny.

★

CONTENTS

★

INTRODUCTION

ONE DRIZZLING DAY in the autum of 1988, I decided to take a break from watching George Bush's campaign machine cut another tightly organized swath across the Ohio countryside. I spent the day instead trailing after CBS television correspondent Bob Schieffer and his producer Janet Leissner. The world I saw changed my view of politics and journalism. Suddenly there were reasons for many of the mysterious details of the campaign I was covering. I could see why candidates' schedules were arranged as they were, why politicians seemed transfixed by violent and malicious language, why campaigns seemed to tend toward certain issues and not others, why politicians had so much control over the media—even as the public decried the power of the press. I saw, in short, that no one could understand American politics without understanding American television first. I also knew that for all their skill and knowledge, most political writers did not know the medium and too many continued to dismiss it as not worthy of their concern.

By 1991, these thoughts evolved into an idea for a book: to follow a network not for a day but an entire campaign. I hoped, in doing so, to see how the media shaped the race from start to finish. By then, the idea had become prevalent that something was wrong with American politics. A few writers had begun calling on the press to act as an agent of reform. I hoped, in the end, to see how politics might actually change if journalism changed. And in the current state of journalism, was change possible? Although more than one network offered the unusual access required, I chose to concentrate on ABC. At the time, it had the strongest combination of resources and commitment to serious coverage. I hoped to see the best of network television.

For twelve months, I had access to the editing bays, the assignment editors, the story meetings, and the thoughts of the principal people deciding how the network would cover the campaign. I traveled with ABC's correspondents and producers as they followed the candidates. I watched how ABC's nightly newscast was assembled by the senior producers and editors and then as it was broadcast on the air. I had access to budget meetings and internal memos. I saw the struggles over personnel and money. I did not see everything, of course, yet, taken together, I was granted the opportunity to watch what most can only speculate about, the process by which the press makes its decisions.

A few people in particular shared their feelings and thoughts with me at each important step along the way. Among them are Peter Jennings, the anchorman; Paul Friedman, the executive producer of ABC's nightly newscast; ABC's principal political correspondents, Jim Wooten, Brit Hume, Jeff Greenfield, and Chris Bury.

What I saw, from the other side of the camera lens, suggests the press has less power to reform politics than many imagine. Yet the press's cynicism has already done great harm. There is reason for leavened optimism. Technology is democratizing the American political landscape. But it is also lowering the standards of American journalism. There is another reason for worry, too. Journalists like to imagine the press to be a great mirror, reflecting the images it sees but not creating them. The metaphor is convenient but wrong. The images in the mirror are magnified and the reflection distorted. The people pictured in the glass now spend too much of their time changing themselves to adapt to the mirror's flaws.

Unlike the fashionable idea of the day, the traditional press are not becoming irrelevant, but their sins are also greater than they recognize and in many ways getting worse.

Most of the conversations quoted here were heard firsthand, but not all. Those that were reconstructed were done so by interviewing the principals directly. Nothing is secondhand. Journalists have a habit of taking notes of almost everything they do on the job, which makes their task of recollection easier. Some conversations are paraphrased to capture their flavor and maintain the pace of the narrative. For critics who deplore the techniques of new journalism, I judged that in this case their benefits in telling the story fully outweighed whatever disadvantages these methods posed to those who might be interested in turning to this book for future studies.

One cannot write about the conduct of fellow journalists without inviting special scrutiny. This is not the work of an historian or an academic, however, but an attempt to capture a moment in time, through the eyes of one reporter. Many things, accordingly, were learned on the basis that their source would remain in confidence. The interpretation of events and their meaning is my own. If readers believe I am too easy on some aspects or too hard on others, it is because I see them that way. In the current climate of the press, praise is often more difficult to bestow than criticism.

★

Roone Arledge
President

Richard Wald
Senior Vice President

Joanna Bistany
Vice President
and
Assistant to the President

Walter Porges
Vice President
News Practices

Robert Murphy
Vice President
News Coverage

Bill Temple
Senior Vice President Finance

Steve Sadicario
Vice President Business Affairs

Jeff Gralnick
Vice President
and
Executive Producer
Special Broadcasts

Stephen Weiswasser
Executive Vice President

WORLD NEWS TONIGHT

Paul Friedman
Executive Producer

Bob Roy
Senior Broadcast Producer

Dennis Dunlavey
Senior Producer

Linda Mathews
Foreign Editor

Jack White
National Editor

Mike Stein
Senior Writer

Carolyn Smith
Director of Political Operations

Jeff Alderman
Director of Polling

Hal Bruno
Director of Political Unit

WORLD NEWS NOW
(overnight news)

David Bohr	Aaron Brown
Executive	*and* Lisa McKee
Producer	*Anchors*

★

ABC NEWS 1992

NIGHTLINE

Tom Bettag
*Executive
Producer*

Ted Koppel
Anchor

20-20

Victor Neufeld
*Executive
Producer*

Barbara Walters
and Hugh Downs
Anchors

Lynn Sherr
John Stossel

Bob Brown
Tom Jarriel

Correspondents

Peter Jennings
Anchor

Brit Hume
White House Correspondent

Jim Wooten
Senior Political Correspondent

Cokie Roberts
Special Correspondent

Jack McWethy
National Security Correspondent

Chris Bury
Clinton Correspondent

Jeff Greenfield
Political Analyst

PRIMETIME LIVE

Richard Kaplan
*Executive
Producer*

Diane Sawyer
and Sam Donaldson
Anchors

Chris Wallace
John Quinones

Sylvia Chase
Jay Schadler

Correspondents

WORLD NEWS
SATURDAY / SUNDAY

David Glodt
Executive Producer

Carole Simpson
Anchor/Saturday

Forrest Sawyer
Anchor/Sunday

THIS WEEK with David Brinkley

David Glodt
*Executive
Producer*

David Brinkley
Host

Sam Donaldson
George Will
Panelists

Cokie Roberts
Guest Panelist

WORLD NEWS THIS MORNING
(and news inserts Good Morning America)

Pat Roddy
*Executive
Producer*

Mike Schneider
Anchor

★

CHAPTER

1

WAITING

★

In the end, they had nothing to do but watch.

The exit surveys began trickling into the computers in the big open room they called the Rim around 1:30 that afternoon. People would still be voting across most of the East Coast for another five hours, in California for another nine. "It's over," said Jeff Gralnick, who would produce ABC's election special that night, wandering into the room, where they produced *World News Tonight with Peter Jennings*. Even with only a fraction of data, the exit survey's computer model projected Bill Clinton's leads in Georgia and New Jersey would be enormous. "It will be an early night." As it turned out, he was wrong.

Around the long formica table in the center of the Rim, the producers and writers of the most popular evening news program in the country turned to their computers to see. Phones rang, desk assistants swarmed with wire service copy and scripts. The tall, slender, bookish man at the head of the long table swiveled around to the computer behind his desk and glanced at the numbers, too, but he said nothing. Paul Friedman had run *World News Tonight* for five years, and he, more than anyone else, had decided how the network had covered this campaign, from the mistakes and hysteria of New Hampshire until today. But, like most in the press, after all that had happened this year he had now little to do but wait.

As the numbers continued dribbling in from ABC's computers over the next two hours, the night seemed to shorten. At 4 P.M., when the news division's senior management gathered around the burled redwood table on the executive level fifth floor, Carolyn Smith, the vice president for polling, said the second wave of polls was even stronger for Clinton. They would probably be calling the election at 9 P.M. eastern standard time. That was when polls closed in Wyoming, Colorado, Minnesota, New Mexico, and New York, and they could declare those states for Clinton, still two hours before the West Coast closed. By this count, Bush would do worse than any incumbent president since William Howard Taft in 1912, said Jeff Greenfield, the bespectacled ABC correspondent, author and columnist, who had sat himself down next to Roone Arledge, the ABC News president.

"How do you know these things, Jeff?" Arledge marveled. "Who needs computers with Greenfield here."

Then Carolyn Smith brought up what everyone around the room knew would come. Since the race was lopsided, she said, what if another network decides to cheat and declare Clinton the winner in a state before voting there had stopped. The networks had pledged in writing to Congress they would never call a state before its polling places had closed. "Gartner is perfectly capable of doing it," she said. NBC News president Michael Gartner was an absolutist about the press revealing what it knew.

No one spoke. Were they willing to allow another network to scoop them? For thirty years, the race to call the election first had driven the networks like a drug addiction. Whose polling unit was quickest? The networks had spent millions to answer that question, both as a matter of pride and a way to lure ratings and charge higher ad rates. But this year, like so much else in television news, the great race had ceased. The networks had joined in one common exit poll to save money. The only way left to compete was to break the rules.

Peter Jennings, the anchorman, finally ended the silence. "Didn't we promise we wouldn't do that?" he said simply.

Were they not gentlemen of their word, Jennings was demanding without sounding demanding. Whatever else one could say about him, Jennings, the Canadian aristocrat, the emotional and endlessly driven star, the voracious but disorganized intellect, was nothing if not a gentleman. He was also the anchor. It was his face up there on the video. His ass on the line. His credibility. Not these people who sat off camera. Did anyone want to overrule him now and argue for doing the sleazy thing?

"I'd rather be on the side of the angels," said Walter Porges, the vice president of standards, who spoke next. "Let them be the creeps."

"If other people are willing to repudiate their promises to the Congress of the United States, let them," declared Stephen Weiswasser, the lawyer whom Capital Cities had installed to look over the shoulder of ABC News's legendary but now embattled president, Roone Arledge. Of course once someone else had broken their word, neither was ABC bound by the terms with Congress, he said.

Arledge, their mercurial leader, sitting in the center seat, just listened. He would overrule if he wanted. He did not. That settled it.

C-Span was already leaking exit poll data, Porges said. It was airing the Jerry Williams talk radio show out of Boston and a guy from the Boston *Herald* was doling out the numbers live.

"There goes C-Span's virginity," Jennings said.

Arledge smiled a little ruefully. "It's about time."

Behind his metal-framed half-glasses and his thin moustache, Friedman was also silent. He looked older than forty-seven and, with his sweater vests and baroque way of phrasing things, he resembled a college professor more than a TV executive. But he was a calculating office politician who talked in meetings only when necessary, and it was not necessary here.

* *

Campaigns seem so public, so much the province of the press and the politicians. Then on election day the press has nothing to do. The awesome exercise does not really belong to them after all. The candidates hide. Reporters sit around and wait. The pictures that come in are the most banal possible. People are voting, just the way they are supposed to.

In many ways for the press, election day in America had become a surreal exercise. Reporters and pollsters and producers and editors had measured and remeasured this election so often from so many angles that the event itself, the act of one hundred million Americans wandering into school buildings and post offices and church basements and casting a ballot and electing a new leader, seemed anticlimactic. And if all the stories and surveys and barroom prognostications during the course of the year weren't enough, there were the exit surveys that began streaming into their computers within hours of the polls opening. It all created the illusion that the wise and waggish members of the press, the pontification class, had this thing wired. Election day felt like a football game you watched on tape knowing who had won.

The sensation was false. The press always knew less than it thought. The assurance with which it had approached the last twelve months was so often faulty. The lessons drawn from the outcome that so many would write the next day were, as usual, overstated. The analysis of the victory was quickly shrouded in myth. For all of the words written and all the tape shot, too much was known, too little understood. And tonight, were the once mighty national media narrating their own decline? Even many ABC stations would preempt them with local election-night shows.

The day had begun, as it always did, at the 10 A.M. meeting held in the little conference room whose glass wall forms the backdrop thirteen million viewers see each night watching *World News*.

Thirty people gathered around the long table. A small gray speaker phone sat in the middle hooked up to the bureaus in England, Los Angeles, Washington, Chicago, and Atlanta—the shrunken universe of the most powerful network television news organization in the country.

Friedman asked the domestic bureaus for clues about voter turnout that he could use on *World News*. His voice was quiet and self-confident. The weather was bad in the upper plains states, the Chicago bureau reported, but the expected turnout in Chicago was "a whopping 79 percent." Atlanta said turnout was heavy. At Harry's Bar in Paris, the London bureau reported, Clinton won the straw poll with 389 votes, versus 341 for Bush and 88 for Perot.

Gralnick, the executive producer of the live election program, had come to the meeting to outline the evening's plans. After Jennings's newscast, he said, the election night program would begin at 7 P.M. and go on until 1 A.M. or later if no winner had been declared. At 1 A.M., the overnight news would take over and be on straight through until *Good Morning America* at 7 A.M. *GMA* went to 9 A.M. All told, ABC News would be on live for 14½ hours.

When the meeting was over, Friedman wandered down one floor to the *World News* offices. His two deputies, his head writer and his foreign and national editor, followed him. They held another short meeting, joined by Peter Jennings, to discuss tonight's show. Then they went out to the long desk in the middle of the Rim and waited. Jennings sat to Friedman's left. Friedman's two deputy producers sat to his right, the foreign and national editors and two writers across the way. Six televisions hung from the ceilings on either side with the sound turned off—ABC, the New York stations, and CNN, a silent parade of video images more similar than different, television's version of peripheral vision.

When White House correspondent Brit Hume called into the Rim at midday from Houston, where Bush was waiting it out, he seemed exhausted and moody. Everyone on the Rim listened in on these calls, ABC's editorial party line. The writers and producers around the Rim had been laughing about Bush going shopping that morning and buying a quail-hunting license. Hume didn't think it was funny. Hume was a vocal conservative, and while his superiors at ABC thought he had been fair in the election, he seemed to be irritable the last few days.

"Bush is really the better story today," Friedman told his correspondent. That's what this election was about, he meant. George Bush's failings more than Bill Clinton's virtues. He was trying to get Hume thinking about the story, to summon another day of energy.

"I don't care anymore," Hume said. "However it comes out is fine with me.

When Mort Dean, the Perot correspondent, called from Dallas he seemed annoyed. Ross Perot had told everyone he had voted absentee, but then went out and voted on election day after all. "He even lied to us about this," Dean said incredulously. Then Perot became enraged at the press for taking the traditional pictures of him doing it. "He's just being a jerk to the end," Dean said.

"Unless you'll give me 'asshole to the end,' " Dean said with unusual meanness. Dean's story that night would be benign. But the antipathy Perot felt toward the press had worn on him.

Nelson Rockefeller had once told Dean that "20 percent of the population will vote for almost anybody."

"Sixteen percent of the population in this country believe in witches," Friedman said. "I hope that's what Perot gets. Sixteen percent."

Ross Perot could have been elected president in 1992, Dean would muse later. "He had something. He still has something." Perot was the man people wanted to talk about. Perot was the one people would have liked to have been able to vote for. Someone who would rescue them. Someone who would fix what was broken. When they couldn't bring themselves to vote for Ross Perot, they settled for Bill Clinton.

Jeff Greenfield felt that way, too. "He could have been Spencer Tracy in *State of the Union*," Greenfield said wandering around the Rim election day. *State of the Union*, a movie about a virtuous businessman who rejects the influence of corrupt political bosses and wins the hearts of the people, had reflected the same image Perot's supporters had dreamed about. But Perot instead turned out to be Humphrey Bogart in *The Caine Mutiny*, the tragic paranoid whose men turn on him.

Perot's candidacy had left Dean with one other thought about campaigns. "I used to think they should be much shorter," Dean would say after it was over. "I am not sure of that anymore. After seeing Perot, I think there's a risk that someone could sneak by using television if we had short campaigns."

Clinton was sleeping, correspondent Chris Bury said when he called in. The likely next president of the United States had come in from a 4,000-mile tour of nine states in the last thirty hours, voted, and took a nap. How long did he sleep, asked Jack White, the producer for national news. "Hillary doesn't tell me when he wakes up," Bury snapped. Desk jockeys are always asking about such foolishness.

"Any nuggets I can use late night?" Jennings asked Bury on a call later in the afternoon. "He was really emotional," Bury said. "He started tearing up. He was overcome by it all."

The Democrats had been so adept in this campaign, Friedman thought. But did it mean Bill Clinton would be a good president? Campaigns are more simple than presidencies. They have one objective, to beat the opponent, day by day, story by story, and finally vote by vote. Governing was harder. For all they had done this year, it was still difficult to know what kind of president Clinton would be. "To understand this presidency, you have to understand our campaign," George Stephanopoulos, Clinton's young communications director would say later. The techniques, the relationship to the press, the change in culture, it was all there, he meant.

When correspondent Cokie Roberts called in from Washington, she said the exit polls now looked so good for Democrats they expected to gain seats in the House, the reverse of what was expected when the day began. As it turned out she would be wrong.

Correspondent Lynn Sherr came down from her office to the Rim to tell Friedman what she would use from the exit polls on World News. People didn't think character was an overriding issue, Sherr said. The economy was. More than 80 percent of voters thought it was in lousy shape. And they blamed Bush.

"If they can't figure out from that who is winning, they're really stupid," Sherr said.

Around 5 P.M., correspondent Sheila Kast called in from Vice President Dan Quayle's headquarters on the 320 line, an open phone line broadcast to everyone at ABC News. The vice president's chief of staff William Kristol had just briefed reporters and conceded the election, she said. "Kristol used the phrase 'failure of governing,' " Kast said. "He said the president had never convinced people he had an agenda for change and he said they had failed to use their power after the Gulf War."

All this was "embargoed" from use until after the President had spoken—probably many hours from now, Kast said. Those were the ground rules of the briefing. Friedman and Jennings recognized they were being used. By holding this briefing so early, the vice president's staff knew their version of events would dominate how the reporters wrote their early analysis tonight of the election. The view of the President and his aides that came later would be inserted into newspaper stories at the last minute. The Vice President was trying to ensure that the press blamed the President for this loss, not him.

The scripts were done early this night, by 5 P.M. Friedman and his team went over every word, a daily afternoon surgery for which Friedman was famous. This was the great irony of how television was put together. The words were pored over, at least at ABC. So were the soundbites, the snippets of the candidates speaking. But the pictures that were so powerful were seen ahead of time only by a few people in the field, an editor, and perhaps the correspondent. In the age of videotape, the people who actually ran the nightly news rarely saw their stories before they went live on the air. This was one of the facts that gave those who wanted to manipulate the press so much power.

When the exit poll data had started coming in, Mike Stein, the head writer for *World News*, drafted an opening Jennings wished he could have used: "Good evening. We know who's going to win the election. But we won't tell you. We do, however, have some neat pictures of people voting."

The only real news would come on Gralnick's election night show to follow. "Our program tonight," Friedman said of *World News*, "is essentially a promo."

Since Gralnick was using the more modern TV Three for his election night show, they ran *World News Tonight* that evening out of the old control room, TV One. As Friedman watched Jennings move through the opening, he looked up at the monitor showing Tom Brokaw broadcasting from NBC's election night set at the Ed Sullivan Theatre. The competitive instincts in television are an unholy passion. One network flourishes by cannibalizing the audiences of the others. Even friends are gut rivals bound by survival to the other's destruction. It was no different with Friedman and Brokaw, who were old friends. "That sets looks cheaper than most local news setups," Friedman said of his former network. The word was that NBC had moved to the Ed Sullivan to save money. "Dumb," Friedman muttered. "Dumb."

Up on the center monitor, Jennings seemed subdued. The anchorman. Certainly the might of being an anchor had waned. Once the central protagonist of the video age, the anchor was now more the narrator to a fragmenting society, his voice one of several, the pictures he described in wide supply, his influence rising and falling depending on events. Yet still no one could match him in audience. He had been a little nervous all day. He would be on camera for six hours straight tonight. Live. No teleprompter. No script. No second chances. Just a few notecards about various states and some key Senate and House races, plus whatever he had written down in his notebook over the last week and what he had absorbed from the election night briefing book Nancy Gabriner had written for him.

Jennings seemed to be thinking about it as he did *World News*.

"Why is Peter talking so slowly today?" Friedman said.

At one point Jennings pronounced the city Sarajevo so deliberately it sounded as if he were talking about a person. "Ah, yes, Sarah. Sarah Yevo," someone said in the control room. "Her middle name is Charlemagne," Friedman said.

"Maybe it is Brinkley. He slows down Peter's speech," foreign editor Linda Mathews suggested.

"He's just getting it out of his system on our time," Friedman assured them.

"Paul?" Jennings asked during the commercial break. Jennings only heard Friedman when the executive producer pushed a button and opened Jennings's earpiece.

"Yes, Peter."

"How we doing?"

"Fine," Friedman said. He saw no point in saying anything about Jennings's delivery. The anchor would just fret about it, and he had a long night ahead. Also, if there was anything Peter Jennings didn't need advice about, it was how to speak on television.

Jennings was supposed to talk to all of his political correspondents on *World News* so that viewers would see them and stay tuned to watch for them on the election night show.

Jim Wooten was in the Capitol rotunda in Washington where he would talk about Senate races. Cokie Roberts was in a Washington studio made with the aid of computer graphics to look like the House of Representatives. Jeff Greenfield was on the set in New York with Jennings working the telephones. Lynn Sherr was on the set to talk about the exit poll.

Jennings started with Wooten, and the correspondent was taking too much time. After a minute he was just wrapping up Pennsylvania and New York.

"Jim Wooten," Friedman said from the TV One control room, trying to cut him short.

"A little further west," Wooten was saying. He was about to start in about a whole new set of races.

"Ahhh," Friedman said, slamming his fist on the desk.

"Thirty seconds," director Charlie Heinz said.

"Wrap it, darn it," Friedman was yelling now.

Wooten was still going.

"Wrap it!"

"He can't hear you," Heinz said.

Friedman pushed the button so everyone could hear him.

"Wrap it somebody," he yelled. Could Wooten hear anybody? "Jeff," Friedman was yelling now to Gralnick up in TV Three. "Tell him to wrap it. He's not hearing me."

Wooten had used up Cokie Roberts's time now, too.

"We go to a commercial," Heinz said.

"Peter, you're going to have to go to commercial out of this," Friedman now told his anchor. "Peter?"

Was anybody hearing Friedman?

"Okay, Jim, thank you very much," Jennings said, when Wooten finally finished. Poor Wooten had been flying solo on live TV without his angel in his ear. Just him, his mouth, his brain, and the freaking red light that told him thirteen million people were listening. "In just a minute we are going to go to Cokie Roberts on the House side," Jennings said. "We'll be right back."

They were off the air now.

"Somebody find out why that fucker couldn't hear me," Friedman yelled. "Peter, we're not going to get to Greenfield."

"You tell him," Jennings deadpanned. Apparently the anchor didn't want to make Greenfield irritable right before they went into the election show. Sitting behind Friedman in the control room, someone from the Rim gave a short laugh.

When they were done, there were no post mortems. There was no time. Television was mostly logistics and machines, and sometimes they didn't work. Friedman and his Rim were through for the day. Their election was over. He would go home and watch the election night special that was about to begin with his kids like everyone else. Most of what ABC would air that night Friedman would not see. WABC in New York, the network-owned and -operated local station, would preempt Jennings almost all night long.

"Hey Peter," Friedman said into Jennings's earpiece.

"Yeah."

"Good luck."

"Thanks. That okay?"

"Yeah."

"Not too hyper?"

It had been just the opposite but Friedman didn't say so. "I've asked Jeff [Gralnick] to check the shot," he said instead. "I think you're slouching a little. I think you may be a little low in your chair."

"Okay."

To most Americans, the election night special about to start is a familiar crawl of spinning graphics, and colored maps and chattering anchormen. The task seems familiar and rudimentary. The anchor calls the states as they come in, the exit poll specialists dissect the numbers, the correspondent comes in from election headquarters and says the mood is subdued for the loser and up for the winner. The differences between networks are a matter of preference.

To people in television, election night shows are the ultimate expression of the craft—the pure adrenaline scream. The months of set design, planning graphics, arranging camera positions, setting up the cast, placing your dozen or so correspondents at locations worldwide, interfacing the computers with the data stream-

14

ing in from every voting precinct in the country, buying the satellite time to feed in the more than sixty images, all click in at one terrifying serene moment. And suddenly the sixty images are all pouring into the darkened control room at the same time, onto the monitors in front of you, into your brain, and then at your command out into America, live. The rival nets are on the monitors above you. And the wits and energy of your hundreds of staff people are matched against their hundreds. It is war—for pride, for money, for the sheer rush of knowing that, in the moment you outdo the other guys, they are sitting in their control rooms seizing up, shouting into the dark.

In 1992, the great competition in network television to see which network could call the race first had ended. It was too expensive, and so the three networks and CNN had joined forces into one exit poll that meant everyone had the same information at the same time. Without any rivalry to call the race, the networks had to distinguish themselves from each other by other means—cast members, graphics, set, the other ingredients that had more to do with television and less with pure journalism.

At ABC, Jeff Gralnick and director Roger Goodman had three special tricks in mind to destroy the competition.

If they all were using the same exit poll, they decided they had to present the data more dramatically. Gralnick and Goodman were fascinated with the idea of holographs, three dimensional photographs that can move in space, created by splitting laser beams. Correspondent Lynn Sherr could be standing in a room, they imagined, and the bar charts could rise up around her. The problem was holographs required a dark place to be projected in. When ABC's British TV partner, ITN (Independent Television Network), figured out a way to make simulated holographs for TV by using new computer graphics, Gralnick and Goodman decided to borrow the idea. Instead of assembling their graphics in advance like posters or charts, ITN technicians used a new generation of computer graphics to create the graphics live, on the screen, while the audience watched. So Lynn Sherr could sit at a desk and the bar charts would rise up in front of her.

Next, Gralnick and Goodman had devised another trick for reporting on the House of Representatives. They had always wanted to report the House elections from the House floor. The government had always said no. So, copying their British ITN partners again, Gralnick and Goodman decided to create a computer version of the House and then project the image of Cokie Roberts inside it. She could wander around, even sit down. This trick was accomplished by taking a photograph of the House chamber, putting Roberts in a Washington studio with a blue matte background, and superimposing the House chamber around her.

Finally Gralnick and Goodman had made one other decision that would prove to be critical. After 1988, the last great expensive election, they had decided to keep their elaborate set in storage. If they reused it this year, they could save $500,000 and have as expensive a set as they had used before, while the others would probably be starting from scratch and spend more to get something considerably scaled down from four years earlier.

Afterwards one of the TV critics would wax enthusiastic about the futuristic set blazing a trail for television in the twenty-first century. Actually it was based on something almost a decade old, the 1983 movie *War Games* version of the North American Air Defense Command Post that Gralnick and Goodman had copied.

The big TV Three control room at ABC looks like a darkened version of the bridge of the Star Ship *Enterprise*. There are three rows of seats that descend toward a wall of monitors. Election night, two other control rooms would feed images to the room, one in New York and another in Washington. Gralnick could choose from sixty-two images in all. He would have correspondents at twenty-six different locations. Altogether, Gralnick could talk to thirty different people at any one time. Roger Goodman, his director, could talk to another thirty.

On the monitor wall, Gralnick had put up a sign that was characteristically cynical: IT'S NOT IMPORTANT. IT'S ONLY TELEVISION.

He knew it would annoy Roone Arledge, who could be endlessly cynical but also strangely innocent. It did.

Jennings, who always worried about how to start, how to get his rhythm, began the election special by talking to Brinkley as if the viewers weren't there. "Well, here we go again, David."

"Here we go again," Brinkley answered.

"Nice to have you," Jennings continued. "We were trying to figure out a little earlier how many votes we'd counted together in the last eight years."

"Millions, millions, I don't know how many," Brinkley prattled.

Then Jennings turned to the audience. "Good evening to you, and welcome to our full-scale election night."

Over the course of eight years, Jennings and Brinkley had an uneasy chemistry on air. They often talked over each other. Sometimes Brinkley sounded as if he were rebuking Jennings for being foolish. At other times Brinkley simply seemed to stop the show cold. People around Jennings thought the anchor was always solicitous of Brinkley and did his best to include him. People around Brinkley felt their man was always carted out like some ornament but never given an adequate role.

This night was average. Gralnick and Jennings gave Brinkley the Senate races to call, which left Jim Wooten without much to do. But Brinkley and Jennings still talked over each other. There were minutes when neither completed a sentence. But Brinkley still had style. He was so much a part of television that everyone in the business imitated him without being aware of it.

Several TV critics used the word "post-modern" to describe the show later—though their usage was so lax that the term was meaningless. Over the course of the night, Jennings, Brinkley, Greenfield, and others simply mocked themselves a good deal. Everyone had been through this so many times, including the audience, that the Olympian tones seemed to ring false.

Jennings at one point talked to director Roger Goodman. He talked about the lines he had blown. He called his analysts members of the "chattering class." Brinkley told Greenfield and Hal Bruno they looked like a couple of wise guys pontificating at a bar the way they leaned against the anchor desk. Greenfield, mocking the phone calls he was making to polling places, said, "We decided to do something new this year and talk to real people."

It seemed urbane, witty, casual.

And mostly it all clicked. The tricks were fine. Jennings was especially loose. Greenfield was clever and succinct. Hal Bruno was good. Although Jennings did not go much to George Will and Sam Donaldson, sitting in a studio in Washington, the two of them, away from the minutiae, offered the best summation of why Clinton won and Bush lost and what Clinton's challenges were now.

But while viewers never really saw it, the exit poll data had been skewing Democratic all night. The numbers had Clinton heading toward double-digit victory and then as the actual vote came in the lead narrowed. Georgia was called for Clinton and then taken back and then late in the morning given back to him. New Jersey was called early for Clinton and then closed to just one point. And then things froze. They couldn't call Ohio. The outcome was never in doubt, but the night kept dragging on. They finally called the race just ten minutes before the polls closed in California.

In Dallas, Perot came out at 9:25 and then led the band in calling tunes until after 9:30 so that the networks were out of their local cutaways and commercials. He got it both ways, maximizing his time on camera and getting the biggest audience.

Bush was stiff, but at his political wake in Houston, where Brit Hume sat on the riser all night saying goodbye to people, the rejected President came out after 10 o'clock and said all the right things. It was Dan Quayle, curiously, who gave the speech of the night, Jennings thought, especially when he told his supporters that if Clinton governed as well as he campaigned, the country would be okay.

The biggest problem was the new president. Clinton made them all wait past midnight, late for his own victory speech. Then he droned on about policy, and Al Gore spoke then longer than the president-elect. Was it a sign that the new government, at first, would be improvising?

When they finally got off the air a little after 1 A.M. Jennings wandered back to the Rim wired. He pulled out a bottle of Smirnoff vodka from the little freezer-refrigerator in his makeup closet, devoured two chocolate-chip cookies and tried to wind down. He looked more serious than on the air, and his features were warmer. He and producer Nancy Gabriner talked politics for another hour. Tomorrow he would ask Friedman how it had gone. And they would begin to cover the transition. There was a press conference scheduled for 10 A.M. This hour would be his only period for reflection.

People always said television had changed American politics. Certainly it had changed its style, but had it changed its nature? Friedman had opened the 10 A.M. meeting that morning with a typically spare review of the year past. "We tried something different during this campaign," he had said. "We were not perfect, but we were, I believe, quite good. It required a lot of cooperation. Required people to often subjugate their egos and their destinies to teamwork, and I thank you for that. I hope that the academics who have made a living criticizing us for the last four years will be among the unemployed tomorrow."

He had thought a good deal more than that. He thought he

had demonstrated this year that the press was not responsible for what was wrong with American politics. He thought he had finally covered this campaign the way the critics always had said he should—and not driven viewers away. And he thought, self-servingly, that it had made little difference. They had much less power than they were accused of. People probably scarcely noticed what they had done. Now that it was over, critics were already proclaiming the mainstream press irrelevant, replaced by talk shows and popular culture and local news. Friedman believed less had changed than people imagined. If anything, the election had reconnected the mass media, not disconnected it. But it would take time for people to see that. He and Jennings were more worried that having finally covered a campaign fairly well, network television might never again have a serious commitment to do it well again.

The Republicans argued, too, that the mostly liberal press had been against Bush all year. The Democrats argued the press had other biases that hurt Bill Clinton—puritanism, sexism, militarism, a lingering distrust of Clinton's character. Friedman rejected most of the arguments out of hand. Television was easy to blame, he thought, but people exaggerated its sway and underestimated its audience. Politics was driven by the invisible engine that had always driven it—whether family or friends were prospering, whether the world was safe. The world mattered, Friedman thought, not what people saw for an instant on television. Television was a flash, and then it was gone. Words and pictures. Writing on the wind.

★

CHAPTER

2

GOOD
INTENTIONS

★

By autumn 1991, the media had enough problems without another campaign to cover. The journalism business was mired in the worst slump of its modern and once wildly profitable history, and now even its own executives were speculating over whether network television and most newspapers were dying industries. The press had spent the previous decade fretting about whether it had a credibility problem. And in the war with Iraq that had ended in the spring of 1991, the public had sided with government censors and against the press having more freedom to learn what was going on.

The prospect of another political campaign seemed almost forbidding. It was going to be expensive to cover. They were going to be hammered afterwards by whoever lost. George Bush was going to win anyway.

In the three years since 1988, a good many Americans had also decided something was seriously wrong with American politics and held the media to blame. Among the critics were some of the most respected members of the press. By glorifying the tactics of politics rather than the substance, David Broder of the Washington *Post* had written the year before, the press was only deepening the public cynicism that politics was shallow and mean. The media had twisted politics into a distorted game, argued Harvard researcher Kiko Adatto, in which candidates were judged not by their qualifications but by their skill at image making—politics as post-modernist art.

Ted Koppel, the anchor of ABC's *Nightline*, even had a theory he called the "Vanna-tizing" of American culture, in honor of Vanna White of TV's *Wheel of Fortune*. Vanna remained enormously popular, the theory went, precisely because she was seen but not heard. Americans could imagine her to be any way they wanted. That was what had happened to American politics. Politicians were rewarded for platitudes and punished for taking serious positions.

Inside ABC News, in reaction, they had prepared for the election year mostly by ignoring it.

Paul Friedman's office at ABC News headquarters on West 66th Street in Manhattan was on the second floor, just off the Rim. There were no photos of his powerful and famous friends—he decorated it mostly with family pictures and notes and artwork penned by his daughters. There was little to suggest that for twenty years, like a handful of other television producers highly paid but scarcely noted, he had had an invisible hand in shaping American culture.

Friedman had been a quick success, mostly at NBC News, turning heads covering the 1972 campaign with Douglas Kiker and then working the weekend news. Tall and polite, the young Princeton graduate had a surprising self-confidence, but he was quiet, nonthreatening, a listener. When he was only twenty-nine, the network sent him to save its struggling New York affiliate's local news, which led into John Chancellor. At the time, 1974, the potential of local news was barely recognized. Only one local station in the country did a two hour show—in Los Angeles. Friedman was sent to build the second. The trick, he quickly realized, was that there wasn't enough local news to fill two hours. So he devised a series of set feature segments viewers could look for instead. There was cooking and consumer news, mixed in with the serious. So began the transition of TV newscasts into highly produced magazine-style programs.

When Friedman left two years later, WNBC's *NewsCenter 4* was No. 1, and local stations around the country were expanding their formats to imitate its success. In short order, Friedman was put in charge of the *Today Show*, NBC's morning cash cow. He was thirty-one, the wunderkind of network television. The high school principal's son from Brooklyn was telling America what books to read and movies to watch and social issues to care about, ten hours of live network TV a week. He would remember those days as his best in television.

By the time he reached thirty-five, it was over. Friedman didn't think much of Bill Small, the new president of NBC News, and he was still young enough not to hide his feelings. Small stripped Friedman of his shows and sent him to the 13th floor, NBC purgatory, with nothing to do but an occasional documentary. A year later, Friedman had had enough. He fled to a modest job in ABC's London bureau and started over.

For most of its history, Friedman's new network was best known for the jokes and the embarrassing numbers. The third of America's two-and-a-half networks, went the line about ABC News. In 1963, when CBS and NBC boasted news budgets of $30 million each, ABC's was $3.5 million. CBS was anchored by Walter Cronkite, NBC by Chet Huntley and David Brinkley. ABC's anchors were Alex Drier, John Seconder, and Fendall Yerxa. As late as 1968, ABC executives considered dumping the evening news altogether.

Things got better in the 1970s when the network lured Harry Reasoner from CBS and Barbara Walters from NBC. In 1977, it finally made its news budget competitive, and that same year ABC named Roone Arledge, the head of its legendary sports division, to take over news. The battered troops at ABC News shivered at the thought. Everyone knew about Arledge. The safari jackets. The gold medallions. The antique Bentley. The women. The guy was a cad. Before long, for godsake, Howard Cosell would be doing commentaries on the news. Former athletes would be anchoring.

Television news was on the brink of massive change. Cable TV was arriving, and the networks were about to see their audiences shrivel by 50 percent. The network oligarchy was dying. By the early 1980s, CBS News's influential president, Van Gordon Sauter, would be arguing that TV news was too oriented toward politics and government. To keep its audience, news needed to focus more on communicating emotion, "magic moments," people crying, laughing, suffering. "Reality-based programming"— shows like *Entertainment Tonight,* then *America's Most Wanted,* were gaining popularity. The philosophies of news and entertainment were merging into something called "infotainment."

Arledge turned out to be a purist against this tide. The gold medallions gave way to blue blazers. And the guy from *Wide World of Sports* and *Monday Night Football* managed the new balance of showmanship and news more deftly than anyone else. In 1978, he launched *20-20,* a prime time magazine aimed at older viewers and modeled after *60 Minutes.* A year later he began *Nightline,* a half hour of news for people who didn't want to watch Johnny Carson. In 1981, he wooed David Brinkley from NBC and launched a new Sunday talk show, *This Week with David Brinkley,* the first real change in the Sunday talk format in thirty years.

By 1987, one thing continued to elude him, being No. 1 in nightly news. *World News Tonight* was respectable enough, Jennings its sole anchor since 1983, but it was dead last in ratings. Jennings and his executive producer, Bill Lord, detested each other, and there were rumors the anchor was toying with leaving. In the fall of 1987, hoping for a radical change, Arledge summoned his executive group to New York's Lowell Hotel to figure out how to save the evening newscast.

* *

Friedman had spent the last five years in ABC's London bureau, as a senior producer and then as director of news coverage for Europe, Africa, and the Middle East. In New York, he was still mostly unknown, but he was just high-ranking enough to be invited to Arledge's summit. With all of ABC News's high command present, the talk went on and on. Should they make stories shorter, longer, harder, softer, more analytical? Friedman listened for two hours before rising from his seat. The network news, he said, had lost its reason for being. By the time it came on the air each night, a lot of viewers already knew the headlines. To survive, and still offer something of value, the network needed to move toward deeper coverage. Friedman then laid out a broadcast that would do it. The show would have four parts. Give the top story five full minutes, two separate pieces. Then a summary of the rest of the news in four-and-a-half minutes. Another in-depth seven-minute piece by Jennings. Then two lighter pieces to close the show.

Arledge, dazzled, appointed Friedman to redesign the newscast and, in January 1988, made the 42-year-old outsider its executive producer. The proposed format by then was slightly altered. The abbreviated news summary didn't work, so Friedman replaced the seven-minute mini-Jennings documentary with a shorter series he called American Agenda focusing on major social problems. But close to half of Friedman's broadcast was still devoted to in-depth reporting about hard news—at a time when the network philosophies seemed to be getting softer.

Within months, *World News Tonight with Peter Jennings* was challenging for No. 1. It secured the spot by the fall of 1989, and had remained there every week without interruption since.

How much Friedman's format accounted for that rise is difficult to know. The research in television is scary: Most viewers barely recognize what channel they watch; what they notice is the anchor. If nothing else, though, even skeptics credited Friedman with one contribution, making a moody, unhappy and valuable Peter Jennings relax.

Success on television is partly gift and partly skill, a voice, a look, a personal style, intellect, charm. It couldn't be faked and it couldn't entirely be learned. The best were naturals, like Mike Wallace or Charles Kuralt. Peter Charles Archibald Ewart Jennings was bred to it.

His father, Charles Jennings, was the first national "voice of Canada" on radio, and later became the anchor and head of Canadian television. Charles was also an idealist. "He hated TV," Peter Jennings would say. "He was not rough enough . . . and in the end it was not kind to him." Charles's only son Peter grew up graceful, popular, athletic, in a world of private schools, artists, and intellectuals. At nine, he was the star of a national Saturday children's radio show. As a teenager, if anything, he suffered from too much style and too little patience. He dropped out of high school and never made it to college. Before he could look back, he had succeeded on his style and instincts. At twenty-one, he was a celebrity on Canadian TV. And in 1967 at twenty-six, only a year after coming to the United States, Jennings was named the anchor of ABC News's struggling newscast. He lasted two years, too young and experienced for the job, and then spent the next decade in Europe and the Middle East as a correspondent learning the business.

Perhaps because he had never had much formal education, Jennings's formidable mind worked in odd ways, restless and open but undisciplined and impressionable—that of the quintessential journalist. In an era of cynicism, Jennings still thought television something magical. The box was sometimes a theater, he liked to say, sometimes a great sports stadium, sometimes a chapel, a place where a nation gathers and communes, grieves and celebrates.

So it wasn't surprising that as the 1992 campaign approached, Jennings was the one disturbed. Over the last three years he had listened to the debates and read the criticisms of the press and the 1988 elections and agreed with them. American politics was never considered his strength, but he thought some of the problems were obvious. One night in November 1991, Jennings sat in his office and watched Tom Brokaw on the nightly news interview live the chairmen of the two major American political parties, Republican Clayton Yeutter and Democrat Ron Brown. Jennings cringed. This was just how a network shouldn't waste its twenty-two minutes a night, he thought. "I hope I never interview a politician on the nightly news that way, because when they're live they just own the fucking time."

Part of the problem, Jennings thought, was that the networks had been so concerned with their financial problems that they had failed to think enough about their journalism. They had allowed themselves to be used and then, in the Reagan years, to be "subdued by a very popular president."

Jennings was unsure how coverage should change, but ideas were plentiful. "Change" had become the current conventional wisdom of the press. David Broder of the Washington *Post* had urged the press to find out what voters cared about, and if candidates ignored those concerns it should wage a "custody" battle for the campaign dialogue on the voters' behalf. Timothy J. Russert, the ambitious young Washington bureau chief of NBC News, had suggested the networks keep their key reporters off the campaign planes as a way to stop airing empty photo opportunities. In the midterm campaigns of 1990, the press had begun policing political advertising, something it had surprisingly never taken seriously before. The press always began campaigns armed with good intentions. But this time, the sense of something wrong, and of the press being responsible, seemed deeper.

It was difficult to believe that, forty years before, people had hoped television would purify American politics. Thomas Dewey, the

Republican nominee of 1948, had called it a political "X-ray," whose "piercing stare" would expose the charlatans and encourage more Americans to get involved.

Politicians quickly adapted to the medium. In 1952, the first TV campaign, Dwight Eisenhower produced TV commercials, which the networks initially refused to air, citing policies against using television to sell ideas. A young Richard Nixon that same season bought thirty minutes of national TV time and asked voters to decide for themselves whether he should remain on the Republican ticket. This was the first case of a politician using TV to go over the heads of the party and the press to appeal directly to voters. Four years later advance men began appearing to stage events for the cameras, and, in 1960, Nixon broke the ban imposed by print reporters against allowing TV cameras at press conferences. By that fall, with the introduction of nationally televised presidential debates, all the techniques of modern campaigning were in use—from staged town hall meetings to telethons, to thirty-second commercials, to call-in shows.

After television's first eight years, politicians also understood the machine had not purified politics, only changed the rules, and through the 1960s an era of growing mistrust toward the press set in. The 1964 Republican Convention erupted into an open demonstration against the press when Eisenhower called on his party to condemn those "outside" the family. With the land war that began in Vietnam a year later, the loathing toward television swelled. In 1968, the Democrats launched a Congressional investigation into network influence after becoming incensed that the networks had exaggerated the riots outside the Democratic convention in Chicago. A year later, Vice President Spiro Agnew traveled to Iowa to launch an open campaign against network influence.

What had changed was the rise in the mid-1960s of the nightly network news. In October 1964, CBS and NBC had expanded their nightly newscast from fifteen to thirty minutes, and within a year television had replaced newspapers as the dominant source of news in America. TV in turn made the press unforgiving.

Reporters could no longer protect a candidate from his odd habits and misstatements. Those things were now on camera. Suddenly we saw public figures in closeup, in a way we once knew only personal friends. Eventually, we also wanted to know personal things about them.

From the 1964 campaign on, politicians, convinced the press was now dangerous and unsympathetic, set out to use television to control the journalists who ran it. Goldwater tried it in the 1964 campaign and Johnson as president. And in 1968, Nixon had raised the use of television to bypass a hostile press to a new level. Nixon's aides limited the candidate each day to a single carefully orchestrated event of invited audiences, cued applause, and a staged mobbing of Nixon at the end. Reporters were usually relegated to anterooms to watch the proceedings on closed-circuit TV.

At the time, political reporting was still modeled on Theodore White's *Making of the President*. White pioneered looking at the backroom strategy and tactics of politics, but he saw elections as heroic clashes of men and ideology that offered insights into the nation's mood. Candidates used words and ideas to appeal to voters, not to manipulate them. The tactics of politics worked in the service of a higher purpose.

After 1968 the press would never again reflect such faith, and White in time was even scorned. The cynicism bred by Vietnam and a year of assassinations and riots was crystallized for the political press in the 1969 book *The Selling of the President* by Philadelphia writer Joe McGinnis. Like White, he focused on the inner workings of campaigns, but, unlike his predecessor, McGinnis had no faith in the ideas and words politicians expressed. As McGinnis watched the rising class of political consultants, admen, and TV specialists around Nixon, he thought he had discovered that in the age of television "something new, murky, undefined, started to rise from the mists." In the age of television, "a candidate's image superseded issues."

Unfortunately, McGinnis's cynicism was chic but wrong. For all Nixon's technique, the Republicans had squandered a 15-point lead after the conventions and defeated the Democrats by barely 500,000 votes out of nearly 73 million cast—against a Democratic party hemorrhaging over Vietnam. But McGinnis's bestseller resonated with the times, and political journalism was never the same.

From then on, the press increasingly saw campaign rhetoric as raw material to be examined rather than simply as information to be communicated. In the network coverage of 1972 the average length of time on television that any candidate or anyone else spoke without interruption shrank by 42 percent from four years earlier, the largest drop in any campaign before or since.* With the party reforms of 1969 elevating public primaries as the means for choosing party nominees, the press's cynicism was also matched by its swelling influence over the process.

This rise in the press's power took its last critical step in 1976, when the network crews first took portable video cameras and satellite trucks on the road. Suddenly they could stay with the campaigns longer each day. They no longer needed to send in film early for developing. They could even go live. Television finally became the dominant force on the campaign trail.

Many of the changes in political strategy were also now aimed at capitalizing on this deepening power. Jimmy Carter set out to win the otherwise meaningless Iowa caucuses so the press would label him as the candidate with momentum so that this recognition would catapult him to the nomination in 1976. By 1980, everyone was playing Carter's game of manipulating expectations, and "spin doctors"—campaign operatives who tried to massage media perceptions—began appearing on the network news.

By 1984, Ronald Reagan had mastered nearly all the techniques, from Nixon's staging of events to Carter's spinning the press. Reagan's team also perfected how to inject their candidate into nonpolitical events, like stock car races and rodeos. Even as

---

*The research on the length of soundbites was done by Daniel Hallin at the University of California at San Diego.

it decried his campaign as phony, the press used the pictures, and the idea became popular that the words spoken on TV didn't matter. The average length of a soundbite dipped below ten seconds.

By 1988, candidates had adapted to the point that even the issues were picked to fit the abbreviated grammar of television. George Bush ran in favor of the pledge of allegiance and against prison furloughs. Here were images quickly and visually communicated that triggered deeper associations in voters' minds—Vietnam, patriotism, the disillusions of the 1960s, crime, race.

In the aftermath of Bush's victory, the press engaged in more than the usual self-criticism. Some of the brightest new political writers began to quit covering politics altogether—at the *New York Times*, the Washington *Post*, the Chicago *Tribune*, the Boston *Globe*, the Philadelphia *Inquirer*, the Los Angeles *Times*. As John Balzar of the Los Angeles *Times*, who fled to Seattle, explained it, "I desperately needed to run off and talk to someone who believed what they were telling me."

Were the press and especially television really to blame? If the piercing stare of television had failed to purify politics, had it trivialized it instead? If the networks altered how they operated, would it make any difference? Jennings wondered. But he had to convince others at ABC to wonder, too, and that had not proven so easy.

Friedman sympathized, but his thoughts were typically complicated. He agreed the press shared responsibility for the public's lack of interest in politics; it failed to make politics interesting. But there was a limit. If the Democrats were too weak to fight for themselves, for instance, the press couldn't do it for them. And if the candidates wanted to talk about symbols, the press couldn't make them talk about something else.

Friedman was not given to elaborate philosophical pronouncements. In the long days on the Rim, he operated by encouraging debate, asking questions and making decisions that provided their own example. He intended to take the same approach with politics. He would change the coverage, he reasoned, by rejecting conventional political stories and challenging his staff to think more creatively. It wasn't that he disliked politics. He had majored in it at Princeton, and they had a responsibility to cover it, "But goddamn it, don't bore the shit out of me."

Network television news organizations are vast collaborative enterprises, where logistics often took more effort than journalism, and whose ranks were filled with people smart about machinery and art as much as news. ABC News produced 35 hours a week of programming now—from *ABC News Sunrise* first thing in the morning to *World News Overnight* airing from 1:00 A.M. to 6:00 A.M.—and Friedman's weekday *World News* accounted for only two and a half hours of that. Much of the effort was focused on producing prime time feature magazine shows.

Most of the 1,300 staffers at the news division were hardly revolutionaries. Even for those who were primarily journalists rather than technicians, indeed, thinking about what was good for the system was controversial. Reporters and editors are taught not to worry about the consequences of what they published. Doing so leads to favoritism, to making deals, holding stories back. Reporters are supposed to tell the truth, without fear or favor, let the chips fall where they may. The press's job was to report what happened, not make judgments about it or try to reform the system. The debate was really a matter of emphasis, for all news involved making judgments, and all judgments began with reporting what happened.

If the network operated differently, Jennings might have had an ally in his desire to change coverage in Ted Koppel. The *Nightline* anchor was uncomfortable with the press trying to shape the political agenda, but he believed the networks had to change their approach. The usual two minutes a day with thirty seconds worth of soundbites served little purpose. But Koppel lived in Washington, not New York, and he mostly worried about his own program, which many at ABC thought had been coasting into bland middle age and could itself use a jolt.

One other man at ABC who might have pushed was Jeffrey Gralnick. He would run the election night shows and the conventions, the so-called special events. Good looking, sarcastic, funny, the fifty-two-year-old Gralnick was a veteran who had done virtually every key job at ABC, including Friedman's, and was one of the few people at ABC who understood all the sides of television, the technical and the editorial. But Gralnick had survived by being relentlessly efficient and by knowing what worked.

People like Roone Arledge and Peter Jennings were dreamers, he said. He was the carpenter. "Roone says, 'I see a dusty truck.' Peter says, 'I see columns of dusty trucks.' I'm the one who says, 'It's not as dusty as you think.'"

Finally there was Arledge. "ABC won't change unless Roone wants it to," one top executive predicted, "and he won't focus."

To outsiders, Arledge was a visionary leader, the man who had seduced America into watching sports by experimenting with cameras and video and inventing programs like *Monday Night Football*, the man who later built ABC News by dreaming up new kinds of news shows and luring away stars like David Brinkley and Diane Sawyer from the competition. If he was not one of the founding fathers of the information age, a William Paley, or a Henry Luce, Arledge was certainly one of its giant innovators. His corporate biography noted that *Life* magazine had called him one of the one hundred most important Americans of the twentieth century.

To the correspondents he had lured to ABC, Arledge was an impresario, a sort of video savant. His gift was more instinctive than intellectual. He had learned somewhere that his tastes and instincts matched those of the American public and so he had learned to indulge them. He had liked watching key plays over again and so helped invent instant replay; he liked to slow them down and helped develop slow motion. When Arledge called from his office down to the control room during *World News* on the red

"Roone Phone," it was usually to warn that Jennings's hair was messed or that manly anchors don't wear polka-dot ties. Yet that was part of Arledge's genius. He saw what viewers saw. He had the eye.

To many of the people on the second and third floors at ABC News, where the editors, producers, and technicians worked, Arledge was a distant figure, socially ill at ease. In January 1992, he hadn't been on the set of *World News* in seven months. "What do I think of Roone? You mean Oz?" said one correspondent.

To the management of Capital Cities Communications, the company that bought ABC in 1985, Arledge was a difficult executive, famous for not answering phone calls, and for ignoring problems until his underlings resolved them. He operated often without leaving fingerprints and was hard to make focus. In the fall of 1991, Cap Cities had installed Stephen Weiswasser as Arledge's virtual equal to co-administer Arledge's division and cut costs. If there were any doubts as to his standing, Weiswasser, a former ABC general counsel, had knocked down a wall so he could enter Roone Arledge's office without people seeing him.

Amid the pressure, Arledge seemed distracted at best. That was one reason ABC didn't hold its first meeting to discuss the campaign until November 1991, about a year later than usual.

They accomplished little: They wouldn't use footage from political ads as "wallpaper" to illustrate a story. They would be careful with polls. But much of what they discussed simply disappeared. To get off the mark, they agreed to do an hour prime time special previewing the election. It never happened. When Friedman later asked Weiswasser what happened, the lawyer just shrugged.

It was a far cry from the days when network television assembled armies of researchers into a political unit, spent millions just preparing, and assigned a correspondent, crew, and producer with every candidate, and sometimes double that. This year, ABC would assign to each candidate a single off-air producer who filed a daily memo to New York. As it would turn out, the other two broadcast networks would not even do that.

The only thing certain to change in the campaign of 1992, indeed, was money. George Bush's election in 1988 had cost ABC $25 million—$18 million for election specials and conventions and the rest for regular news coverage. And that was less than the $30 million it had spent in 1980, the peak of network profits and expenditures, an era when CBS even sent its own shoeshine man to the conventions. No one had the money anymore, and they had just spent more than they had on coverage of the Gulf War, by best estimates $30 million to $40 million for each of the three networks. For 1992, ABC hoped to cut spending in half from the four years before.

Another sign of change was the scramble among the correspondents to cover the campaign. There wasn't one. Correspondents who once angled and maneuvered to cover the election now preferred to stay home. Friedman and Jennings decided they would use a core group of four people—a large change from the days when every candidate had two correspondents trailing him from day one. Brit Hume, who covered the Bush White House, would be the lead correspondent on Bush. Jim Wooten, the senior political correspondent, would cover Democrats. Jeff Greenfield, the former Robert Kennedy speechwriter, author, columnist, and Yale law school graduate, would do political analysis.

The last member of the team would be Cokie Roberts, Arledge's current trophy correspondent. Roberts covered Congress for National Public Radio and worked also for ABC with a special parttime status. Widely respected among virtually everyone at ABC, Roberts had deftly kept Arledge's fascination going by her unwillingness to fully leave NPR. "Somehow she knew what the rest of us learned the hard way—that after you finish with the negotiations Roone loses interest," said one colleague.

In late November, still trying to get ABC organized, Jennings decided to call in outsiders to talk about how they should improve coverage. The first invitation went to Bill Kovach, the tough, uncompromising former *New York Times* Washington bureau chief and Atlanta *Constitution* editor-in-chief.

It ended in disaster. Sitting down for lunch with Arledge, Greenfield, Jennings, Friedman, and others, Kovach accused network television of superficiality and lack of courage. Television, he said, had the capability to do some things far better than newspapers, like biography, but the networks failed to take advantage of the medium.

When Kovach condemned television's approach to issues, Friedman lost his temper. Covering issues was one thing Friedman took pride in, because of his American Agenda segment, which looked at one issue a week for three nights. Perhaps Kovach had not seen it, he said.

"I'm not going to sit here and argue with you," Kovach said, staring at him.

People left the meeting angry. "What a fool to take a day and talk to these jackasses," Kovach fumed later. "They invited me and then started a damn argument. . . . After lunch they jumped up and left. I was left there alone. I didn't know how to get out of the damn building."

Jennings's plan of inviting outside guests to appear ended with this one experiment. The campaign had already begun, and ABC had not yet begun covering it—or figuring out how to start.

Elsewhere, planning in the press was only marginally more organized, though the desire for change was a little more focused. The most prepared was NBC. Under the guidance of Washington bureau chief Tim Russert and political director Bill Wheatley, it intended to keep its top correspondents away from the candidates' planes to avoid becoming imprisoned by campaign photo opportunities, and to begin policing not only ads but speeches for honesty. NBC's plan also served its corporate parent's desire to cut costs. What was less clear was whether NBC had the people left to make the coverage plan work. The network had lost a significant percentage of its talent in recent years: Roger Mudd to PBS, Ken Bode to CNN, Chris Wallace to ABC, Connie Chung to CBS, and others off camera, like Joe Angotti, who ably produced its political coverage in 1988, and George Paul, one of its most talented directors.

CBS had Susan Zirinsky in charge of politics, the hard-charging producer who had been the prototype for the lead character in the hit movie *Broadcast News*. By November, it had aired some interesting pieces, including analysis of the candidates' early stump speeches. But CBS also had serious tension over the future of its news division. *The CBS Evening News with Dan Rather* was now in the hands of local news veteran Erik Sorenson, and he and CBS News President Eric Ober seemed to be taking CBS down market for bigger ratings. Politics, many at CBS feared, might not be part of that plan, regardless of Dan Rather.

Then there was CNN, Ted Turner's Atlanta upstart, the star of the Gulf War. It was a popular notion outside television to think of CNN as the network of the future. Inside television, and even inside CNN, the cable network was best known for copious but often sloppy coverage. Privately, many at CNN were often still embarrassed by what they put on the air. The network too often was epitomized by Miami correspondent Charles Jaco, who had lost his composure on the air during Scud attacks in the Gulf War, thus playing into Iraqi hands. For the 1992 election, CNN was trying to assemble a more impressive group than in the past, led by former NBC chief political correspondent Ken Bode, former chief ABC documentary maker Pamela Hill, and NBC's former weekly analyst team of David Broder and Jack Germond. It also had high hopes to try all the new techniques for covering politics advocated by the reform-minded.

Where did that leave newspapers? Many were imbued with a greater desire to change than any of the networks. The Washington *Post* was among the most aggressive. "We do have to have our own agenda," political editor William Hamilton said, to find out what concerned voters and "call into question any candidate" who ignored it. In November 1991 the *Post* embarked on a series of polls and interviews to register the electorate's mood, which it said would serve as a "guide" for the rest of its coverage.

The *New York Times*'s intentions were less certain. It, too, wanted to focus more on voters this year, managing editor Joseph Lelyveld explained before the campaign began. But he also thought it was "unrealistic" for the press to think it could "take a leadership role shaping the campaign."

Some of the most imaginative work was being done at local papers. In the 1990 Kansas governor's race, the Knight-Ridder-owned Wichita *Eagle* had focused its coverage around ten key issues considered most important to its community. It ran long stories on each one, and, for the six Sundays before the election, devoted a full page to outlining all the issues and where the candidates stood on them. Its research later showed that 80 percent of readers read the repetitive Sunday pages and 70 percent read the long issues stories. Far fewer read the traditional coverage. Voter turnout in the county also had increased, contrary to statewide and nationwide trends, and for the presidential race several papers in the Knight-Ridder chain planned to imitate the *Eagle*'s approach.

Not everyone in the press was pleased. Some journalists considered the whole idea of reform naive and misplaced. It presupposed that people cared about issues and that the press was to blame for candidates ignoring them, a false assumption. And it presupposed that politics was meant to be rational, positive, and substantive. It wasn't.

And, of course, everyone knew this wasn't going to be that much of a race anyway. George Bush was going to roll over whatever sacrificial lamb the Democrats threw his way. The major Democrats weren't even running.

* *

Then by January, things seemed a little more interesting. Pat Buchanan was posing a serious challenge, and people smelled blood. ABC News was caught short.

The first week of January 1992, Peter Jennings trudged into Friedman's office to try one more time. He pulled off his thick aviator glasses, the ones viewers never saw, and stood over Friedman's desk. His tie was pulled down to its usual length six inches below an open collar, his sleeves rolled up.

"New Hampshire is becoming a much bigger story than we had ever imagined," he argued. "We have to profile the candidates."

From behind his desk, Friedman looked up at his anchorman and gave a wry smile to indicate he was unconvinced.

After four years together, the two men were close. They were neighbors on weekends in the Hamptons and few at ABC knew where their ideas diverged. But at this level in television, people always held something back. Especially Friedman. Jennings was beginning to wonder whether his executive producer was succumbing to one of the most sad and dangerous notions he had encountered. No one talked about it out loud, not at the networks. But it was there, below the surface. Politics was a turnoff. Americans hated it. It was bad for ratings. There was even the theory that the network news needed to blend in more with the shows that preceded them—meaning local news—so they didn't alienate the audience they inherited. The local shows, in turn, would resemble in tone their lead-ins, tabloid programs like *Hard Copy* and, at a lot of ABC stations, gawk-show mistress Oprah Winfrey.

Friedman was far from subscribing to this theory, Jennings knew. But not wanting to cover a presidential election was a step down that road.

"The usual candidate profiles on network TV news are next to useless," Friedman answered Jennings. Here's a man and every-

41

thing he believes in two minutes, and then a commercial. If they were going to do profiles, Friedman said, he wanted something different. The pieces had to be narrowly focused. And they would have to be long, four minutes at least. But ABC didn't have the time, not on the nightly news, not with six Democrats in the race. And it was January. No one was paying attention anyway. What was the point?

Because we have to, Jennings argued.

By now, Friedman's office was beginning to fill up. If there was a debate going on in there, people wanted to hear it. Nancy Gabriner, Jennings's political producer, had come in. So had Friedman's two deputies, Bob Roy and Dennis Dunlavey.

Doing something dull was worse than doing nothing, Friedman said, because it would turn people off. Dunlavey and Roy were appalled. How could they cover the race without profiling who was running, Dunlavey argued. Friedman eventually gave in, mostly out of guilt. But the profiles would have to be tightly focused, he instructed—why is each of these men running—not how they were doing. And Jennings would do them. If the anchor was involved the stories would be longer.

Jennings decided to begin with Paul Tsongas, the least important candidate, but the profiles never aired. Before Jennings could finish the first one, all hell broke loose. And they were off and running.

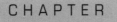

CHAPTER

NEW HAMPSHIRE DEMOCRATS

In the bar of the Sheraton Tara Wayfarer in Manchester, where the wisdom of the press corps was poured, Jim Wooten looked in disbelief at the cocktail waitress who had told him she was out of Stolichnaya. Then he turned back.

"It'll be cliché stuff," Wooten was saying, referring to the story he had come to do. "The perils of being the front-runner."

The Wayfarer hotel was an old mill converted into a hotel and then surrounded by a shopping mall. For years, it had also been the unofficial press headquarters of the New Hampshire primary. It was here, especially in the bar, that reporters, pollsters, and campaign operatives drank after deadline, exchanging information and impressions of the candidates and their chances, deciding who was "resonating" with voters, who had a "message," exchanging word of the latest polls, playing the elusive game of expectations.

"CBS used to own this place," Wooten said, looking around. "They booked every parlor and suite and a block of about five hundred rooms." Tonight, late January 1992, there were only a handful of CBS technicians in the back.

Wooten had considered skipping this campaign, too, which would be his seventh. At fifty-four, he was a grandfather with silvery straight hair that he wore long in the style of television and a droll courtly southern manner that came across the screen as a gentle irony. He was the network's most gifted writer, but he had an artistic temperament, intuitive, painstaking, and strangely wise, and he was viewed by his employers as moody. He had worked at the *New York Times,* where he was White House correspondent and covered national politics, and he had moved to ABC in 1979 because he saw newspapers becoming less hospitable to creative spirits and more corporate. Now, with the networks' cutbacks and their move away from covering politics, TV was changing, too, and his enthusiasm was uneven. The last campaign four years ago had been hard. He had drunk too much, and afterwards he was bored. Then the Gulf War had come. Wooten did work that he was proud of—"not just television." And in early fall, he had written Friedman a memo that said he wanted to cover the campaign after all and explained how he thought television could do that and still keep its viewers.

The network should discover the underlying theme that takes shape beneath every presidential campaign, he wrote in the spirit of Teddy White, the theme that teaches Americans about themselves. This year, he predicted, might be a watershed moment for the Democratic party, trying to take a new direction, away from interest-group politics. Now, a few months later, he also thought the Democrats had the best chance to win the White House since 1976, when Wooten had covered Carter and written his biography. The end of the Cold War had eliminated the reason to vote for Republicans, he thought, and the recession had given people a reason to vote Democratic. The Democrats might win, he thought. More likely they might screw it up.

Wooten had produced three pieces so far, one about the economy, another about Buchanan, and a third about the mood of the state. Now he was back for another trip to New Hampshire, hunting for the theme of the campaign. This time he was here to do a story about Bill Clinton, the young Arkansas governor. Clinton had broken from the pack. The New Hampshire primary was still a month away and already the horse race was taking over.

* *

Clinton's ascendance, like too much of what was about to happen, revealed more about the press than it did the candidates. Clinton had become the front-runner by having already won the invisible primary, a critical event conducted by a closed circle of journalists and Washington insiders that decides which candidates could raise money, build an organization, and win party support. The press drove the invisible primary by insisting on writing about who was ahead or behind before most voters knew who was running. And the 1992 campaign demonstrated not only how embedded the press were in the process, but the extent to which some journalists exploited their influence.

Clinton's rise began in late November 1991. The Democratic candidates were speaking to an otherwise obscure meeting of the Association of State Democratic Chairmen in Chicago. Once-mighty state party chairmen now had only limited direct power. A good measure of their influence was derived from reporters using them as sounding boards; if a candidate could woo these party chairmen he could get an early headline. The day after the Chicago meeting, the Washington *Post*'s Dan Balz quoted several chairmen as saying Clinton had given the most thoughtful and impressive speech. On the same evidence, the *New York Times* account by Robin Toner called Clinton "the candidate most ready for prime time." Even Balz was alarmed by the response. The coverage of the Chicago meeting catapulted Clinton as front-runner among party activists, financial donors, and reporters.

Two weeks later, Clinton won a straw poll at the Florida state party convention, the first exercise that even vaguely resembled an election. He won it, like most straw polls are won, because he had a better organization. And in the weeks following, Clinton surged ahead in fundraising, particularly after December 18, when New York governor Mario Cuomo announced his decision not to run.

Then Clinton began making the covers of key magazines, first *New York*, then *Time*.

"We didn't anoint Clinton," Baltimore *Sun* columnist Jules Witcover said in the Wayfarer a few weeks later. "We didn't invent the money-raising, the superior organization. We just reported them."

True enough, Clinton did have the best combination of organization, strategic plan, and message. Young Arkansas pol, Rhodes scholar, class president, governor at twenty-nine, Clinton had actively been preparing for this race for more than a decade. He had used his state as a lab for new ideas, and he had wooed intellectuals and Washington power brokers, positioning himself.

Compared with Clinton, the other candidates considered seriously by the press paled badly. Nebraska senator Bob Kerrey's campaign was so hastily arranged he did not have media consultants or his final team of advisers set until after Christmas. The stories about his lack of knowledge of the game were so numerous they became barroom humor. Then there was Iowa senator Tom Harkin, who struck many reporters as mean-spirited and careless. On one particularly sorry day in New Hampshire, Harkin tried to attack all of his rivals by reading to them from the Boston *Herald*, a Rupert Murdoch tabloid, as if it were an authoritative source. "This is pathetic," one said loud enough for Harkin to hear. Then he claimed his private polling showed him moving up in the race. You aren't conducting any private polling, a reporter reminded him. Harkin suffered, too, because reporters were persuaded that few voters had strong ties anymore to the New Deal spirit he was trying to evoke. They believed Gary Hart's neoliberalism was slowly prevailing. The reporters were young, mostly under forty-five. Harkin represented "unrepentant liberalism," wrote Robin Toner in the *New York Times*.

Paul Tsongas was exempt from this group. Although he thought about why he wanted to be president, the press had already dismissed him as unelectable, as it had Jerry Brown.

The press had not just reported Clinton's virtues, however,

as Witcover thought. It had created them, too. For all the publicity Clinton enjoyed, for instance, Tsongas did not see his name in even a subhead on page one of the *New York Times* until January 18. By then it was nearly too late to build an organization beyond New Hampshire.

The problem with the invisible primary is that the magnetic pull of the press and other insiders to define the race had occurred prematurely, on evidence that was too scant, and without any substantive input from voters. At a time when politics was only marginally relevant to many citizens anyway, the press's aggressive involvement in the invisible primary only ate away at its credibility with the public.

And in the meantime, the press wasn't telling people what the candidates stood for. When the candidates spoke to the party chairmen in Chicago, for instance, the *New York Times* and Washington *Post* did not offer any outline of what they had said. It merely used the occasion to frame who was ahead or behind.

One other factor also influenced the process. Clinton's candidacy was aided by a clique among newspaper and magazine reporters who not only liked Clinton personally but had an affinity for him ideologically.

Few reporters believe in objectivity—the idea that a journalist is neutral. They strive, rather, to be fair, to have their biases and affinities overmatched by the responsibility to tell all sides, by the pull of a good story, by being true to the facts.

But by 1992 the press's devotion to fairness was giving way to something else. Journalism was becoming more subjective, and, in politics, the distance between journalists and intellectuals involved in reshaping the Democratic party had narrowed.

The shift had begun in the 1970s when American newspapers had quietly moved from being a medium for the masses to a medium for the elite. Most large metropolitan newspapers, such as the Chicago *Tribune*, Boston *Globe* or Los Angeles *Times*, only reached about a quarter of the households in their regions, usually the most affluent. Only 10 percent of the households in the New

York metropolitan area bought the *New York Times*. Newspapers became more analytical, since the networks were providing the headlines. And newspaper reporting became less influential.

Then, as the speed of information accelerated in the age of twenty-four-hour news and cable channels, newspapers found themselves challenged even further. Information was becoming the cheapest currency of all. By the time the morning newspaper arrived, some people had heard the story several times, or maybe seen it happen live on C-Span or CNN. Old-fashioned gathering of information was becoming a skill less valued, and newspaper reporters were turning to other outlets for recognition.

Plenty of people still made their name digging for news—Ed Pound of the *Wall Street Journal*, Ronald Ostrow and Doug Frantz of the Los Angeles *Times*, Charlie Babcock and Mike Isikoff at the Washington *Post*, David Johnston and David Rosenbaum at the *New York Times*, to name just a few.

But many top print reporters, particularly in Washington, had moved from being purveyors of information to plying a different craft. Some made their biggest reputation by being TV pontificators—staking out provocative positions and doling out advice on TV talk shows. Others did it by writing essay-like features, more personal than even straight analysis stories, which were now being played on page one.

And some of the best print reporters in Washington increasingly turned for fulfillment to writing books aimed at shaping policy. In 1992, many of the ideas that would influence the political debate came from their work. And the line between policy analyst and reporter inevitably blurred. Bill Clinton, in particular, cited in speeches the work of the Washington *Post*'s E.J. Dionne. The candidate referred to Dionne as "my friend." Clinton similarly cited a book by *Post* writer Thomas Edsall, who with his wife had written a powerful book about race.

Dionne himself hoped that readers distinguished between what he hoped was his neutral daily journalism and his subjective books. "The one beauty of our business is there is total truth in packaging because everything we write is in public." And Dionne's writing was fair and perceptive.

Still, Clinton in private sought Dionne's advice, as he did many other members of what his staff called "the new breed" of journalists. Dionne, according to Clinton aides, was loath to give it. With others, though, the line between gathering information and sharing it was difficult to discern, and Clinton exploited that.

Another of those accused by colleagues of being close to Clinton was Joe Klein of *New York*, who later moved to *Newsweek* and became a political analyst for CBS. A squat man with a long dark beard and permanently rumpled look, Klein was one of the most eloquent and provocative political writers in the country. His clear prose harshly criticized what he perceived as the failure of Johnson's "Great Society" liberalism.

As the race in New Hampshire began to take shape during the second week of January, Klein profiled Clinton in a *New York* cover story. He was the first candidate to be granted this influential boost, and it came at a crucial time. Klein's feelings about Clinton were evident in his conclusion. Clinton was a rare politician, he wrote, who appeared to care about the deeper issues facing a troubled nation—black family disintegration, "the debilitating consequences of racial preference"—while "making clear that he stands for social justice." He was capable of "summoning a national altruism that was assassinated a quarter-century ago in Vietnam and the streets of our cities," and it was high time "some politician tried."

Was Klein being biased? The writer conceded he did see himself "as part of a group of intellectuals working to reshape policy." But Klein defended himself on the grounds that he was a columnist paid for his opinions. And he said candidates in both parties had borrowed from his ideas, including Clinton, and "that doesn't mean I have become anyone's advocate."

Klein also did keep some distance. By summer, he had written pieces that had bedeviled and angered Clinton. By fall, he was openly contemptuous in print and in private that Clinton had abandoned his big ideas and calls for personal sacrifice.

But Klein and Clinton also talked regularly, and Clinton usually asked his advice. "These were not so much interviews as policy discussions," one Clinton aide said.

Amid the criticism directed at him, Klein also saw something he considered more serious than blurring the lines between columnist and insider. Somewhere along the way the press shifted from a natural skepticism to a strange cynicism. He was praised if he called Clinton too clever, but he was accused of being in the tank if he lauded Clinton's education proposals. The press, he said rightly, had to be able to "write positive things, to acknowledge that these are serious people engaged in something important."

Clinton also tried to cultivate Michael Kramer at *Time*, Clinton aides said. Kramer is billed as a columnist, but he has strong influence at the magazine. Kramer lobbied for Clinton to be on *Time*'s cover in January, *Time* staffers said, and following the New Hampshire primary, Kramer wrote an analysis of Paul Tsongas's and Clinton's economic programs that within three days became the basis of a Clinton advertisement entitled "Time." Part of Kramer's analysis—that Tsongas was advocating building hundreds of new nuclear power plants—was something he had inferred. Tsongas never advocated this. Yet that inference also played a pivotal role in costing Tsongas the Colorado primary.

Kramer defended the invisible primary. "We are paid as professionals to make some judgments," he said, to inform voters of a candidate's strengths, not simply record words. But it is a matter of reporting, he said, not personal or ideological affinity.

At the Los Angeles *Times*, reporter Ronald Brownstein worried that he "was on the fringes" of the Clinton clique. As with the others, Brownstein stood out as a reporter who wrote seriously about political ideas, not just technique. He liked to place candidates' positions in the context of their ideological history as well as talk about their political advantages. Yet as he did so, he felt himself being drawn into what he called "the invisible circle" of complicity.

He could sense Clinton and his advisers' reactions. "You are a little bit ahead of them, and they start incorporating what you write into their thinking." At times Clinton would call him at home at night to pursue some idea, a habit that seemed sincere but nonetheless flattering and seductive.

No one, however, wrote about Clinton with more enthusiasm than Sidney Blumenthal of *The New Republic*. Bill and Hillary Clinton, Blumenthal wrote in a particularly fervent cover story the last week of January, were in the center of the "Conversation" among intellectuals to rethink liberalism. In Blumenthal's mind, the Conversation was a heroic endeavor that placed "why one should get elected" above personal ambition. Clinton's nomination might "solidify an epochal change." Reaganism was about the end of policy. "Clinton is about the renaissance of policy, informed by the Reagan years but clearly moving away from them."

Clinton aides were using Blumenthal, making him feel like an insider. "He was thought of as something of a liberal, and we needed support from that part of the party," one senior Clinton aide said.

The press has fallen in love with candidates before—Bruce Babbitt in 1988, for instance. Babbitt's political liabilities overwhelmed even the press's adoration, offering proof that the media's influence has its limits.

But the problem for the new breed of analyst/journalist/insider is not the degree of their influence. The problem is that readers can't distinguish what role is being played. Although their power may be limited, the media still should not play kingmaker. By doing so they risk their credibility, the only quality of value the press possesses.

The invisible anointment of Clinton in the media preprimary had also taken place entirely in print, revealing another misconception about politics. In these early stages of presidential campaigns, the network nightly news programs were largely irrelevant. Print was dominant, the low-rated Sunday talk shows were important, and in New Hampshire the process was driven by the local press, which took its cue from the major papers.

And that trend was almost certain to grow, as the networks cut their investment in political coverage. The more reporters a news organization sends out on a story, the more stories it will come back with, regardless of the news value.

The press did not control this alone, however. No one factor controlled anything in politics. That was why Paul Tsongas still had a chance.

Sad-eyed, underfunded, and laughed at by reporters in Washington and New York, the former Massachusetts senator had been a rising star of the Democratic party a decade ago, one of the first politicians to call for the change in direction of the Democratic party in his 1980 book, *The Road from Here*, before Ronald Reagan, before Gary Hart, before Bill Clinton. For his return to politics in 1992, after battling cancer, Tsongas was campaigning by the oldest techniques in the book. He had hired a state organizer who plastered the state with banners and house signs, and worked the suddenly more diversified local press.

And he had a message—that the problems of New Hampshire were too serious for the kind of promise-everything-politics of the past, or the antibusiness view of the traditional Democratic party. In his own way, Tsongas used the press as well. Campaign manager Dennis Kanin found out when major newspapers would be conducting opinion polls, and timed the first Tsongas commercial in December to air just before them to influence the results. The trick pushed him into an early tie for first place. But Tsongas's lead looked shaky. He had been campaigning there longer than anyone, and even New Hampshire voters were telling reporters they doubted he could win in November, the same message they were hearing in the press.

In their focus groups, Clinton campaign advisers like pollster Stan Greenberg, media adviser Frank Greer, and strategists Paul Begala and James Carville could see Tsongas's message was striking a chord in the state, and part of what they did was imitate him.

First, they molded Clinton's message into a booklet, like one

Tsongas had produced six months earlier, and beefed it up by adding his Georgetown speeches in the back. They also decided to look like a nontraditional by beginning their ad campaign with something other than a conventional biographical ad. They began instead with a sixty-second commercial promoting Clinton's plan to fix the economy, and made the plan available through an 800 number or local libraries. Over the next six weeks, 18,000 people called for the plan. Although the press had tried to anoint Clinton, it was this ad begun on January 6, that catapulted his campaign. Within a week of the ad going on the air, Clinton jumped from 16 percent and fourth place to 33 percent and a clear lead.

The people of New Hampshire were paying astonishingly close attention, the questions were remarkably sophisticated, and Clinton in particular handled them well. Wooten watched in Concord one day as the governor, when asked what he would do to improve education, said he saw four necessary steps and ticked off three of them. The next question from the audience asked him not to forget to mention his fourth solution.

Jeff Greenfield, the *Nightline* correspondent, author, attorney, and former Kennedy speechwriter, was working on a story about young people's perceptions of what the Democratic party was. And he sensed far less pessimism about the process than he had in years.

On January 20, WMUR held a debate, and for the entire two hours, the proceedings were watched by an extraordinary 140,000 people in the state. As Greenfield watched the debate in the press filing center in an empty warehouse below the WMUR studios, he kept commenting, "I think this is really an excellent debate. Really substantive." All this detailed policy discussion was difficult for the press to fit into stories, however. Watching in his hotel room, Los Angeles *Times* correspondent Bob Shogan at one point even shook his fist at the screen during the debate and yelled "Less substance damnit. More fireworks."

In the three days after the debate, Bob Kerrey's pollster, Harrison Hickman, conducted his first major survey of the race.

By Wednesday afternoon, Kerrey adviser Michael D. McCurry saw time running out for Kerrey and everyone else.

"You can't print this until the campaign is over," McCurry told a reporter Wednesday, January 22. "But Clinton is running away with it. I mean like twenty points ahead." Unless some candidate decided to take him out with a scorched-earth attack, "this whole campaign could be over two weeks before people ever vote."

That afternoon, Wooten arrived from Washington to do his profile of Clinton the front-runner.

Within twenty-four hours, everything changed.

Wooten arrived about 2 P.M. the next afternoon at the American Brush Company in Claremont, New Hampshire. He was looking for B-roll, background footage, of Clinton meeting voters, "Just some gripping and grinning," Wooten called it, and maybe a quick interview.

With him was his producer, Michael Bicks, an MIT graduate in economics who became a TV producer because it was more fun. "Correspondents don't know anything," Bicks had explained from the front of their rental Taurus as Wooten drove. "Correspondents are meat puppets." Just good-looking beef who performed what their producers told them, Bicks joked. "Michael is my producer shit," Wooten explained.

Wooten knew Clinton vaguely. He had sought out the young governor a few years earlier, having heard the Arkansas reformer was an interesting man, which Wooten thought many politicians were not. He had found Clinton extraordinarily bright and a hard worker, but as of a year ago he didn't consider him among the top Democratic prospects for president, and he had heard considerable talk that Clinton had affairs with women. It was mostly gossip among reporters, but there was a lot of smoke.

Clinton was late, and in a company dining room stocked for reporters with cider, cookies, and coffee, Wooten found a pay phone to call the Rim. Something had happened, Friedman said. A supermarket tabloid called *The Star* was publishing a story next Monday in which a sometime cabaret singer and state government employee named Gennifer Flowers claimed that she had an affair with Clinton for twelve years. ABC had an advance copy of it. Significantly, an ABC producer had also shared the story with the Clinton press corps.

Wooten and Friedman agreed the Flowers story had two elements that made it something they at least had to evaluate. Flowers was not a secondhand witness, but the woman in question. Second, the *Star* said it had tapes of Flowers and Clinton talking on the phone about the allegations, Clinton assuring her not to worry because no one had any proof. Unsubstantiated rumors about Clinton had been circulating about him for years. When Clinton gets here, I'll confront him, Wooten agreed.

For as long as there had been presidential campaigns, someone had to decide who was allowed to run and who wasn't. The job used to be handled by party officials behind closed doors. After the party reforms of the 1970s, and the elevation of presidential selection through public primaries, vetting candidates had to be somehow handled in public, which meant via the press.

The problem was that the press no longer knew how to distinguish private from public. It probed for virtually any information it could find and then purported to let the public decide what is relevant and what is not—as if the act of reporting has no consequences on its own.

When he reached the tiny vestibule, Wooten saw a group of young Clinton volunteers waiting for their candidate. A feeling of helplessness and sadness swept over him. Five years before, twenty miles away, in a town called Lebanon, he had seen another group of young volunteers watch Gary Hart fly away in a small plane through the fog, amid allegations of marital infidelity, his political career in ruins. The real victims here today, Wooten thought, would be these kids. The idealists. They were the ones who came to this state every four years and made politics seem worthy.

What was about to happen had a lot to do with the Gary Hart story. Before Hart, the unspoken consensus among journalists was that a public figure's private life was relevant only if it intruded on public conduct. This was the more subtle side of pack journalism. The press operated by rough rules of consensus, rules not so much taught as enforced by practice and hardscrabble editors. Those lines were once clear. When Ohio Congressman Wayne Hays in the 1970s hired a secretary for something other than her typing, that became a story because she was on the public payroll—not because he cheated on his wife. The lines were pushed after Vietnam and Watergate, when politicians were more easily suspected of lying and corruption. They were pushed by television, where asking a question on camera itself made news.

But what happened to Gary Hart drew a new line. The Miami *Herald* had followed a woman to Washington to catch Hart cheating on his wife. Now private conduct inferred something about what was loosely called presidential character. Committing adultery during a campaign was a sign of recklessness, perhaps a desire for self-destruction.

One reporter had taken it even further. During a televised press conference, the Washington *Post*'s Paul Taylor asked if Hart had ever committed adultery. In doing so, especially on camera, Taylor made adultery per se an issue. It was not necessarily disqualifying, the question implied, but people deserved to know.

In the four years since, while the press dithered about the propriety of the story, Taylor's radical view became the unspoken standard of American journalism. It was not uncommon for local reporters now to ask politicians Taylor's adultery question. It had already happened to Clinton the week before on the local New Hampshire TV station, WMUR. Afterwards, the Washington *Post* wrote about the media wrestling with the adultery issue. The Los Angeles *Times* wrote about the allegations, it claimed, to note the charges were unsubstantiated. All this was enough for ABC's Cokie Roberts to raise the adultery charges later in the week in the televised debate on WMUR. That in turn prompted more coverage. The Los Angeles *Times* even made it the lead of its debate story.

It was a textbook illustration of how the media worked. This faint buzz of coverage gave the allegations of infidelity enough weight that reporters saw them as a potential political liability for Clinton—even though they had no substantiation. And this buzz, largely unknown to the public, made possible what was about to happen.

When Clinton entered the vestibule of the American Brush Company, Wooten's camera was sixteen inches from his face. The vestibule was the size of a foyer of a large home, about 8 × 8, and it was packed with more than thirty reporters. "It was the worst gang bang I had ever seen," thought Mark Halperin, the twenty-seven-year-old off-air producer ABC had assigned to travel with Clinton. Yet it was here that Clinton first would respond to the Flowers allegations.

Wooten began. A woman named Gennifer Flowers was alleging that "she had a longstanding affair with you," he told Clinton. "And she says she tape-recorded telephone conversations with you in which you told her to deny you had ever had an affair."

"Well first of all, I read the story," Clinton said. "It isn't true. She has obviously taken money to change the story, a story she felt so strongly about that she hired a lawyer to protect her good name not very long ago. She did call me. I never initiated any calls to her. And whenever she called me she basically wanted reassurances. Like a lot of people do when they have to face this and they aren't used to it. And I told her over and over, just tell the truth. Tell the truth."

Clinton seemed so calm, Wooten thought, as if he had been preparing for this moment for years.

"When did you call her?" another reporter asked.

"I don't remember," Clinton said, "but whenever it was, she always called—"

"Was it in the last week?" someone asked.

"No. She called my secretary in the last week. She would always call my secretary—"

"Did you tell her this could cost you the nomination?" another reporter asked.

The next question came before Clinton answered. It went on, chaotically. Most of his answers were interrupted by other questions.

"Do you think you can persuade people you are innocent? Will people be able to believe you?"

"I don't know if I can," Clinton answered. "The other charges I have been able to actually affirmatively disprove. I don't know if you can disprove this. All I can tell you is we have a letter from her lawyer that she sent protesting her innocence to a local media outlet. . . . And she's admitted taking money to change her story. So it isn't a true story. I've read the article. It's not true. And—"

"But did you have these conversations with her but the meanings are distorted?"

"Absolutely," Clinton said. "The meaning is distorted. She called me. I never called her—"

The whole thing lasted about seven minutes. Then Clinton and his aides fled to a room upstairs to hide and evaluate what to do.

In the car, with Bicks driving the hour and a half back to Manchester through heavy snow, Wooten called Friedman on a cellular phone. He would try writing a script in the car, he said, but he didn't think they had enough substantiated material for a story. Not tonight. But the story would not hold for long. Too many cameras were there. And there was just enough that was true—the existence of the tape for one.

In New York, Friedman, Jennings, and the others around the Rim had been hashing out the horrible story all afternoon. Friedman mostly listened, as usual, but it was clear he thought they shouldn't touch it. Jennings agreed, but he also felt helpless. He thought the story was unsubstantiated. And, somewhat angrily, he could see again the potential of being trapped into doing something if everyone else was. On the other hand, he said, if everyone else does do something, "we can't ignore this without looking pretentious."

"Here we go again," thought Nancy Gabriner, the producer who had as much influence with Jennings about politics as anyone. "Let's not do this," she argued. "Why are we being trapped by the *Star?*"

Jeff Greenfield made the argument for running the story. If there are millions of Americans for whom adultery is a disqualifying flaw, what is the press's responsibility, he asked? What information are voters entitled to know? If he were a deeply religious person, he said, someone who is bothered by adultery, he would want to know if this man cheats on his wife. "This is a mortal sin. For Catholics it's the sixth commandment." And in a lot of ways, he argued, Clinton had already conceded the issue. Months ago Clinton and his wife had told reporters they had problems in their marriage, that the candidate, as he had put it, was "not perfect."

Greenfield's arguments yielded a familiar set of responses. So only men who would never cheat on their wives can be president? How do we know this will really disqualify him? Maybe, just as Americans came to accept other political taboos—a Catholic Kennedy and a divorced Ronald Reagan—they would accept a wife cheater.

No one knew what was right. There were no rules anymore. Each case struck them as different. But Friedman and Jennings had agreed this time to say no. They would not air this.

Finally, the two of them went up to the fifth floor to talk to Arledge in his office. Jennings showed him a copy of the *Star* story and argued against their going with it. "We don't go with stories that are not substantiated," Jennings lobbied. Arledge agreed.

"You've got guts," Greenfield told Friedman. "I'm not sure you're right, but you've got guts."

The scene was similar at the other networks. The executive

producer of the CBS evening news, Erik Sorenson, took one look at the *Star* and threw it in the trash. "This is what I think of the story," he told senior producer Brian Healy. Sometime later, Sorenson fished the story out of the garbage. At NBC, the absence of network correspondents and cameras in the field showed. Relying on a local affiliate to provide footage, Steve Friedman, the executive producer at *NBC Nightly News,* did not see a clean video feed of what Clinton had said until about 6:50 P.M., ten minutes before the network's broadcast was ending. Since the network was profiling Clinton that night, Brokaw, working off the Associated Press account, mentioned the flap in his introduction. The network newscasts that night had all said no to the Flowers story.

But that decision began to break down almost immediately. At the Washington *Post,* editors had much less hesitation. A major reason was that Clinton had answered reporters' questions about Flowers. "My sense is that the key event was his ready willingness to discuss it himself, which is sort of a copout answer," Robert Kaiser, the managing editor of the *Post,* said a few days after the incident. "I am not sure that had he refused to talk about it, we would have refused to write about it. But his willingness to talk about it made it easy."

There is an obvious circularity to this. Reporters raise the issue by asking questions, and then say it is news because the candidate answered.

That answer is especially troubling given the crass nature of the scene in the brush factory. Had Clinton not answered questions in that tiny room, would he have had any other option but to flee? Hypothetically, he could have refused to answer, but even Kaiser admits the *Post* might have written the story anyway. Knowing that, Clinton might have looked worse not answering.

The Los Angeles *Times* ran the story, too, and editors argued a key reason was that the story had been circulating for some time. And some people in the media simply waited to see what others did. *USA Today* called the Los Angeles *Times* to find out if it would run the story the next day. *Wall Street Journal* Washington bureau chief Al Hunt said he wanted to see if the networks and the Associated Press ran the story before deciding how the *Journal* would react.

What happened next revealed how the great journalistic institutions had lost power. While the three networks' evening newscasts refused the Flowers story, most of the local news stations around the country ran hard with it on the 11 o'clock news—including those owned by the networks. Watching the NBC-owned New York affiliate at home that night, NBC political director Bill Wheatley winced. They couldn't keep the lid on this garbage can.

Before 1980, the networks still had a hand on the lid. Back then, the networks controlled all the pictures of national news their crews shot and would not distribute them unless they had first appeared on their newscasts. The arrival of CNN in 1980 dramatically altered the nature of news in America. To make a profit, the cable network began selling its pictures to local stations worldwide, and to keep its affiliates happy the networks gradually had begun to do the same. With that, the networks lost their oligopoly over national news, and their ability to set journalistic standards.

Then, in the late 1980s, the values of entertainment and news began to mix into "infotainment" and "reality programming" in shows like *A Current Affair, Geraldo,* and *Cops.* These shows reflected a change in culture, certainly, but also a change in technology. They grew with the expansion in the number of independent TV stations and the rise of syndicated programming. As the spectrum of media expanded, the main media institutions began to lose audience share. In response, the editors and producers in charge of the establishment press felt compelled to react. If it was on *Hard Copy* it might make it on the local news, and if it got on there, it became difficult for the networks and the morning papers to ignore. In effect, the Flowers story was the most powerful demonstration yet of what amounted to a tabloidization of the press in general.

The most telling facet of the Flowers story was the degree to which by 1992 the elite national press felt it had no choice but to allow the supermarket tabloid to set its agenda. Even at the *MacNeil/Lehrer Newshour* on PBS, anchorman Jim Lehrer told his troops Friday afternoon they had to cover the story that a day earlier he had denounced. "It is out of my hands."

It was a form of Gresham's law: When the number of journalistic outlets has so proliferated and each has access to the same information, the bad journalism drives out the good. Since technology and economics have democratized the information flow, the media are now only as good as the worst member of the press.

With a strange passivity, journalists sense that they do not control what they put on their broadcasts or in their newspapers.

Greenfield put it aptly, "There are no gatekeepers anymore."

The one paper that tried to resist was denounced for it. The *New York Times* tried to deal with the Flowers story over the next several days by writing brief factual accounts, placed below small headlines at the bottom of its political page. "We don't want to stick our heads in the sand about anything, reliable or unverifiable," *Times* executive editor Max Frankel explained a few days after the Flowers story broke. "But in the only language we have, where we play a story, how big we play it, we are telling the reader what we think of this stuff and whether we can vouch for it or not."

Sadly, even many *Times* reporters criticized the paper for not running the story in the same detail as the competition. The criticism was misplaced. The compulsion in the press to match the competition on every story had become mindless.

At ABC, only five hours after Friedman resisted, the Flowers story broke on the air. There were two other ABC News shows on that night, *PrimeTime Live* and *Nightline*, and under Arledge they each operated independently. "You do what you think protects your broadcast best," Jennings said.

At *Nightline*, anchor Ted Koppel and executive producer Tom Bettag had already called Clinton headquarters in Little Rock inviting Clinton to appear and answer the charges. And they were told he was considering it.

At *PrimeTime Live*, executive producer Richard N. Kaplan had a more complicated situation. Kaplan had been a friend of Clinton's for more than a decade. "There is no way to avoid relationships with politicians," Kaplan explained later. "I knew that he was not 'Slick Willie' and not a scourge and really a terrific, terrific person."

When the Flowers story broke, Kaplan called Clinton adviser Susan Thomases, a mutual friend. "Bill has to come out and do something about this," he told her. Why not his show, *PrimeTime Live*. Since it was live, the candidate would have some control. And they should have Hillary on, too, he told Thomases, appearing alongside her husband. Kaplan received a tentative yes. But don't start promoting it, he was told.

These private negotiations, in their own way, invisibly altered how the Flowers story played out.

Soon Clinton called Kaplan for advice from upstairs at the brush factory. "I am really torn. You know her story isn't true," an obviously frightened Clinton said. "But I don't want to get into a situation of 'no not this one but another one.' "

Clinton was also getting conflicting advice about what to do from his own staff. James Carville was arguing they should confront the story before it took on a life of its own. Frank Greer in Washington was arguing that they should stick to the schedule, another event that night in New Hampshire. This was a fundamental rule of the Clinton campaign. Always stick to the schedule or the media would think the campaign in crisis. Managing perceptions, particularly the media's, was a cardinal principle in the magic craft of creating impressions for the public.

Before long, George Stephanopoulos in the brush factory was on one phone talking to Koppel of *Nightline* while Clinton was on another with Kaplan of *PrimeTime* weighing competing offers to appear that night on ABC.

"Do the toughest interview you can," Kaplan advised Clinton. "If you want to prove your credibility, you don't want to do it on *Good Morning America* or the *Today Show*. And you won't get the ratings in the morning. You have to go for the largest audience."

On the other line, Stephanopoulos was telling Koppel that Clinton would consider *Nightline* on two conditions: that he appear on the same set with Koppel—not isolated in some remote studio able to hear but not see—and that Hillary Clinton appear on the set as well. Koppel agreed.

When Koppel hung up, he turned to his staff and said, "The price of poker has just gone up." The story was no longer a question of what was in the tabloid, he argued. The story now had enough substance Clinton felt he couldn't sidestep it anymore.

Compared with most in the press, Koppel's view of the adultery question was clear. Some percentage of voters still felt adultery disqualified someone from the White House. That made it a story. What the media thought about it was irrelevant.

But whether this story had enough substantiation to go on the air with tonight was not yet clear. Koppel's view then changed about 7:15 P.M. when Clinton and his aides bolted from the brush factory and headed off in their van at breakneck speed through heavy snow. Like characters from a screwball comedy, the press corps still waiting in the brush factory foyer now followed, piling into their own vans and then chasing him. Clinton was heading toward Manchester, they could see. He was abandoning the next campaign event. Abandoning the sacred schedule. Maybe he was even going on the air that night. Mark Halperin, the ABC off-air producer with Clinton, called into ABC headquarters in New York and announced over ABC's internal intercom system that the candidate was headed to the Manchester airport—apparently to do *PrimeTime Live* or *Nightline*. Halperin was wrong. Clinton at that moment was on a cellular phone with Kaplan and he was nearly paralyzed by doubts. But no one else at ABC knew that. The fiefdoms were separate.

Halperin's call sealed Clinton's fate. Koppel and his producer Tom Bettag decided to devote *Nightline* to the Flowers story, and when they found out around 9:30 that they were wrong about Clinton appearing, they decided only to shift the focus slightly to the debate inside the media over whether this was a legitimate story.

In addition to Koppel's view of the pertinence of adultery, he and Bettag had two reasons for staying with the story. "He was going to discuss this, and whether he was going to do it that night or the next day, that made it a story," Bettag reasoned.

And Koppel liked *Nightline* to make news.

Friedman was incensed when he heard, especially when he discovered that Koppel was going at it sideways as a media story. He buttonholed Greenfield, who was doing the *Nightline* story. "I hear you're sneaking this through the backdoor," he said.

"Yeah, maybe," Greenfield acknowledged.

Thus the story had broken onto network television, on *Nightline* of all shows, and gained further momentum.

The night ended for Kaplan at 4 A.M. when Clinton called one last time. The candidate, Kaplan thought, was distraught. He was considering doing *60 Minutes*. If you do, Kaplan said, it should be with Mike Wallace or Morley Safer or Ed Bradley. Otherwise tell them forget it. People aren't going to be impressed that you went on *60 Minutes* with somebody whose name they couldn't recall. They are going to remember that you stood up to Mike Wallace. It was advice Clinton ignored.

"That was why," Kaplan would say later, "the *60 Minutes* interview was a failure. It wasn't a good interview, and it didn't do for him what he wanted."

Later, Clinton's aides would say they should have seized more control of the *60 Minutes* interview by agreeing to talk for only as long as the interview would air, thereby eliminating the show's ability to edit it. They were wrong. Clinton's mistake on *60 Min-*

utes was that he tried to admit to adultery without clearly admitting it. He had "caused pain" in his marriage, he said. "If the standard is perfection, I can't meet it," but Gennifer Flowers's story was not true. That slight tremble would haunt him.

60 Minutes executive producer Don Hewitt had his own agenda. Twice during the taping he kneeled by Clinton and exhorted the candidate to admit to adultery. He had helped make a president in 1960 as producer of the Nixon-Kennedy debates, he said. He could do it again now. People would love the candor, he was suggesting. They could create a president here, he said.

By the time Clinton did *60 Minutes*, the press felt relieved of any responsibility for judging the story. The next day, the morning shows reverberated with the *60 Minutes* story and reaction. That afternoon, Flowers held her press conference, which CNN carried live. That night, the networks led with the story, twinning *60 Minutes* and Flowers's response that Clinton was lying.

In retrospect, the press has fallen through an intellectual trapdoor on private character. Once entering, it cannot get back out. Since journalists feel unable or unwilling to judge for themselves what areas of inquiry are legitimate, they publish material they consider improper on the grounds that this information will shape the outcome of the race. Gennifer Flowers was a story not because it was true—that was not established—but because it had become a political liability for Clinton. Six months later, the same criteria was used to publish even less substantiated rumors about George Bush.

The root problem is this: The press has so oriented coverage around predicting who will win in politics that anything which might influence the outcome is relevant—whether or not it helped voters decide who would be the best president. In this way the political press have begun to lose touch with their readers, to become too focused on strategy and minutiae rather than the policy basics that move voters. This is also why rumors, innuendo, and gossip all become stories now—but not until they gain momentum in the least responsible press first.

What now is the press to do, especially in an environment in which the whole culture has undergone tabloidization, in which a paper that ignores a story is accused of being self-indulgent? Where does the press now draw the line of privacy?

The media have two choices. The first, the favorite of press critics and academics, is to return to the previous standard, that private conduct is relevant only when it demonstrably influences performance in public office. This would cut off discussion of most types of sexual behavior and private morality. Unfortunately, turning back is probably impossible. In the era of tabloidization and diverse information systems, the mainstream press simply lacks the power to impose that standard anymore. Also, the culture has changed enough that voters do demand more intimate information about candidates than they did before. The genie on this issue is out of the bottle.

The other choice is for the press to take Koppel's view and publish everything without hesitation—including questions of adultery—but in a different context than it currently does. This approach has two virtues. By publishing this information first, rather than waiting for the tabloids to develop it to a point of political harm, the mainstream press would have to take more responsibility for what it airs. And by treating subjects like adultery more matter-of-factly, the press might help move the culture to a point where voters can deal with these questions in a reasonable way. As it is, however, by letting the tabloids set the agenda, the mainstream press are merely hypocritical. They ignore stories they consider illegitimate or unsubstantiated. But only until they appear somewhere else first. The standard is simply dishonest.

If politicians knew they were going to be pressed, however, they would have to become more matter-of-fact about discussing these concerns. They would know that Clinton's subtle dissemble on Gennifer Flowers was not enough. And they would know the public can be trusted with the truth.

Over the next few days, tracking polls in New Hampshire suggested that the majority of people—eight out of ten in an ABC poll—thought the press had no business poking into Clinton's private conduct and had heard enough about it. Only 11 percent thought the information relevant. To the amazement of some in the press corps, Clinton's support actually rose.

At ABC, Cokie Roberts thought most people were misreading the polls. Even if adultery would offend only 15 percent of the population, that meant you were now trying to win an election by contending for only 85 percent of the vote. Clinton was damaged goods. He was flawed. He might survive and win the nomination. But he probably could not win in November, she figured.

Such calculations hold subtle sway over the media. The press, in a sense, is engaged in a continuing three-way conversation, between its sources, its audience, and itself. If any of the participants no longer seem interested—if, for instance, the press writes about something but experts consider it insignificant, the story will soon die. If the press believes people no longer want to hear about a story, or that its coverage has gotten too far ahead of its audience, it similarly tends to stop. When polls suggested the majority of people did not consider the Flowers story a decisive factor in their vote, the press backed off.

But something lingered. The story felt unresolved.

Most in the press, including many at ABC, believed that Clinton had been dishonest about the Flowers affair. At NBC, one correspondent watched the Flowers press conference and sent anchorman Tom Brokaw a message. "Clinton lied," it said. Watching the Flowers press conference at WMUR, Wooten and Bicks thought Flowers seemed credible. "Maybe not twelve years. But twelve minutes," someone said. Or at least credible enough. "He did her," said Ronald Brownstein of the Los Angeles *Times*.

What they were engaged in was a form of literalism that is common among journalists. While Clinton had acknowledged problems in his marriage, he had equivocated about Gennifer Flowers.

This, in the end, was the larger ironic meaning of the Flowers story. It depicted Clinton as dishonest, not because he cheated on his wife, but because he agreed to talk about it but then didn't really do so.

Nothing ever really ends in the press, not until all sides have exhausted the topic. If the Flowers story was unresolved, journalists would find another way of getting at it.

The call came a week later. The affiliate service forwarded it to Tory Smith on ABC's national desk in the room called the Bubble, the one viewers saw over Jennings's shoulder on the news. She didn't want her name used, she said. But she had something they might want to know about Bill Clinton.

The previous morning, the *Wall Street Journal* had published an account of how Clinton had survived the Vietnam-era draft without serving in the military. Others had covered the ground before, but the *Journal* story, by Jeffrey Birnbaum, quoted Col. Eugene Holmes, then head of the Army ROTC recruiting office at the University of Arkansas in Fayetteville. Holmes said he thought Clinton had managed in 1969 "to manipulate things so that he didn't have to go in." Holmes had never said this before. He'd always said there was no problem. And this was after that Gennifer Flowers mess.

On the stump the day of the *Journal* story, Clinton was barraged with questions, and every major paper would do a story, using the same syllogism as in Gennifer Flowers: While the truth of the allegations was unclear, it was news because it was affecting his campaign. Television was not so involved, again. NBC and CBS would not touch the story that night, and on the Rim at ABC, too, many wanted to let it pass. It smelled of a leak, perhaps by Republicans, at a time when Clinton was vulnerable.

But Friedman disagreed. The Gennifer Flowers story was

garbage, but this was not. "Now look, we climbed all over this fella named Dan Quayle because of the draft thing," he yelled. "We have to look at this as hard as we did that." So that night ABC was the only network to do a piece about the draft controversy, and the result was significant.

The caller said she had seen the ABC story, and it jarred loose a memory. The caller had worked for the ROTC in the 1960s, and when Clinton pulled himself out of the program in 1969, he had written a letter to Col. Holmes at the ROTC, the caller said, a disturbing letter. In fact the caller had kept a copy of it for twenty-three years. The caller then read the letter, which was transcribed into the ABC computer.

Friedman was alerted, and soon producer David Peterkin from Atlanta had interviewed two people who had worked in the ROTC confirming that the letter was legitimate. As it turned out, one of the two, Clinton Jones, who had been No. 2 in the ROTC office, had kept a copy of the same letter to Holmes because he thought Clinton's evasion offensive.

What kind of person inspires such animosity in people, Friedman thought, that they would keep a letter for twenty-three years?

The letter was an astonishing document:

I am sorry to be so long in writing. I know I promised to let you hear from me at least once a month, and from now on you will. . . .

First I want to thank you, not just for saving me from the draft, but for being so kind and decent to me last summer, when I was as low as I have ever been. . . . Had you known a little more about me, about my political beliefs and activities . . . you might have thought me more fit for the draft than the ROTC. Let me try to explain. [When he had worked in Washington for two years, Clinton wrote, he] worked every day against a war I opposed and despised with a depth of feeling I had reserved solely for racism in America before Vietnam. . . .

Interlocked with the war is the draft issue, which I did not begin to consider separately until early 1968. . . . I came to believe that the draft system itself is illegitimate, [in part because the war] does not involve immediately the peace and freedom of the nation. . . .

The decision not to be a resister and the related subsequent decisions were the most difficult of my life. I decided to accept the draft
in spite of my beliefs for one reason: to maintain my political viability
within the system. For years I have worked to prepare myself for a
political life. . . . It is a life I still feel compelled to try and lead. I do
not think our system of government is by definition corrupt, however
dangerous and inadequate it has been in recent years. . . .

But the particulars of my personal life are not nearly as important
to me as the principles involved. After I signed the ROTC letter of
intent, I began to wonder whether the compromise I had made with
myself was not more objectionable than the draft would have been,
because I had no interest in the ROTC program in itself and all I
seemed to have done was protect myself from physical harm. . . . I am
writing [now] in the hope that my telling this one story will help you
to understand more clearly how so many fine people have come to find
themselves still loving their country but loathing the military.

Clinton was spending the weekend in Arkansas. The campaign had
conducted hastily arranged focus groups in Manchester on Friday
and found that people had liked Clinton's answer on the draft. As
a result, he and his aides decided that he had put the story behind
him and that it was safe to leave New Hampshire. They were
wrong. Over the weekend, half of Clinton's support in New Hampshire evaporated, from 33 percent to 17 percent, his private poll
showed. When Clinton returned to New Hampshire on Monday,
he believed Paul Tsongas was now ahead.

Jim Wooten and Michael Bicks of ABC were waiting at the
tiny suburban airport in the southern New Hampshire town of
Nashua when Clinton's small charter plane landed from Arkansas.
They confronted him with the draft letter, and in the cramped,
charmless waiting room, Clinton's composure astonished them
again. He seemed not to have seen this letter in twenty years, and
yet no emotion showed. Clinton read the letter and then retreated
into a tiny men's room, along with advisers Carville and Stephanopoulos, and a half hour later emerged agreeing to talk with
Wooten later in the day. Carville, a Cajun lawyer and former

marine, had argued they should take the offensive and release the letter to every newspaper in New Hampshire. "This letter is your best friend," he told Clinton.

On the Rim in New York, Friedman, Jennings, Bob Roy, Dennis Dunlavey, and Nancy Gabriner were debating whether the letter was friend or foe, as well.

One passage particularly bothered Jennings: Clinton's saying he was accepting the draft for one reason, to maintain his political viability within the system. Jennings thought the quotation unmasked a man, even at age twenty-three, astonishingly calculating.

Correspondent Jeff Greenfield argued the opposite. The reference to political viability within the system has to be looked at in the context of the whole document, Greenfield thought. And remember this was 1969. When Clinton said he wanted to maintain his viability within the system, he was saying he wanted to work within the system, not referring to his own ambition. In 1969 choosing to accept the viability of the system was a significant issue.

In his interview with Wooten that afternoon, Clinton interpreted the letter the same way Greenfield had. There was a lot Wooten was trying to discern. Why was the letter dated December 3, 1969, two days after the federal lottery was held, in which Clinton, with lottery number 311, escaped the draft? Had he known his lottery number when he wrote the letter? Clinton claimed not to have. And what made Clinton so sure he would be drafted? Had he received an induction notice? No, Clinton answered. That answer, Wooten would discover three months later, was a blatant falsehood.

Finally, Wooten asked everyone else to leave the room so he and Clinton could be alone—no cameras, no tapes, no handlers. They were both Southerners, and they knew each other as friends. Wooten was counting on that, on all those cues. He leaned close to the Arkansas governor and asked quietly, "What the hell is going on here?"

"Jim," Clinton said, "I promise you. There is nothing going on here. This is exactly what it looks like."

It didn't look like anything at all to Wooten, at least nothing that was clear. "Well there is so much happening," Wooten said, pointing to the letter. "It's really hard for me to figure out what's true, what's fantasy and what's politics."

Clinton looked at Wooten and bit his lower lip, and then he spoke to the reporter in the intimate way that only a Southern politician ever would, and only a Southern listener would understand.

"Jim, you've always been very fair to me," Clinton said, touching him. "And I've loved you for that."

As Clinton rose to leave, Wooten was overcome by one pure instinctual reaction:

Clinton was lying.

He told this to no one, not even Bicks. But they both agreed they were confused. There were too many discrepancies, which could help or hurt Clinton but needed to be resolved, he thought. Why, for instance, had Clinton said last week that he had reentered the draft because he didn't "feel right" having a deferment when friends from high school had died in the war; that played no part in his "one reason" mentioned in the letter. A week before, Clinton had said, "I put myself in the draft when I thought it was a 100 percent certainty that I would be called." If this letter had come as a shock to Clinton Jones and others at the ROTC office, when and how had Bill Clinton earlier removed his ROTC application? They needed to talk to the head of the ROTC office, Colonel Holmes.

In time, Wooten would come to suspect something even more serious, though over the next ten months he could never prove it: Clinton had never actually reentered the draft or withdrawn from the ROTC—at least not until the lottery had already saved him. Almost everything Clinton had said on the subject, Wooten feared, was a lie.

In New York, Friedman did not want to go with the story yet. Jennings was worried about ABC "piling on," thereby "manipulating the process." They also kept looking to see if the letter "altered the public record. . . . Did it contradict the truth as he had stated it before?" Not yet, at least not clearly. Another problem, Jennings and Friedman thought, was that the letter was simply too complicated for the nightly news. How much of this dense three-page letter would you have to put on the air to be fair, or for it even to make sense to viewers? It was hard television.

Wooten wanted to pursue Colonel Eugene Holmes, the recipient of the letter. His family said only that he had "gone fishing." As it turned out, he would remain silent for another seven months.

Within twenty-four hours, any chance of pursuing the letter further and perhaps clarifying Clinton's draft experience was destroyed—by competition within ABC.

The same day Wooten and Bicks had confronted Clinton with the letter, Ted Koppel had obtained another copy of the letter from a man named James Tully, a longtime Republican with business ties to Watergate conspirator and Nixon administration attorney general John N. Mitchell and IranContra conspirator and former air force Major General Richard Secord. Tully's closest friend was Jack Brennan, now an employee of the Bush White House.

While Wooten was interviewing Clinton in New Hampshire, Koppel was calling the Clinton campaign in Little Rock, inviting Clinton onto *Nightline* to discuss the letter. And during that conversation, Koppel indicated that his source for the letter had connections to the Pentagon.

Clinton refused *Nightline* in order to ponder his options. His campaign was in free fall. And he had now been contacted by two competing ABC news shows about the letter. James Carville was arguing Clinton had to go on the offensive. He should release the letter himself. And citing Koppel as the source, he said, Clinton should say the Pentagon had leaked it in order to destroy him. Clinton's candidacy hung in the balance, Carville said. He was that close to being politically dead.

After sleeping on it, Clinton agreed to release the letter. And after hearing Koppel repeat that the Pentagon may have had a role in the letter's release, he agreed to appear on *Nightline*.

The Clinton news conference was a classic. The candidate arrived, released the letter, blamed the Pentagon for trying to get him, and cited Koppel as his source. He was trying to get out in front of a story and put his own spin on it. It was an exercise in damage control. In the political wilderness, where handlers believe perception is reality, Clinton was trying to manage reality. By their clumsiness, ABC had allowed Clinton to steal their scoop and obscure the meaning of the story.

Afterwards, a furious Wooten called Friedman. *Nightline* must have stolen the letter from *World News*, he argued. How else could this have happened? Friedman agreed to conduct a discreet internal investigation.

Koppel and Bettag were meanwhile conducting their own investigation about where the letter had come from. Koppel had now become part of the news for partially identifying a source. What they learned, or at least what they told Friedman, was almost too strange to be made up.

When the ABC crew took its second copy of the letter—the one provided to it by Clinton Jones—to a nearby hotel in South Carolina to be photocopied, a hotel clerk had kept a copy and then faxed the letter to Tully, a friend whom the clerk knew was involved in Republican politics and had ties to the military. Tully in turn had given it to Richard Secord. And Secord had given it to *Nightline*.

Not everyone at ABC believed Koppel and the bizarre story of the hotel clerk and the fax machine. Whether Tully had ever contacted the Bush administration about the letter was never clear, and never pursued.

But all that was lost in the crush of events. In large part, television dispatched this story by labeling it another controversy surrounding Clinton. On NBC's WBZ-TV (Boston), for instance, the story ran under the logo NEW CLINTON CRISIS while the anchor failed badly at trying to describe the letter.

Later that evening, *Nightline* would prove a turning point in saving Bill Clinton as a viable political figure, a dramatic illustration of the occasional power of television to alter the course of politics. Koppel treated the letter thoughtfully but gingerly in a unique forty-five-minute program, which included a ten-minute segment with Koppel simply reading the whole letter aloud. In the era of trash television, nine-second soundbites and heavily subjective news, the *Nightline* program was extraordinary. It allowed viewers to hear and decide a complex issue for themselves.

As Clinton's key campaign aides watched the show in a makeshift office in the Days Hotel in Manchester, they felt their fate was in Ted Koppel's hands. They watched, powerless, their expressions ranging from ecstasy to fatalism. As Koppel described the letter and asked Clinton a few questions, Clinton aide Mark Gearan slumped on the sofa and said solemnly, almost whispering, "We could be watching the end here." After Koppel read the letter, James Carville leapt out of his seat, shot a fist into the air and turned to the others. "He was fucking great to us! We got no complaints!"

In the fragmented media environment that now existed, rarely do the nation and the press watch the same news at the same time. But with its then unchallenged 11:30 P.M. time slot and the freedom to try things no other show would, *Nightline* still had the potential to create that kind of singular coverage of an event. In this case, Koppel helped end the media feeding frenzy at just the moment when the press could have ended Clinton's candidacy.

No reliable figures are available to estimate how many New Hampshire residents watched *Nightline*, but the next day tracking polls there suggested that the slide in Clinton's support had stopped.

The press also reacted. On the stump the next day, Clinton

for the first time in two weeks was allowed to discuss what he wanted. When the *New York Times* followed with a story probing more deeply into the ROTC questions, some reporters even argued with Howell Raines, the paper's Washington bureau chief, that he was piling on.

Clinton's letter may simply have been too complex, and too ambiguous, to have any specific political meaning. Some accounts saw the letter as evidence of an impressive and thoughtful young man, like many in his generation, tortured by the war. Others saw the letter as a powerful example of the politician they called "Slick Willie" Clinton in the making, a boy too clever by half, overly concerned with his political future even then and trying to have things both ways, to dodge the draft without admitting it.

In the remaining days of the primary, Clinton tried to fight back by borrowing from Nixon's Checkers speech forty years earlier. He produced two thirty-minute TV shows in which he faced a live audience and viewer call-ins. Afterwards, pollster Stan Greenberg's polls showed Clinton support climbing back above 20 percent.

What was worst about all this is how little the press had told us about Clinton. What had been learned about the candidate or the future president? During the dark moments in New Hampshire, intimates described Clinton as a man lost, despondent, not angry. "I wondered about whether I had totally failed to see a part of myself I should have seen," Clinton would say later. The comment was revealing. Like many politicians, Bill Clinton is a man of unfinished and contradictory character—scholarly and shallow, outgoing and shy, principled and craven, the mood depending on the motive. He possesses extraordinary talent and a fierce thirst for knowledge and insight, but above all approval. One reporter who spent time with him shortly after the incidents in New Hampshire found him one of the most outwardly directed people she had ever met—as if he had little inner sense of self at all. He is also a man, friends would say afterwards, who is capable of deceiving himself. In the best profile written of him during the campaign, Clinton told David Shribman of the *Wall Street Journal* that character was "a quest." The choice of words was curiously apt. Character was something to be searched for. Something not held. But Clinton would learn from New Hampshire, as he would learn from its aftermath, and he would adapt.

The press would learn, too, but not about its own mistakes. The lesson it took from New Hampshire was that the draft story and Gennifer were not resolved. Wooten and other reporters thought too many questions were unanswered. Clinton had gotten away with lying, twice. "He should have just come clean and said, 'Like the majority of Americans in 1969 I opposed the war and did everything I could within the law not to die in it,' " *USA Today* reporter Adam Nagourney stated. In the end, the Gennifer and draft story blended into one incident, an example of a man who would not level with people, and perhaps with himself.

Not long after, Democratic National Committee strategist Paul Tully, who would later die of a heart attack working for Clinton in Little Rock, told Walter Robinson of the Boston *Globe:* "Clinton's biggest problem now is that 90 percent of the press corps think he is a liar."

★

CHAPTER

4

**NEW HAMPSHIRE
REPUBLICANS**

★

"What the hell are you doing here?" Brit Hume whispered.

Jack Heath just grinned.

Hume was taller than the young local news director and better at intimidation. He pulled Heath into ABC's soundproof office in the back of the White House press room and closed the door. "Tell me what is going on here?"

Every presidential campaign features some new strategy that later politicians call decisive. In 1976, Jimmy Carter had manipulated media perceptions about which candidate had momentum. In 1980 and 1984, Ronald Reagan had controlled the pictures voters saw. In 1988, George Bush had campaigned on values, something soft and unassailable and easy to communicate on television.

In 1992, many in the press thought bypass would be the winning theory: Candidates would use technology to avoid the national media and rely instead on local. The local guys were easier to manipulate. And they had altogether more audience.

Bypass, Friedman figured, threatened to diminish network television's relevance even further. And it would probably thwart the press's good intentions about doing things differently. "And I don't think we know what to do about it."

The master of bypass would of course be the Republican

White House. In the 1988 primary season, Bush had already used what he called "regional media" strategy. The Vice President's press conferences were open to reporters from local media only. A lone member of the national press corps was allowed in to take notes and distribute them to the other national reporters as part of a pool, but the reporter was forbidden from asking questions.

This year, the administration was planning on going even further. In the Old Executive Office Building next to the White House, Bush had already built a special TV studio to do satellite interviews. Then he hired Dorrance Smith, the former executive producer of *Nightline,* to manage the operation. While Ronald Reagan had Michael Deaver stage photo opportunities for the national press, George Bush had Dorrance Smith trying to set up interviews and teleconferences around the country that the national press did not even know were taking place.

By the time the New Hampshire primary had finished, the rest of the nation might have thought that George Bush made just three campaign trips to the state. The truth was he had campaigned more vigorously for reelection in New Hampshire than any incumbent president in history. But most of it was invisible— on drive-time radio shows, via teleconferences with business groups, in interviews with local television—much of it on the phone, or via satellite from Washington.

And it didn't work.

Instead, the invisible gears that drive politics—economics, ideology, and character—overwhelmed the theory right from the start.

The studios of WMUR-TV, the state's lone television network affiliate, now stood in one of the century-old red-brick textile mills along the Merrimack River in Manchester. Its blue call letters on the roof were visible from the interstate. The little ABC station was begun in 1954, but as New Hampshire had grown in the economic boom of the 1980s, so had WMUR's fortunes. By 1992,

WMUR, with its five half-hour newscasts each day, had become the most important conduit for news in the state. More state residents, over 80,000 people, watched its 6 P.M. news than all three newscasts of the neighboring Boston stations combined.

The station had eclipsed even the influence of the Manchester *Union Leader*, the flagrantly conservative local paper that had berated its way into American political mythology back when William Loeb was still alive and running things. In 1972, Loeb had attacked Edwin Muskie's wife as part of a Nixon White House dirty trick. The incident provoked Muskie into what looked to reporters like crying and helped end his dreams of being president. But Loeb had died in 1981, and New Hampshire's influx of new residents was not so conservative. The *Union Leader* had not noticeably helped a candidate win election since it championed Ronald Reagan in 1980. In 1988, it had backed former Delaware governor Pierre DuPont. He finished fourth.

By 1992, WMUR had thirty-two news employees and broadcast five half-hour newscasts each day. And some of the people who once saw small stations like this as places to start and then leave were staying. Jack Heath had been a reporter there who moved on to the Boston ABC affiliate, but he had come back to WMUR to become news director in 1990. "I'm thirty-one, and the most important thing to me is my wife and kids. And here I work till 6:30 and I'm home in ten minutes, and my life is better."

WMUR's quality under Heath careened between the competent and interesting to the earnest but meaningless. The stories were short, usually only a minute-thirty, but they covered everything, including the state economy. And Heath could rightly say, "We are less sensationalized than we were," less sensational than many big city stations.

WMUR was also not alone. There was cable Channel 60 delivering a newscast, plus an hour-long interview program, and the three network affiliates in Portland, Maine, and the three in Burlington, Vermont, and the three Boston stations. Rather than just the Manchester *Union Leader*, there was now the Nashua

Telegraph, the Concord *Monitor,* the Portsmouth *Herald,* the Laconia *Citizen.*

The theory behind bypass was simple. Politicians believed they could control their message more completely with local news outlets than national. Local reporters weren't necessarily dumber. But they were not steeped in the subject of national and international affairs. They also weren't used to talking to the President of the United States of America and leader of the free world, or his cabinet. And that made them easier to snowball.

Technology made bypass possible. With satellites, a candidate could sit in his office and campaign anywhere in the country. One needn't necessarily stage elaborate photo ops. Satellites made politics something that happened in the air rather than in physical space.

WMUR was the White House's first target, but it also proved to be where Friedman, Jennings, and Hume first glimpsed the depth of George Bush's ambivalence about his reelection campaign.

The first week in December, the White House called Heath to say it had decided to grant the station a months-old request for an interview with the President. In Washington, the pundits were saying the President was in a political free fall. Bush's popularity had dropped to 50 percent. Worse, conservative talk show commentator Patrick Buchanan had announced he would challenge the President in the New Hampshire primary. Suddenly, the audience of Heath's little station had become important.

For the next two days, Heath was besieged with calls from four different White House offices. For the two weeks after that, the White House tried to control every aspect of the interview. It first tried to make WMUR hold off airing the interviews till January. Bush would be in Japan, and airing the special reports that week would counter the image of a globetrotting President who neglected domestic policy. Chief of staff John Sununu called to make the request personally. Though flattered to receive a call from "a famous household name," Heath declined.

Then the White House tried to manipulate WMUR into giving the President more time on the air. It offered Heath more access than he had asked for. Then it told him to bring a second camera crew, which would have nearly doubled WMUR's cost. The greater Heath's expense, the more time he would likely devote to the project on the air to amortize his costs. We're setting up a whole day for you, a White House aide argued, with a photo op every hour, plus Mrs. Bush. Again Heath declined.

Finally, the White House called saying it was becoming displeased with Heath's attitude. The young news director, overwhelmed by the crush of political news at his tiny station, just snapped. "I am getting tired of hearing from six different people every other hour about this trip. All we want is ten minutes with the President, ten minutes with the First Lady, and we'll fly home. If you guys aren't interested, that's fine." And with that, Jack Heath of WMUR-TV hung up on the White House.

The next day, Bush's aides became more compliant, though they vainly attempted one last pass at control: to get WMUR to reveal its questions in advance.

When Heath, a cameraman, and another reporter arrived in Washington for "a day at the White House," something unexpected occurred. Heath's questions were not soft. And his inquiries had a certain authority coming from a New Hampshire local that they might have lacked coming from Sam Donaldson or Brit Hume. "Do you regret not coming out sooner and talking about the economy, because in New Hampshire there is a lot of hurt?" Heath began.

Reading from talking points in his lap, Bush ticked off his answers by number. "One, I know there is a lot of hurt. Two, I think you're right about the perception (that I have been late on the economy). Three . . . people in New Hampshire may not know that for the last three years I have presented in the State of the Union message a growth package to stimulate this economy."

Heath's second query was more of a statement from a local resident than a question. "If you had come out and talked about the economy a little more, maybe people in New Hampshire would feel a little better."

Bush answered as if he were reading jumbled cue cards. He invoked the Gulf War, then suggested the economic problems in New Hampshire were being exaggerated by the press. "In Desert Storm, we did what we had to do, got the job done. American people saw it ex post facto. Here, I have been concerned. We have been making proposal after proposal. But I'm the guy who has to share the blame for their not knowing that I know that they're hurting. I can't blame somebody else for that. But we get pounded every night in the media by the bad news." Bush concluded by referring to the pork barrel he was showering on the state. "I signed a good jobs bill that will mean $200 million to New Hampshire over the next couple years. That means jobs for New Hampshire. I hope that got through to the people there."

If anything, Barbara Bush's interview with reporter Karen Appel was even worse for the White House. When asked about condoms in schools, a major issue locally, the First Lady seemed lost.

"I'm too old to believe that's right," she began hesitantly.

When Appel asked about "parental consent for AIDS tests," another major local issue and something required in thirty-four states, the First Lady stared blankly at the camera. "Parental consent. Never even thought about that." Sensing that she might be coming off miserably, Mrs. Bush added, "You're making me sound like a 1920 grandmother."

Then, curiously, Mrs. Bush said that though of course it would be "great" if her husband won reelection, frankly, "If he loses, that's even better for me."

Some of her children "might feel that life would be easier if their father wasn't president," the First Lady explained. "I know his brothers might feel that way."

In the White House elevator, the First Lady's press secretary Anna Perez was ashen. "You're not going to use that, are you?" she asked of the AIDS questions.

Later, Perez repeated the demand three times.

The stories Heath and Appel produced from this were not as tough as their interviews. The two local newcasters lacked the skill to control their material or the confidence to challenge the President and First Lady on the air. But the morning was a warning to the White House. The First Family had to do better.

What happened next revealed how the White House communications machinery had to do better, too. For his "day at the White House," Heath was given five minutes every hour in the Oval Office to tape the President at work. In between trips, Heath and his team were left to wait in the pressroom with the regular White House press corps. If the White House was trying to bypass the national press, Heath thought, stashing him among them was a hell of an incompetent way to do it.

ABC White House correspondent Brit Hume spotted Heath almost immediately. He had met the young ABC affiliate news director before.

"You doing a story about Sununu?" Hume asked when he got Heath inside the cramped privacy of ABC's workspace.

"We're here doing interviews with Bush and the First Lady," Heath told him, grinning. "We followed Bush from the residence to the Oval Office this morning, and we're spending the day with him at the White House," Heath said.

"You're what?" Hume said incredulously. Hume had covered Bush for three years and never been granted such access.

"Then we went over to this studio they built in the Old Executive Office Building, with the fireplace, did the interview."

Hume had never seen the studio. How long was Heath's interview with Bush?

"About fifteen minutes," Heath said.

"Fifteen minutes!"

"And then Barbara Bush joined him and we did six more, and then another twelve with Barbara." He had asked why Bush had broken his no new taxes pledge and why, after thanking New

Hampshire in his victory speech in 1988, Bush had never again visited the state.

We want a copy of that interview, Hume told Heath.

Heath needed footage of Barbara Bush visiting a children's hospital. Maybe they could make a trade, Heath said.

Hume called Friedman in New York and arranged the swap, and that night, even before Heath and his crew could get back to New Hampshire to put together their special packages of stories, Hume aired the New Hampshire video in a biting piece. If you want demonstration of White House worry about the President's political standing, Hume narrated with his trademark sarcasm, "Look at this: The White House allowed . . . WMUR-TV in New Hampshire . . . unprecedented exclusive access to Mr. Bush today."

Rather than slick, the White House looked desperate and clumsy. A Bush aide called Heath the next morning to argue the President had been betrayed. "How the hell did they get that?" the aide demanded.

Look, Heath answered. "If you think we want to be scooped by our own network you're mistaken. If you're pissed off at somebody, why don't you ask your media affairs people why they put us in the pressroom on our down time. You were asking for trouble. It took three minutes for the network guys to hit on us. If you wanted to pull off some exclusive incognito deal, you should have hid us away in some office."

In New York Friedman was gleeful.

Four weeks later, newly appointed White House chief of staff Samuel Skinner reorganized the communications department, though he had problems doing it. Prominent Republicans turned down the job and finally Skinner centralized control of the communications under press secretary Marlin Fitzwater. The WMUR incident was not the cause of the shakeup, though surely a symptom of why it happened. Nor did it destroy WMUR's relations with the White House. Bush needed the station, at least until February 18, 1992. When the President came to New Hampshire in mid-January, in large part to shoot footage for a New Hampshire campaign commercial, the lone interview he gave was to WMUR.

Brit Hume, the ABC White House correspondent, had doubts about whether George Bush could succeed bypassing the national press even before the WMUR mess.

In his first three years, Bush had governed unlike any president in the television age. Since the Kennedy years, presidents had learned to use television to communicate directly to the American people—over the head of the press. It had made politics a more intimate and direct transaction between the man and people in their living rooms. And traditional press conferences had gradually devolved into anachronistic staged performances, infrequently held, featuring the president in combat with reporters. The press functioned almost as props. Even reporters were wondering whether the institution had outlasted its value.

In a secret memo in the early days of his administration, Bush and Fitzwater had developed a plan that changed this—and in a way that offered special insight into Bush. The centerpiece of their strategy was to resurrect the presidential press conference. In his first three years, Bush would hold 114 press conferences, more than three a month, six to every one of Reagan's, three to every one of Carter's. And their manner was tailored to fit Bush. Most were held in the mid-morning, when only CNN would air them. Their principal target was newspapers, not television. Bush usually did not prepare, and the press conferences were usually held on a few minutes' notice. In most, Bush rambled across many topics with no particular message he wanted to deliver. Their aim, mostly, was to satisfy the press and maintain rapport. Every week or so Bush would come to Fitzwater and say, "Is there any pressure building out there? Let's go out and have a press conference and relieve the pressure."

The strategy demonstrated Bush's penchant for informal,

unpressured events, and his command of detail. And they were built around what Bush considered his greatest political asset—his skill at face-to-face personal contact with people he knew, in this case the White House press corps. Holding them with little or no warning meant there were no expectations for Bush to live up to, no carefully prepared questions and less chance of another Bush problem, getting nervous, and freezing up on TV. And with only CNN airing them in the morning, Bush was communicating through the press, not around them.

The only message to the public was a general one, that things were okay, that Bush was in control. He was managing the in-basket.

They revealed a basic truth about Bush as president. He did not derive his power from his relationship with the American people. He derived it from his ability to make deals with people in person—foreign leaders, Congress, the press, audiences he could reach without television. He trusted that this stewardship was what the public wanted. In short, Bush was a print president in a television age.

His limitation was obvious. With only an indirect link to the public, could Bush weather a crisis of confidence?

Hume recognized this about Bush even before the campaign began. "He is at his best here with us. Doesn't matter what the questions are. When he is in a huge impersonal atmosphere or worse, behind a desk with a camera in his face, he is often terrible."

Technology, in other words, did not dictate what worked in politics. The politician did. Roger Ailes, Bush's friend and former media adviser, had even written a book on this principle—that "the man is the message." Yet surprisingly few in politics understood this, perhaps even in Bush's own team. The months to come only proved it.

ABC had three correspondents at the White House—one more than the other two networks. Kathleen Delaski handled weekends.

Ann Compton covered the beat for the morning news and handled supplementary stories Friedman wanted for *World News*. Brit Hume was the senior White House reporter, most nights the face for ABC from the White House lawn.

Tall, ramrod straight, with a slight boyish pout and a bellowing voice, Hume was the man who had replaced Sam Donaldson on the White House lawn when Bush replaced Reagan in the Oval Office. At forty-nine, he was more contemplative than Donaldson, and a more subtle analyst of the White House. That level of nuance, perhaps, made him a less famous TV personality. But Hume had nonetheless developed an ability to write to his video, and a strong enough persona that his words broke through the predominance of the pictures and added something to his pieces.

He came from "old family, no money," Hume told an interviewer once, though his inventor father had put him through private school in Washington and the University of Virginia. And he was one of the few in the White House press corps who openly considered himself a conservative. He saw the Republicans often as victims of an unfair liberal press and he loved haranguing his colleagues whom he saw as reflexively liberal.

In private, Hume also railed at what he thought of as Jennings's knee-jerk New York liberalism. But he respected Jennings's talent. Peter, he thought, was a master at television.

Friedman's politics were harder to read, Hume thought, which was a compliment. The executive producer was fair and listened and Hume had flourished under him.

If Hume thought he detected a liberal bias from his colleagues at the White House, many, in and outside ABC, were even more suspicious of him. "Maybe *he* has the bias," said Ann Devroy of the Washington *Post*. Friedman and Jennings were not so harsh. They had called Hume on the carpet for being too soft on Bush a few times, and Jennings joked that occasionally Hume wanted his stories to correct the perceived sins of the rest of the press corps; Jennings called these Hume's "fair" days. But as the campaign approached, the issue seemed to have ebbed. They considered Hume an unusual talent who could be caustic about Bush when necessary, and off the air a corrective voice with whom they could argue to make sure they were not being biased themselves.

Hume also passionately disagreed with the current conventional wisdom in the press that reporters should function as a truth squad against politicians' claims. Truth, Hume thought, was too subjective for the press to discern. "Our first responsibility is to report what happened and what is happening, not to say who is right."

Bush had resisted beginning this campaign. He did not even formally decide whether to run until a family meeting at Camp David at Christmas. When the campaign team finally began to organize in January, "It was all hands on deck," as one senior member of the campaign put it. "Let's react to New Hampshire. It was such an ad hoc, ill-prepared operation, it was shocking." By that time, of course, talk-show personality Patrick Buchanan had entered the race and moved to New Hampshire.

From Bush's first trip to New Hampshire the second week in January, the campaign's problems were obvious—even from the distance of the press bus. Hume was taking a few days off. So Compton handled it for *World News*.

To manipulate press coverage, one trick the White House often played was to keep certain events off the official press schedule. Suddenly, the motorcade would stop and the President of the United States would bolt from his limousine. What's that? Let's go! The press always took special notice. And even though most of these maneuvers were carefully planned, the reporters could never be sure which ones. Reporters called these events "impromptus." White House aides called them "off the records."

Along Bush's motorcade route that day in New Hampshire, the White House staged a stupefyingly ill-conceived impromptu so Bush could pet a cow named Holiday. But this time the press corps instantly recognized that the local farmer who owned the cow was actually the Republican leader of the New Hampshire House, proof that the event was staged. The blatantly political photo op only reinforced the image on the network news that Bush was rushing up to New Hampshire for political need, not, as his handlers wanted to suggest, because he cared about the state.

In her piece that night, Compton assumed the stunt was for a Bush TV ad but had simply been too blatant. The truth was worse. Holiday the cow was never intended for a Bush commercial. "The cow shot," as one aide called it, was a favor for a local politician. When the President's advance staff, media advisers, and secret service had rehearsed the cow impromptu the day before—every move a president makes is rehearsed the day before—Bush's political aides were appalled. White House TV adviser Sig Rogich looked over at advertising consultant Don Sipple with a sick look on his face. "You guys want this?" Rogich asked the President's ad maker.

Not only did they not want it, Sipple said, but this shot was so stupid it would only embarrass the President if it made the evening news.

Rogich ordered it off the schedule, but the next day someone had ordered it back. To accommodate it, Rogich had to eliminate another impromptu that was for a Bush commercial and that would have made a good moment on the TV news—the President jumping out of his limousine and meeting with voters. The party that invented the carefully controlled picture was now the party trying to please local politicians at the expense of its own interests.

Bush's ambivalent campaign was only part of the President's problem, and the other was more powerful. ABC producer Michael Bicks saw it in the parade of people who came out to see candidates, people who had lost their homes, their jobs, their insurance, their confidence in the future. Correspondent Jim Wooten saw it in the padlocked shops and empty malls he passed as he drove to campaign events. Jeff Greenfield saw it in the serious, focused, and surprisingly substantive questions candidates faced at the senior centers in Nashua, the high schools in Manchester, the auditoriums in Concord. Videotape editor Judd Marvin felt it sitting in his editing room reviewing the network pool footage of the candidates on the stump. "I don't know how these guys could not be deeply affected by what they've seen here after all this time. I have been."

In New York, Peter Jennings received a letter in the mail from a Laconia, New Hampshire, man named Philip A. Dyment.

I am writing this letter because my wife and I have had such a hard time recently, and . . . I have little else to do these days. Nineteen ninety-one started with the loss of my job as marketing director and the unexpected death of my mother on the last day of my job. . . . My wife was an executive secretary at a local clinic and lost her job after two years due to budgetary constraints.

[Dyment wrote about how he and his wife had lost their health care, and then discovered a rash of new medical problems. They had moved to New Hampshire two years earlier to realize their dream of living on a lake with a boat, so they would not have to wait until retirement. Now they were living on his unemployment check, and borrowing against his life insurance.]

We are in the midst of losing everything we have spent the last twenty-eight years working so hard for. We realize there are a lot of people much worse off than we, but when you are having such a difficult time in your own life, it is hard to keep this in mind much of the time. . . . We hope the presidential candidate that wins the election is capable of turning the economy around and bringing this country back to the prosperous nation it once was. America is the greatest country in the world, and it hurts us to see its people and the economy struggling so. Thank you for taking the time to read this. I guess I just needed to tell someone who cares.

Jennings might have cared, but he did the only thing he knew to do. He had his producer Stewart Schutzman interview the Dyments and add a few dozen seconds of their plight to a piece Jennings did on election eve. In the month he had been there, producer Michael Bicks told Schutzman he had seen hundreds of people like the Dyments.

Against this sad stage, George Bush's campaign act paled. One afternoon in January, Bush advertising consultant Mike Murphy went to Manchester to shoot a commercial of voters on the street endorsing the President. Murphy spent five hours on the street, shooting roll after roll of film, but he couldn't get enough Bush supporters to make a coherent ad. The President was in deeper trouble than he thought, Murphy realized.

Murphy put five and a half minutes of the footage together for campaign chairman Teeter. "We're here trying to make a commercial for President Bush," Murphy told voters in the film. "Do you like him?"

"No."

People laughed at him. Some cursed him.

"George, we're tired of ya."

"Not votin' for Bush," said a man in a business suit. "The economy is Bush."

"We have no voters here," Murphy said on the film.

It was a precinct Bush had carried in 1988 by 60 percent.

Buchanan's appeal was obvious. So was its significance. ABC did just one piece about the talk show personality. Wooten did it the night Bush came in early January, but it avoided the trap of overstating Buchanan's chances. He "offers few solutions himself [but] it doesn't seem to matter," Wooten's report said. "He is primarily a vehicle for the rage and worries of many New Hampshire voters." Yet "there's a very real question now as to whether the President has enough time to soothe the anger and anxiety that seem to be fueling Buchanan's challenge."

ABC did not explore Buchanan's ideas any more than that, nor anyone else's particularly.

One more thing magnified the weaknesses in Bush's campaign. New Hampshire was supposed to be a simple primary—easily understood and easily managed. This was a state where voters could still meet candidates at coffee klatches, house parties, and cafes, and make personal judgments about them—the art of so-called retail politics. This was why early primaries were held in states like New Hampshire, so some element of old politics was still part of the process.

As they wandered across the shimmering snow-carpeted towns of the state, Wooten and Jeff Greenfield and others in the ABC team saw the theory of the New Hampshire primary no longer held. There were simply too many reporters standing between the candidates and the voters. Candidates still held house parties, but the living rooms were bright with the hot stare of klieg lights, and voters had to fight for standing room with reporters. When Greenfield watched Bob Kerrey go to Dan Callaghan's home in January, Kerrey stopped talking after only twenty minutes to do a live interview with WMUR on the Callaghans' front lawn for the six o'clock news. Callaghan's guests watched on the TV in the den.

Compared with campaigns of the past, campaigns framed by a few national media organizations and in-person campaigning, what came through the more complex media filter of 1992 was more confusing, more disconnected, and certainly harder for politicians like Bush to control. On the same day, a poll by WMUR and the Manchester *Union Leader* declared Bush as having a "commanding" 60 percent lead, while one by the Boston *Herald* and Boston's WCVB-TV had "Buchanan gaining momentum." The noise created by all this media was an obstacle, not an aid, to candidates conveying their ideas to voters. In one particularly grotesque press conference in Manchester, correspondent Jim Wooten watched as Kerrey spent a half hour fending off questions from local reporters trying to get him to respond to polls conducted by their stations. "Do you think you're dead in the water," the reporter from Boston's WCVB-TV asked after learning the station's latest poll had stuck Kerrey at 10 percent.

"No," Kerrey answered.

"Would you elaborate?"

He wouldn't.

"Is your support eroding?" asked the WMUR reporter whose station also had a poll.

"I like where we are," Kerrey lied.

"If you don't do well, is there anywhere else you can go?" the reporter followed up.

Twenty minutes passed before Dan Balz of the Washington *Post* asked Kerrey the first policy questions, but by then, the local TV crews had moved outside to do their live standups for the noon news.

In an odd way, the networks added to the incoherence of the expanding media environment by cutting back on their coverage.

Bob Murphy, the ABC News vice president who controlled the equipment and the people, was trying to cut his costs in half from four years earlier. Using off-air reporters rather than correspondents was one way. Another was by keeping tighter accounting of costs. He now had a piece of paper on his desk every morning and another every night that told him how much ABC News had spent in the last twelve hours.

The competition was doing even less in New Hampshire than ABC. CBS had off-air producers only with the major candidates. NBC did not have staff traveling with anyone—at least not yet. Its political correspondents, Andrea Mitchell and Lisa Myers, stayed in Washington most of the time and also had to cover other stories, like Congress and the Supreme Court. For its on-site reporting it relied on the wire services and one researcher, Collette Rhoney, who doubled as the research department for *Meet the Press*. The cuts made a difference. Not long ago, even print reporters like Dan Balz of the Washington *Post* conceded the networks helped drive the campaign dialogue. With shared cameras pools and stenographic off-air researchers instead of correspondents, the networks were becoming passive recorders of a campaign driven by local press.

* *

Bush had two weapons with which to fight back, his advertising and the power of the presidency.

The commercial produced from Bush's troubled trip—showing Bush listening to people in New Hampshire, many of them angry—proved to be one of the campaign's most effective maneuvers. In the days after it ran, Bush pollster Fred Steeper's internal surveys for the reelection campaign showed the President's support moved above 60 percent. Buchanan's dropped to below 30 percent.

Having established that Bush understood voters' problems, the next step in the Republicans' vaguely conceived strategy was to lay out what the President would do about it. For that, incredibly, the Bush campaign put nearly all its hope on one moment, the State of the Union address in late January.

Hume viewed the President's economic policies with sympathy. A year and a half earlier, Bush had agreed to raise taxes in exchange for spending caps from Congress. The Federal Reserve could use monetary policy to stimulate the economy instead.

But the economy did not recover on the timetable expected in the fall of 1991. And Bush got conflicting advice how to react. Political advisers urged him to bundle various growth packages and throw them at Congress. Economic advisers told him to wait, avoid action that would spook the markets, scuttle the budget deal, and inhibit the Fed. In other words, "Just don't do very much," Hume said. "Economically it was good advice, but politically it was lethal." And now the President was going to have to deal with the whole thing in his State of the Union speech.

On the air, Hume went down the middle. "Despite the intense buildup the President has given the speech on the campaign trail and elsewhere, the address represents a decision basically to do nothing major on the economy," Hume reported, because economists told him that was the prudent course. Even some conservatives thought Hume's analysis charitable. They argued that Bush had squandered an opportunity after the Gulf War to turn to domestic affairs. But no one could argue the President had been politically inept to put so much stock on a single speech.

The focus group the Bush campaign assembled that night— thirty undecided voters who had supported Bush in 1988—were unimpressed by the speech. All the lines the White House thought would get a big response, like mention of the Gulf War, and statements of sympathy for Americans suffering hard times, registered little or nothing. Only attacks on big government and welfare got the undecided voters to move the dials on their hand-held Perception Analyzer meters.

Armed with the data, the next day, the Bush campaign shot its second television ad, Bush in the Oval Office explaining his economic plan:

> I've given Congress a deadline of March 20 to pass my plan for economic growth. It will cut taxes for families, encourage investment . . . and restore the values of homes and real estate . . . without big government spending. But I need your help now to send a real message to Congress to get this job done.

In Bush's internal polls, the ad drove Buchanan to as low as 18 percent. Bush aides began to leak to the press that Buchanan was fading.

Not privy to the focus group or polling data, Hume could still sense what followed. After producing one ad showing Bush being sympathetic and another reprising the slim proposals in Bush's speech, "We didn't have anything more to say," one aide said later.

Bush's campaign turned into a series of internal arguments over what to do next. The President's advertising team advocated attack: since "Buchanan had the message," the only choice was "discredit the messenger." Campaign chairman Teeter refused, trying to avoid the patina of attack politics.

Bush instead chose to campaign on his proudest achievement, the Gulf War, another move that proved politically foolish. The voter research said it would only remind people that Bush had neglected the economy, and it turned out the White House had never shot any film footage of Bush with the troops in Saudi Arabia. "All we had was some beta cam shot by a Navy crew . . . barely a grade above home video," one Bush aide sputtered.

The President's fortunes sliding, the White House added an extra trip to New Hampshire—this one with actor Arnold Schwarzenegger—the weekend before the primary, which backfired badly. A new Buchanan ad accused Bush of already reneging on promises from his State of the Union speech. The package Bush sent to Congress, the ad said, did not include a promised $500 tax deduction for families with children. The State of the Union was "just a speech for New Hampshire," one Bush aide had even conceded to the Washington *Post*, the ad said. Bush spent the weekend griping that Buchanan was telling "outright lies" about him.

ABC, meanwhile, had belatedly begun to cover the campaign more seriously. Jennings had never found the time to do the profiles he and Friedman had intended. It was another good plan gone awry, like Greenfield's attempts to do a story about the substance of the campaign here, or Wooten's intention to do a piece about the growing centrism of the Democratic party. On Friday, ten days before the primary, Jennings and Friedman regrouped and decided to dispatch two more reporters to New Hampshire—Judy Muller from Los Angeles and Chris Bury, the lone correspondent left in the once-huge Chicago bureau.

In the course of five nights, Bury did quick snapshots of Brown, Tsongas, and Clinton, while Muller did Kerrey and Harkin. They were precisely the kind of quick and dirty profiles Friedman had wanted to avoid.

The final weekend Jennings himself arrived to report a piece with his producer Stewart Schutzman about the sadness of the

New Hampshire people. Cokie Roberts returned, along with Jeff Greenfield and correspondent Jack Smith for the Brinkley show to join Wooten, Bury, and Muller. Suddenly, the tiny ABC workspace in the mill below WMUR-TV brimmed with the activity of sixty people. They were shooting four and five pieces each day and another half dozen for the affiliate feed *ABC News One*, the overnight *World News Now*, and the morning shows *World News This Morning* and *Good Morning America*, out of the workspace, through the satellite truck in the parking lot, up into the satellite in outerspace, then down to New York, each one taking a moment or two to make the trip.

Since Buchanan couldn't win, the Republican race came down to something other than votes. On the day the people of New Hampshire cast their ballots, and those days following, the press rendered a more elusive verdict than who won: it decided what the returns meant.

This was the real primary of New Hampshire—the fragile game in which the media set expectations and then interpreted the vote by watching who succeeds or fails to meet them.

In politics, where perception is reality, history suggested this media ruling could profoundly influence who would be president of the United States. When Lyndon Johnson—running as a write-in—won the 1968 New Hampshire primary by eight points the press deemed second-place finisher Eugene McCarthy, the anti–Vietnam War candidate, to be the real winner because his showing was so unexpected. Embarrassed and vulnerable, Johnson dropped out of the race before the next primary. When Ronald Reagan came within one percentage point of defeating sitting President Gerald R. Ford in 1976–48 percent to Ford's 49.4 percent—the press deemed it a blow to Reagan because the week before most had expected him to win.

This game of setting expectations and seeing who succeeded or failed to meet them was, in effect, a long alchemic conversation between reporters, campaign operatives, and pollsters, that occurred each night, usually after deadline, in the bars and restaurants of Manchester—Athens, Holiday Inn, Back Door, Bedford Inn, and most of all the Wayfarer, the headquarters of spin and speculation—as the political bedouin class compared impressions and data about who has a solid message, who was raising money, whose events seem well managed, who would likely be appealing in other states, who had a good organization, who was resonating, who was not.

Various bits of data went into the calculation. Campaign operatives worked feverishly to shape prevailing perceptions by arguing—and lying—about what they expected to happen. Historical precedent played a part, too. Most reporters thought that Bush would be devastated if Buchanan got 40 percent, since Eugene McCarthy had ended Lyndon Johnson's presidency by getting 42 percent in 1968. Public opinion polls played a role, as well, even though most reporters claimed they thought the polls unreliable. Each night in the Wayfarer, reporters from *USA Today* and the Boston *Globe* would rush to the phones to check the latest movements in their paper's notoriously risky nightly tracking polls. These results then spread like a virus through the bar.

Finally, all this was balanced against that intangible last ingredient—the gut instinct a reporter derives from watching candidates on the stump interacting with voters. Instinct was part of what doomed Bob Kerrey. Reporters talked constantly about how, as the Washington *Post*'s Lloyd Grove put it one night, "He doesn't seem to want to be doing this." The story spread that Kerrey would head to his van after campaign stops and watch movies on his VCR, including *Being There,* the Peter Sellers film about an ignorant cipher raised on television who is nearly elected president.

"How do we decide this?" Jack Germond, one of the deans of the press corps and the Wayfarer, asked while discussing the expectations game the weekend before the 1992 primary vote. "Arbitrarily."

In the end, it was not necessarily voters in other primary states who were influenced by the media assessment. It was the campaign contributors and party insiders who paid heed, by rushing to the perceived victor and abandoning the perceived losers. And the loss of financing, rather than lack of appeal to voters, is what kills campaigns.

Most of the veteran reporters like Wooten and Greenfield did not seriously question whether the expectations game distorted the process. They believed the press's act of measuring votes and giving them a secondary meaning was not only inevitable but legitimate, or at least semi-legitimate. "Presumably, we bring some knowledge and history to this," said Germond.

One of the few reporters who expressed serious doubts about the expectations game was William Greider, the former Washington *Post* editor who was now the Washington editor of *Rolling Stone*. Greider thought it created a false pack mentality and intruded on the process. "The coverage of politics would be better," he said, "if you could get these people to stay in separate hotels and forbid them from drinking together." But it was a fact of life that the campaigns understood and tried to manipulate.

For Bush, the question of expectations was simple: How big a margin would he need to avoid humiliation, and what percentage of the vote would Buchanan need to be able to press his challenge in other states?

Bush's slide in the last days had hurt. Suddenly his aides had to try and lower expectations at the last minute. "If we could put him away with 60 plus, the press would say he weathered the storm and handled it pretty well," said one senior adviser. "We thought if we were below 55 the feeding frenzy would be on."

On election day, a mistake by the media pushed Bush below that magic 60 percent level, altering how the press perceived the results and damaging Bush further.

To save funds, the networks had agreed to conduct a joint exit poll under the control of former CBS pollster Warren Mitofsky. But the exit poll had a faulty design. Mitofsky failed to build in the possibility that Republicans would write in the names of Democrats out of disaffection toward both Bush and Buchanan. So when people left the polling place and told network pollsters that they had written in the name of Paul Tsongas or in some cases even Ralph Nader, those votes were not counted.

As the press watched the first third of exit poll data trickle in around midday, Buchanan was above 45 percent. "Bush is barely above 50 percent," Cokie Roberts marveled as she tracked the data. Though she had no way of knowing, Buchanan's numbers were inflated. He had pushed his get-out-the-vote organization to move early to inflate the numbers. And those crossover voters for Tsongas and others weren't being counted. (The press also leaked its exit poll results to the campaigns, and the Bush campaign started pushing to get women out in the afternoon with the argument that Buchanan was doing better than expected—a further press intrusion on the process.)

When the networks went on the air, the joint network exit poll was still projecting Buchanan at 41 percent and Bush at 57 percent. "Buchanan gets the boost," Jeff Greenfield said during ABC's 11:30 election night show, "because 40 percent was the high water mark, that's where the bar was set and he hit or passed it."

This hurts Bush, David Brinkley explained on the air, because "it was something we didn't expect, and I don't believe George Bush did either."

Only the day after did it become clear that Buchanan had not passed the magical 40 percent line. Ten percent of the voters had voted for write-in candidates. Buchanan only reached 37 percent. That was still remarkable. No president in this century had won in November if a challenger in his party had earned 37 percent or more. But the difference was enough to change how the press viewed the race—and how the Republicans behaved.

As they prepared to go to Greenfield for analysis around midnight at Bush headquarters, Gralnick in the control room in New York noticed that the Bush victory party had ended. The room was empty. One security guard waited in the back of the room for Greenfield and his crew to leave. "Look at that," Brinkley said during a commercial when he saw it on the monitor. "Let's use it," Gralnick said from the control room and cautioned Greenfield to remain patient while they panned the room first.

When they went on the air, Brinkley hammed it up. "Jeff, are you there?" he kept saying as the camera moved across a room without a single person in it. It wasn't even midnight and even Bush's supporters had abandoned the game. The shot told the story, a story created in part by the press's expectations and its errant poll. New Hampshire had been a disaster for the press as well as Bush.

★

CHAPTER

5

THE CLOCK

April 22 8:57.12 A.M.

Lee Kamlet stood in the lobby of Philadelphia's Warwick Hotel looking at the windy rain streaking against the windows and thinking they would have to account for it.

He had to call Washington about arranging an interview with that environmental lobbyist. Get tape of pollution in Little Rock. Check the schedule for where to pick up the campaign tomorrow. Wake up correspondent Chris Bury. Load the crews into their spots in Bill Clinton's motorcade, and off into the Pennsylvania drizzle.

So it began, again.

There were moments, in the spaces between the exhaustion and the adrenaline, when one could feel the phantom that was still haunting American politics in the spring of 1992. The ghost was the memory of Ronald Reagan's successful presidential campaigns, and its black-sheep child, George Bush's campaign of 1988. The prevailing theory learned from those years was that the presidency was won by controlling the images and soundbites that appeared on television. Control the image—rather than answer journalists' questions or lay out a comprehensive agenda—the thinking went. Stay on message, the political operative would tell his candidate. Drive the agenda, the historians would write later of the winning campaign.

A few days before George Bush's 1988 election, campaign chairman James Baker III delivered a speech in Washington arguing that campaigns were run that way not by choice but because the breathless abbreviation of television required it. If politics seemed trivial, he contended, it was because of television's strange compression—in which events were turned into TV segments, speeches into soundbites, life size into screen size. Able candidates crafted their rhetoric to fit the way television stories were put together, he argued. They packed their speeches with key sentences designed for soundbites, using instantly recognizable references from movies and television. And they proffered ideas digestible into a minute thirty of TV time. "If summing up our case in thirty seconds or less, preferably with some allusion to a figure in popular culture, is what it takes to get on the evening news, then a winning strategy simply requires that we do this," Baker said. "It is simply a fact of life, ladies and gentlemen, and not one of our making, that the American people get most of their news from television's evening news programs."

Was Baker making excuses? Was television really the reason that the public sensed the political process had been reduced into something less than it was—and something not quite real?

If the question could be answered it was in the decisions and concerns each day of people like Kamlet. He was the ABC field producer assigned to Clinton, the second half of the team with correspondent Chris Bury. They were the people, in consultation with the Rim, who built the most basic unit of American politics, the TV story.

9:13.27 A.M.

The day would test Baker's theory as much as any in the young campaign. Clinton was going to deliver his major address of the primary season about the environment, a day of substance, detail, policy.

The event had a political context, of course. Clinton by now was on his way to securing the Democratic nomination, but not the public's confidence. People didn't trust him. They didn't even like him. He seemed like just another slick politician, they told his focus groups. So Clinton had embarked on a series of substantive speeches challenging Bush directly to demonstrate his seriousness. And today he hoped to distinguish himself from past Democrats one other way: He would show that, while his environmental record was shaky, it was better than Bush's and he was tough enough to prove it.

9:31.23 A.M.

Neither Bury nor Kamlet had intended to cover this campaign. They were ordered to New Hampshire on two days' notice in February when Jennings's plan to profile the candidates collapsed and, before long, had become the Clinton team, though they were never given any outline of what ABC expected.

Bury was from ABC's Chicago bureau, a redhead with a boy's face and a crisp baritone from his days at WLCX-Radio in La-Crosse, Wisconsin. Like most of the new generation, he had come up through local television and made it to the network when he was thirty. Now, ten years later, he was favored for his uncomplicated and competent style. He did not "punch through" the screen to people like ABC's stars yet, Jennings would admit later. In time that might come.

Kamlet, from the Denver bureau, was a particular favorite of Friedman's. A man with a gentle open face and dark intelligent eyes, he was unusual among field producers, whose world is a perpetual wave of small details easily but dangerously forgotten. Kamlet rarely lost his temper and had an eye for the larger implications of a story. Friedman, in return, had won Kamlet's loyalty by allowing the producer to move to Denver for the sake of his children.

Titles are confusing in television, but at ABC, roughly, the correspondent handled the words, in consultation with the Rim; the field producer handled the pictures and logistics, which meant supervising the camera crews, logging the pictures and managing the editing. In terms of hierarchy, the correspondent was in charge. "The correspondent is never wrong," was one saying in television. "No matter how wrong he is."

9:38.17 A.M.

Because of the clock, there are two realities in the world of television politics—network and local.

Network reality is the early part of the day, everything before roughly 2 P.M. eastern time. Anything after that is unlikely to make nightly network news, because Bury and Kamlet and their counterparts will have broken away from the campaign to produce, edit, and feed their stories to New York. Usually, candidates deliver their most substantive speeches in the morning, so the press has the most time to digest them, and the second event around noon offers pictures, or wallpaper, to illustrate the morning's message.

Then the candidate enters local reality—usually a rally staged around 6 P.M. so that it will be carried live on local news for five minutes or more.

Clinton's environmental speech was scheduled for between 10:15 and 10:45, network time. Afterwards he would rush to Johnstown, east of Pittsburgh, to hit the western side of the state while the networks stayed behind. In the evening, after neither the networks nor most local crews cared, he would run for Florida for an evening fundraiser.

9:49.14 A.M.

The national traveling press was gathering in Philadelphia, in the Warwick lobby: E.J. Dionne of the Washington *Post*, Gwen Ifill of the *New York Times*, Joe Klein of *Newsweek*, John King of the Associated Press, Paul Richter of the Los Angeles *Times*, Maura Liasson of National Public Radio, Adam Nagourney of *USA Today*. Many of the supposed stars of the media, however, were noticeably absent. The people surrounding Kamlet were young, most of them scarcely forty, most of them unknown.

Absent, too, were the television networks. Only two of the four networks had correspondents traveling regularly with the candidates anymore. The other one besides ABC was CNN, which had Gene Randall on Clinton.

10:05.28 A.M.
In New York, Paul Friedman and Bob Murphy were holding the ABC News morning global conference call in the Crazy Eddie conference room. The room took its name because it featured an entire wall of TV sets, like the one in television ads for a now bankrupt New York discount appliance store named Crazy Eddie's. Someone from each ABC News program was always present at these sessions. And as always, Friedman began by reviewing what he liked and didn't like about last night's *World News*. Then Murphy asked for reports about today from each of the ABC News bureaus—first the national desk in New York, then Washington, Chicago, Los Angeles, and London. There were once many more bureaus, but technology had allowed television to be more centralized, and declining profits had accelerated it.

Kris Sebastian, the assignment editor for the national desk, explained that Clinton aides had leaked an advance copy of the speech to the Los Angeles *Times* to get an extra day's press coverage and it condemned the President fairly harshly. The Washington bureau said it would wait to see what, if any, response the White House had.

10:07.01 A.M.
In Washington, correspondent Brit Hume was arriving in the closet-sized cubicle in the White House pressroom. His producer, Terry Ray, was already in his office at the ABC Washington bureau, where he had the full complement of equipment needed to handle the pictures, the satellites for receiving video, the editing bays for cutting it, the assistant producers needed to conduct any extra interviews for Hume, the crews to shoot any video from elsewhere besides the White House.

10:12.27 A.M.

Clinton was late, as usual. Inside the Drexel University auditorium, Kamlet's two camera crews synchronized the clocks on their video equipment to the watch on Kamlet's arm, which he would glance at every few seconds whenever they were rolling. This was crucial.

When Clinton spoke, Kamlet would write down the exact time of day to the second at which he began and ended each paragraph. This is the strangest of television's ironies. It is the medium most committed to real time—every second of the day, every moment of tape, was measured and logged to the tenth of a second. And yet it is the medium that compresses time the most.

The contradiction is like the irresistible flickering deception of television itself. The images seem so near to reality—and the easy confusion is what critics find so troubling.

On a typical day, ABC crews easily shot three hours of tapes, recording virtually every moment a candidate or his motorcade was visible in public. Yet the longest story Bury and Kamlet were likely to get on the air was two minutes and fifteen seconds. A minute and a half was more common.

10:19.48 A.M.

Clinton's speech was a mix of policy and politics. The Republican dichotomy between protecting the environment and protecting the economy was a false choice, he argued. In the end, the same policies benefited both. He endorsed a series of environmental policies and then defended his own record by saying it had been better than the Republicans' anyway.

Clinton is not a great orator. He has the mind of a policy grunt and the heart of a politician but he lacks the soul of either a poet or a performer. Few politicians were orators anymore, however, if they ever were. It wasn't necessary. One needed to master sentences nowadays, not paragraphs.

Was the nightly news responsible for that? Had two minute news stories made twenty-minute ideas unnecessary? Peggy Noonan, the great Republican speechwriter, argued that a great speech still had to be a coherent argument, full and whole. Paul Begala, Clinton's speechwriter, believed the teachings of Republican strategist Roger Ailes that the press was mostly interested only in conflict, scandal, polls, process, and gaffes. So to get coverage of a speech, he usually included attack lines, making his speeches more malicious than they would otherwise be. But he agreed a speech had to be a full, coherent argument, since it had to please the high-brow columnists as well as the local news. Certainly television also required soundbites or summary lines that captured the essence of an argument. But that predated television. Roosevelt and Churchill were masters of the art. The irony of television—especially in 1992—is that reporters demanded politicians deliver serious speeches if they wanted coverage, and then reduced them into soundbites so that is all the public ever heard.

10:38.13 A.M.

Clinton's advance team had staged the Drexel speech to look presidential. He would stand in front of a blue curtain as Bush often did and use the same kind of fancy teleprompter Bush had for the State of the Union address. The stage was filled with lush green rented ferns to complement the Earth Day theme.

The placement of the camera platforms also said something about modern politics. They were located in the middle of the auditorium, splitting the room in half. Anyone behind them barely saw the stage. But since they were unnecessary as props for the TV picture, they were irrelevant to the event.

10:51.28 A.M.

In Washington, George Bush wasn't much interested in Bill Clinton or the campaign—as usual. The White House had released a written statement in the President's name listing his accomplishments on the environment in honor of Earth Day, the minimal White House effort to say the least. When Bush emerged to see off some visiting foreign dignitaries on the South Lawn driveway, a reporter in the bleachers set up for the press had shouted a question about the speech Clinton had just given. Bush seemed to think about answering briefly and then stopped himself. "That is apparently as good as it gets at the White House today," Hume told the Rim when he called it in.

11:01.23 A.M.

When Bury called the Rim from Philadelphia, he told Dennis Dunlavey that he saw two items as news: Clinton's admitting his mistakes in Arkansas and his vow that he would not let his record there be used as a smokescreen to cloud George Bush's environmental record the way Michael Dukakis had in Boston four years earlier. Politics, not policy. Dunlavey agreed, and Bury and Kamlet were on the early rundown for *World News*.

Inside the Drexel auditorium, Clinton deputy campaign manager George Stephanopoulos was spinning reporters about what in the speech was important, to ensure Clinton got the soundbites he wanted. "The politics of 1988 won't work in 1992," Stephanopoulos said. "If Bush wants to come to White River, we'll be on the banks waiting for him." From the campaign's point of view, ABC was already on message.

Bury and Kamlet were also done with Clinton for the day. Network time had ended.

When they arrived around noon at WPVI-TV, the local ABC affiliate in Philadelphia, to edit their story, Bury, Kamlet, and the second camera crew knew they were not wanted. Though WPVI, like ABC, was owned by Cap Cities, they were left to wait in the lobby for thirty minutes, and then they were given workspace in a hallway. Relations between the networks and affiliates had deteriorated over the years as the networks declined in ratings and influence, and the locals grew in profitability.

1:04.15 P.M.

Someone, most think it was Fred Friendly, the famous producer for Edward R. Murrow, once called television an 800,000-pound pencil. For all of the money, the speed, the dizzying confusing influence, the business from inside was a conspiracy of logistical details, of plane schedules and satellite coordinates, overtime pay, and trying to get trucks and people to a certain point at a certain time.

When ABC News had determined a few days earlier that it probably wanted a story from Clinton's speech, it decided to send a videotape editor to Philadelphia to put it together. To arrive in time, Herb King, a small bearded man who had wanted to be a filmmaker, had gotten up at 3:30 A.M., picked up his portable editing equipment at ABC, and driven to WPVI-TV in Philadelphia to cut the piece.

In all, King's portable "edit pack" consisted of eleven fiberglass packing cases of equipment totaling 1,500 pounds, valued at about $70,000. To edit this single story, he would need, at minimum, two editing machines, two monitors, an audio sequencer, a sync generator, an audio mixer, and an oscilloscope to analyze the video images. This was the eraser of the 800,000-pound pencil.

1:29.14 P.M.

In New York, they had to decide how much time to give Clinton's environmental address. Around the Rim the discussion took about four seconds. In network television, political stories ranged from 1:30 to 2:15. The longest news story might go 2:45. Clinton got 1:45.

Time was television's demon, its crack cocaine. The networks had twenty-two minutes to tell the news. The dream of winning an hour was gone. Local stations had become too powerful, local news too profitable, to relinquish the time. And television was so cumbersome that producing long stories took enormous effort. Friedman's Agenda pieces could take weeks. Telling the news in 1:30 was efficient. And finally there were habit and cynicism. The public wouldn't pay attention if stories were too long, the argument went. Look at *MacNeil/Lehrer*. It had long stories and low ratings. Local news stories were especially short, and local execu-

tives defended their case with balance sheets and ratings statements. But the fact was longer required more intelligence and
skill.

1:34.18 P.M.

In their hallway editing bay, Kamlet and Bury were reviewing
what pictures they had before the correspondent went off to write
a script. King, their editor, was playing Clinton's speech at double
speed—lip lock speed—the fastest rate possible in which speech
was still intelligible. Kamlet logged the shots he liked, marking
them by time of day, and then transcribed, or "verbated," the
soundbites he and Bury liked, measuring their exact length in
seconds. Bury would pick from them when writing his script.

Clinton had this habit of grinning after he delivered a good
line. "I just think he's immature," Kamlet said.

"He's the kid in the front row with his hand up in class,"
Bury said.

They had the power to control this. King could cut the
soundbite tight, right at the end of the last word of the sentence,
and make Clinton's annoying grin disappear. Eventually he
would, mostly because the piece was long.

1:43.18 P.M.

To add balance and context, Kamlet had arranged for the Washington bureau to interview environmental activist Bill Matty of the
League of Conservation Voters reacting to Clinton's speech.

Experts like Matty play a clearly defined role. Journalists use
them to mouth criticisms they cannot raise themselves, in this
case, the conventional view that Clinton had a poor environmental
record in Arkansas, which made Clinton's rhetoric on the environment suspect. But as Kamlet read the quotes from Matty's interview out loud, it was clear that Matty had liked Clinton's speech.
Whatever Clinton's record, Matty kept saying, it would be better
than Bush's.

"What's the most critical thing he had to say?" Bury asked.

"I would say most environmentalists are not satisfied with Bill Clinton's record on the environment in Arkansas."

"Darn it," Bury said. It was fifteen seconds, too long in such a short piece for a soundbite from a critic.

Kamlet disagreed with Bury on the length of soundbites, but he kept his silence. Bury was the correspondent.

The shrinkage in soundbites was strange. The academics had made a lot out of it. When Kamlet had begun in the business more than a decade ago, soundbites typically had been eighteen seconds long. Why had it changed? "I just think the culture has speeded up," Kamlet said. "When you watch it, eighteen seconds just seems really long now." But it depended on what someone said. When the Gulf War ended, Friedman had let General Norman Schwarzkopf roll for several minutes.

In this case, Matty was gone from Bury's piece.

1:57.22 P.M.

In Washington, the Bush campaign had had a change of heart. Michael Deland, the head of the President's council on environmental quality, had sent word to the White House press corps that, if they showed up, he would have a statement on Bush's behalf reacting to the Clinton speech. He couldn't be sure, but Hume thought that the Bush campaign was only responding because Deland had volunteered, a sad commentary about the aggressiveness of the Bush reelection team.

Deland handed out something called the Green List, with the relevant pages highlighted, that showed Arkansas near the bottom of all kinds of environmental categories and forty-eighth overall. Then he fired off one of the most malicious soundbites Hume had heard in a while.

"Make a snappy piece, an easy piece," Hume said.

In New York, the Rim was now eager for a story. They could package the two pieces together.

2:11.37 P.M.

Bury would pick three Clinton soundbites—nine seconds each, twenty-seven seconds combined—comprising a quarter of his piece. It was the same ratio as almost every television story in America.

Three soundbites, connecting narration, an open and a close.

"Under the last two presidents, leadership on the environment has become an endangered species."

Bury thought it the best soundbite in the speech, pithy, glib, sardonic, so he had used it first.

"I've made the choice, from time to time, for jobs, because my state was a poor one without either enough jobs or enough federal help to clean up the environment."

Clinton's confession. Forgive me my sins because they were George Bush's fault. It had to be there.

"I will not let this become the Boston Harbor. So, Mr. President, if you want to place the blame, you're gonna have to shoulder some of it, too."

No Michael Dukakis he, no Greek from Massachusetts, and this, no repeat of 1988.

All three bites were political. To the extent it was possible, Bury could handle the substance of Clinton's proposals in his narration.

2:17.23 P.M.

There were several ways to start a television piece visually.

The most common was to open with the most arresting pictures to grab the audience—"especially if it reinforced the story you had to tell," said Kamlet. This was why the Reagan White House's visuals were so successful.

If politicians supplied pictures that reinforced their words, they could gradually control the stories that the TV correspondents produced.

The Reagan administration also fervently believed that if the pictures and words clashed, only the pictures counted. So he who staged the pictures controlled the message. The White House spokesman during the Reagan years, Larry Speakes, even kept a sign on his desk that read "You don't tell us how to stage the news, we won't tell you how to cover it."

Reagan's approach was an oversimplification. It suited a man who delivered speeches well, and a president who was popular. But Friedman was also convinced that meaningless pictures disappeared, and powerful words survived.

Clinton today had not supplied much of either, so Kamlet and Bury would take another approach, the most basic kind of TV story. Write to and from each soundbite. Clinton came and gave a speech about the environment. Here is what he said (soundbite). He also said this (soundbite), and this (soundbite). Summary close.

In the speech, Clinton laid out his environmental plan, Bury's piece would say. To illustrate that, Bury had decided to use a "tick list," a graphic in which the key phrases of Clinton's proposals were written on the screen in text.

Then Clinton defended his record, so Kamlet would show pictures of Arkansas pollution.

Finally, Clinton said he would not let his state be turned into a Boston Harbor, so Kamlet would show pictures of Bush's trip to Boston Harbor.

3:06.17 P.M.

New York had assembled the footage Kamlet wanted—Boston Harbor in 1988, Arkansas pollution, Matty's interview—and ordered time on the satellite, given Kamlet coordinates. In a few minutes, the video had moved into outerspace and bounced back down the satellite dish in the parking lot of WPVI, into the video switching room and onto a videocassette recording by King.

3:45.27 P.M.

After Bury had finished his script, and Kamlet and King both suggested changes, Bury began reading for time. He was twenty seconds too long, and the arduous process of cutting began. If nothing else, television was the tyranny of seconds.

Most days, each piece seemed to lose good portions of its texture, bits of business that gave the pieces verisimilitude, as the stories were reduced to the common grammar of 1:45.

"So much for any touch, huh," Bury said after fifteen minutes of cutting. They were still long.

They cut for another ten minutes, compressing, reducing, not making it worse, nor better. A good network TV script is adequate to the time allowed. Only rarely was one memorable, and then usually because of the way it interacted with the videotape. But few correspondents wrote well to pictures anymore. That had been a requirement in the days of film, when one waited for the pictures and cutting them was painstaking. One could see the difference between some of the older correspondents and the younger ones. With videotape, it was easy to take the pictures for granted. And a lot of veteran correspondents thought television was becoming closer to radio with video wallpaper.

4:50.03 P.M.

When the script was at time, Bury hooked his Toshiba into the telephone and shipped the script via modem to New York for Friedman's approval. The script would be passed around the Rim, and everyone would take a crack at it, including Jennings if he was inclined. Until the script was approved, they could do nothing.

"I worked for ITN, the British independent news agency," Herb King said. "They don't have script approval."

"You know how they work at the BBC," Kamlet said. "Completely differently than we do in American television. The correspondent says what footage he wants, and what soundbites in what order, then the editor puts it together however he likes. The correspondent comes back and reads to the pictures, changing the script to fit the images the editor has come up with."

It was, King thought, a system that led to a more visual kind of television and kept the BBC from becoming a hybrid medium—radio with pictures—that had neither the power of radio nor the strength of real television.

Script approval, however, allowed Paul Friedman in New York to weave stories so that *World News* had a uniform style, which was crucial in the era of magazine-style news.

In twenty minutes, word came back that New York had approved the script with only minor changes. This was far easier than it could have been. Friedman is a stickler, particularly with closes.

5:42.19 P.M.
After Bury had recorded his soundtrack through an old-fashioned "lip mike," a radio microphone like Ed Murrow used during World War II, Herb King began to lay down the first piece of video. They had forty-five minutes before *World News*.

Kamlet ran through his list of shots, being careful not to pick consecutive pictures that had drastically different points of view, which would jar the audience.

The cutting in television has become very quick, a few seconds per image. King laid in three shots to cover Bury's first two sentences.

6:05.22 P.M.
They had missed their feed time on the satellite and New York wanted to know what was happening. Bury also read his close too slowly, so they were now three seconds over.

6:25.47 P.M.
King had laid in the last shot, and it had been sent to New York, four minutes before the broadcast, about nine minutes before it would air. The timing was typical.

6:36.21 P.M.
King, Bury, and their camera crew now crowded into an engineering room to watch the program. Their piece came right after the first commercial.

Jennings and Friedman had chosen to package them in a way that gave the environmental speech an even more political tone.

> In presidential politics today, a fairly broad hint of what the fall campaign might look like between George Bush and Bill Clinton as Democratic nominee. First Governor Clinton chose this Earth Day to make a major speech about the environment, a subject on which he clearly believes that Mr. Bush is vulnerable. And this time the White House decided that the likely Democratic nominee shouldn't be ignored. First, here's ABC's Chris Bury.

Bury watched himself without expression as the piece began:

> Clinton's Earth Day address was aimed straight at President Bush. [The picture showed Clinton walking on stage at Drexel University, giving the speech, the audience reacting.] He accused Bush of ignoring his pledge to be the "environmental president" and called the White House record, "reactive, rudderless and expedient."

Then the first soundbite: "Under the last two presidents," Clinton was saying, "leadership on the environment has become an endangered species."

> Clinton promised he would create a national energy policy. [Here text popped up on screen to reinforce the key points.] It would seek to raise auto fuel standards to forty-five miles per gallon by the year 2020. Buy government vehicles powered by natural gas and offer business tax breaks for recycling. It is possible, Clinton said, to protect the environment and have a healthy economy. Yet in Arkansas, the Governor conceded, he had traded environmental protection for jobs.

"I've made the choice from time to time for jobs," Clinton was admitting, "because my state was a poor one without either enough jobs or enough federal help to clean up the environment."

Then Bury was moving into the third soundbite, covered by pictures of chicken guano in Arkansas and a river that did not look particularly dirty.

In Arkansas, critics claim Clinton has been too willing to accommodate powerful polluters like the chicken industry. Animal waste from farms has contaminated parts of the once pristine White River. Clinton remembers the 1988 photo opportunity attacking Democrat Dukakis for the pollution in Boston Harbor. So, today, he invited Bush to help clean up the White River and pointed out the lack of federal standards on farm pollution:

"I will not let this become the Boston Harbor. So, Mr. President, if you want to place the blame, you're gonna have to shoulder some of it, too."

The standup close was shot with Pennsylvania foothills in the background.

On the environment, Clinton hopes to take the offensive, by acknowledging his mistakes, and spreading blame to President Bush. To establish early on that pollution is too complex a problem for photo opportunities to fix. Chris Bury, ABC News.

The screen cut back to Jennings, then to Brit Hume's White House piece.

In a moment they saw that the White House had switched gears and responded after all. Hume's piece caught it well.

"At the White House today," Hume narrated over pictures of Bush, "reporters tried to get the President, who was seeing off some foreign visitors, to answer Governor Clinton's scolding of him on the environment." There was a shot of reporters shouting. "The President seemed momentarily tempted to respond then thought better of it." Bush on screen was hesitating, then kept walking. "The job of answering Clinton fell instead to the head of Mr. Bush's Council on Environmental Quality that sounded almost like the text of a thirty-second attack commercial."

"Bill Clinton's record on the environment as governor of Arkansas is the worst in the nation," the bureaucrat Michael Deland was saying. "His slippery attempt on Earth Day today to gloss over that deplorable record gives new meaning to the word oil slick."

"Oh Jesus," Kamlet said after hearing the finely crafted line. Bury, who was looking at his watch, announced to the group assembled at WPVI, "eighteen seconds." An extraordinarily long soundbite. And one that was so outrageous that it was guaranteed to get on air. It was the only soundbite Hume used, and Hume had built the piece around it and Bush's walk through the White House lawn. Hume continued:

> Deland also had ready copies of an independent study called the Green Index that ranked Arkansas forty-eighth overall in a state-by-state analysis of the nation's environmental health. The White House, meanwhile, released a written statement in the President's name on the environment, consisting mostly of lists of all the things he claims to have done or tried to do for the environment.
>
> One of the President's claimed accomplishments is calling for the worldwide antipollution treaty that's to be signed at the international conference in Brazil next month. But at the moment, it's unlikely the President will even go to that conference because the administration thinks the treaty language, which is still being negotiated, is too strong. Brit Hume, ABC News, the White House.

It was an equal match. Clinton's speech and Deland's attack bite.

Yet blaming television, or even short soundbites, would have been an oversimplification.

The *New York Times* story the next morning by Gwen Ifill used the same quotes from Clinton as Bury had, and the same attack bites from the White House.

Side by side, her story and the combination of Bury's and Hume's script tracked closely, though she had longer quotations and included a reaction from an environmentalist and then comments from Jerry Brown.

The same was true of the story by E.J. Dionne and Tom Kenworthy in the Washington *Post*.

Both the newspapers and the networks had focused on the political fight rather than the philosophical argument Clinton was making about the false choice between economic growth and environmental protectionism. The political story offered conflict and projected something about the race to come—features of modern journalism. Clinton had anticipated that, too, and tailored his speech to fit. His spin doctors had then pitched that, too.

What had changed was not that television was hiding the real substance of Clinton's speech. Clinton's speech had been so tailored to the grammar of journalism—especially but not exclusively television—that the candidate himself had made this the primary element of the speech.

Curiously, Clinton had taken his philosophical argument about false choices from a book written by one of the reporters covering the speech, E.J. Dionne. But Dionne's story was as political as ABC's.

On the 11 P.M. local news that night in dozens of markets around the country, ABC affiliates would rerun Bury and Kamlet's piece, shortened and with Bury's narration removed, the local anchor or correspondent reading an abbreviated version of the script. More people watched local news than network now. But network remained the root.

6:51.13 P.M.

Kamlet got another call from New York, probably his fortieth that day. *Morning News* wanted another piece, to run on *Good Morning America*. They had to do it all over again.

8:49.14 P.M.

It was done. The second piece actually looked fairly good on screen. Sometimes the ones done in an hour are as good as the ones done in five.

Now if they could find a cab, they could get back to their hotel, dump their equipment, and have dinner. They might get to bed by midnight. Tomorrow they would catch up with Clinton again in Florida.

★

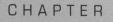

CHAPTER

THE REMAINING PRIMARIES

On one of those numb, three-hours-of-sleep mornings before the New York primary in early April, Jim Wooten had wandered into Friedman's office, lit a hated Marlboro, and offered a weary smile.

"This whole thing has gone kaflooey," he began, landing onto Friedman's sofa. "I don't know what's wrong. How did we do this?"

Friedman turned his desk chair to face the correspondent and nodded. He had always been skeptical they would be better this year, but he shared the sense of something wrong. The feeling of failure was in the air.

At the White House, Brit Hume thought the press had turned against the President in its simpleminded focus on a single story line—a campaign in disarray.

And the younger correspondents, like Chris Bury covering Clinton for *World News*, and Kirk von Fremd, handling the campaign for the overnight and morning shows, thought the press had turned Clinton into a kind of caricature. "I just don't think I have communicated what a serious guy this is," von Fremd confessed.

In the two months since the New Hampshire primary, even Jennings, so interested at first, seemed distracted and unhappy. "We have just kind of been swept along on the ocean," he said.

Worst of all, he thought the press had gotten in the way of the process.

Everyone had done what they thought they were supposed to. The press, having learned from 1988, had conducted fewer polls, tried to focus on character more, and didn't just emphasize the horse race.

For his part, George Bush and his aides had waited for the economy to improve, as instincts and his economists had told him it would, if he were prudent, and stayed out of the way.

And Bill Clinton did what he was supposed to, like the A-student who read the whole course syllabus. He had learned all the things Michael Dukakis had failed to do four years earlier and made sure to do them. He defined himself ideologically, defined his major opponent, Paul Tsongas, and made sure he fought back whenever he was hit—all the things George Bush had done in 1988. And the strategy succeeded; he blew Tsongas away.

Yet somehow, none of it was working. The more primaries Clinton won, the more people had doubts about him. The economy seemed to be getting better, a little, yet for the White House things got worse. And everyone thought the press was doing a miserable job. "It is coverage wanting humanity, common sense and not, incidentally, news," wrote author Ward Just. He was partly right, but the problem went deeper than the press.

The primary process was cockeyed. Party leaders had so front-loaded the schedule after New Hampshire—there were twenty-eight contests in twenty-eight days—that candidates had to campaign on stupefyingly simple messages communicated mostly in two brief ads for each state, one positive, the other attacking their opponent. The press was writing about matters unrelated to anything voters knew or cared about—focusing on tactics and the horse race with one hand, and with the other scrutinizing for disqualifying flaws any candidate they mistakenly assumed voters already knew something about. The campaign was functioning on a logic all its own, providing answers to questions that voters had not heard, about controversies they knew nothing about—a traveling cloud of klieg lights, TV spots and motorcades disconnected from real life.

You could see what had happened the moment people left New Hampshire. On his flight to Maryland the next day, the winner of the New Hampshire primary, Paul Tsongas, wandered at one point to the back of his new chartered jet to talk to reporters. As he chatted, one of the journalists leaned over an airline seat and asked him, "Senator, what would you say is your biggest character flaw?"

Photographers pushed forward to capture his answer. Tsongas thought a moment and then offered a characteristically candid and self-mocking reply: "There is a tendency to cross the border into being moralistic. It is not very pretty. I plead guilty."

Reporters called it the phenomenon by which the media eat their young. Once the press had participated in the birth of a front-runner—inevitably echoing the polls by exaggerating the man's virtues—they turned to examine their discovery for blemishes. They had done it in short form already with Clinton. They would do it later with Ross Perot. Now as the race began to sort itself out, they waited for a true front-runner on whom to fix their gaze.

The press seems able to scrutinize only one candidate at a time, which further tilts the coverage out of balance. One journalist described the press as "a campaignapede," a sort of giant insect connected by wires, with hundreds of legs and one brain. Another imagined the press during this time as a kind of cyclops, a monster, powerful, dangerous, with only one eye.

Tsongas was mostly spared. He never enjoyed as much bounce from the press as one might have expected, and never suffered any real scrutiny. The day of the primary, Friedman asked Wooten, the chief political correspondent, which candidate he wanted to travel with after New Hampshire. Wooten picked Clinton. "I just don't see Paul as the real story," Wooten told him.

Over the next two weeks, as the race sorted itself out, Friedman ordered just one story specifically about Tsongas, a feature the day after his victory in New Hampshire. Otherwise Tsongas was covered in general campaign stories, usually horse-race pieces. Friedman was waiting for the former Massachusetts senator to establish himself as more than a regional candidate. Tsongas accomplished that two weeks later on March 3 by winning the Maryland primary, and Friedman finally assigned a correspondent, Judy Muller from Los Angeles, to Tsongas's campaign plane. Two weeks after that, Tsongas dropped out.

In all, *World News* did just eight pieces specifically on Tsongas's candidacy. None of them focused on Tsongas's proposals or ideas.

It wasn't appreciably different elsewhere. *NBC Nightly News* did only two stories about Tsongas, a profile and an analysis of his economic policies. Nor was it even that different in print. The only paper that looked seriously, if gently, at Tsongas's record was the *New York Times*. The reason was simple. "I don't know ten reporters in one hundred who think he can be the nominee," Jack Germond had said in New Hampshire.

George Bush, too, was largely spared the monster eye. The incumbent President had already been through this process, the press rationalized, and the investigative work, if any, would come in the fall. The job of covering the President was more routine, partly transcriptive, partly intuitive. One waited for the President to act, then called various friends and sources to get an explanation about what he was up to. In the case of Bush, the White House press corps defined their task mostly as watching the President veer in all directions and demonstrate an even deeper political ineptness than he had in New Hampshire.

The days after New Hampshire were almost difficult to watch. First Bush said he would confront Buchanan. Then he tried to ignore him. Then the President couldn't control his own party. A week after New Hampshire, Republican senator Connie Mack of

Florida called on Bush to fire old friend and treasury secretary Nicholas Brady. Mack even held a press conference to say on camera that "the economic team has failed."

Mack wouldn't get Brady fired, Hume boomed from the White House lawn that night. "What's important is that it suggests that things down south may not be as good for the President, either politically or economically, as the White House thinks."

Four days later, Bush went to call on Ronald Reagan, and the Washington *Post* had a welcoming gift for him. It quoted Reagan that morning as saying "Bush didn't seem to stand for anything." At Reagan's house, the fence was covered with brown paper to stop photographers, and the press was kept locked outside so there could be no customary photo op. The Gipper wouldn't even have his picture taken with Bush.

And it got worse from there. In the South Dakota primary the next day, running unopposed, Bush managed only 69 percent of Republican primary voters. By March 2, a week later, Hume thought the White House was in a state of near paralysis. It released a photo of Bush working in the Oval Office, but the picture was ten days old, "and there was no explanation of its release," he marveled on the air. Bush had no speechwriter, he had no plan, he had no stomach for the campaign. Hume was disgusted.

The next morning, as Ann Compton prepared for a piece on *Good Morning America*, she got a call from the White House press office alerting her to an interview that day in an Atlanta newspaper. The President had conceded that breaking his no-tax pledge was the biggest mistake he had ever made. And he had buried this major announcement in an Atlanta newspaper! It was bizarre.

By mid-morning Bush was backing off the statement. "Well, I don't know about the biggest, but, yes, I . . . see, I'm very disappointed with Congress. I thought this one compromise—and it was a compromise—would result in no more tax increases,"

Bush said. The day after, White House aides told Hume the President's admission of error did not mean he was prepared to make another tax pledge.

This ship had no captain, no charts, and no direction. Only three weeks since the New Hampshire primary, and Hume could already see some of the President's men despairing. On March 6, the unemployment rate hit 7.6 percent, its highest point in six years.

Bush was campaigning in the south that day for Super Tuesday, enjoying a tremendous rally at a Christian college in Oklahoma. The Baptist kids in the crowd, fresh-faced, clean-cut, never having seen a presidential candidate before, let alone a president, were going nuts. "Four More Years. FOUR MORE YEARS." The press for days had been writing about the President getting lackluster crowds, and press secretary Marlin Fitzwater thought it was garbage. This day he snapped. In the middle of the rally, Fitzwater suddenly ordered the Wocka boys, the White House Communications Agency, to turn off the loudspeakers piping the sound of the event into the press filing center next door. Make the "lazy bastards" come out and see the crowd reaction for themselves, the press secretary sneered.

Fitzwater deserves to be remembered as one of the better presidential press secretaries. He served six years under two presidents, at times functioning as an aggressive surrogate attacking the president's opponents, yet managing throughout his tenure to maintain the press corps's respect. He had a sophisticated understanding of media, especially print, and usually maintained his composure. The evidence of White House disarray and strain didn't get any more obvious.

Beating Buchanan did little to help. Reporters knew from their own polling and reporting what the Bush campaign was discovering from its focus groups in Maryland and Georgia: the President's problem was not Buchanan, it was Bush. Some of Buchanan's ads in Georgia—particularly one featuring pictures of homosexuals dancing—had actually helped Bush. Once Bush fi-

nally started running ads attacking Buchanan—first over Buchanan's protectionism and attitude toward women, then for own-
ing a foreign car while preaching America first—the commentator's campaign collapsed like an empty suit.

But the President's problems remained. Four days after Buchanan stopped campaigning, Bush bowed to conservatives and
started attacking Congress. But the decision to do so was so con-
tentious, aides started leaking to reporters everywhere to undermine the message. On the air that night, Hume was merciless.
"Officials said today's speech was the product of a week-long series
of highly unfocused meetings presided jointly by the President's
chief of staff and his campaign chief," Hume reported. "One top
official said it was the most chaotic process he'd ever seen in ten
years of government."

"This place is like Noah's Ark," Hume said to Compton by
summer. "There is two of everybody."

Because of the chaos, Bush couldn't buy a positive story,
regardless of the substance of his message. Of the 417 stories on
Bush in the Washington *Post* and *New York Times* between June
1 and the Republican convention in mid-August, only twenty-
three had a decidedly positive tone. More than three hundred were
negative.

One day in early summer, Fitzwater even called Hume into
the office. "Why do reporters hate Bush," he asked. Hume did not
argue with him. He concurred that Bush was suffering an incessant
negative press, at times unfairly. And privately he thought some
of it was liberal bias: Reporters wanted to see government be used
for great works. Otherwise, why cover it? But bias was not the
whole of it.

Bush also brought some of the problem on himself, he told
Fitzwater. Maybe the problem is that the President seems weak
and indecisive in response to the attacks from the right and the
left, Hume said. The press secretary simply nodded. He looked
sad.

Hume was partly right: The criticisms of Bush's White

House in disarray were political judgments, not ideological. They reflected the bias of Washington insiders who cared about political technique, and consequently probably did Bush less harm than other sorts of criticism might. Would voters care come fall that Bush had been politically inept last spring?

Nor was this investigative scrutiny. The press did little to probe Bush's record beyond some obligatory summaries. (The one exception were a few reporters, including Doug Frantz and Murray Wass in the Los Angeles *Times* and Koppel's crew at *Nightline*, who focused on Bush's secret buildup of Iraq before the Gulf War.)

What the President suffered from, rather, was a kind of tyranny of consensus, a subtle form of pack journalism that afflicts the White House press corps in particular. The dominant newspapers and the networks set a story line, and it becomes difficult for any White House correspondents to deviate from it without being second-guessed by colleagues or editors.

Early on in the campaign, a reporter from Knight-Ridder newspapers was even put on notice by the editors that they thought the reporter was too tough on Bush. They would be double-checking the adjectives and vetting the stories for bias, they told the reporter. A few months later, when the story line elsewhere had changed, the reporter was told to toughen it up.

Hume felt the tyranny of consensus too. "The only story I can sell is disarray at the White House," he grumbled one day in early summer.

In part, the consensus criticism of Bush was a function of incumbency. Friedman and Jennings, for instance, had consciously worried about a sitting president's power to manage the news during a campaign. And they decided to balance it by treating Bush like a candidate more than a president. And when measured on political technique, Bush was doing a horrible job.

Two nights after the Los Angeles riots, when Bush decided to briefly address the country, Jennings even decided to invite Bill Clinton on for a response.

When executive vice president Richard Wald heard, he summoned the anchor and Jeff Gralnick to the fifth floor. Wald, the balding veteran news executive who was normally a quiet Arledge loyalist, was presiding over news while Arledge was recovering from colon cancer surgery. With Stephen Weiswasser, the lawyer installed by Cap Cities functioning as a kind of moderator, Wald stunned nearly everyone by shouting down his anchorman.

"This is wrong!" he yelled at Jennings. "This is a presidential occasion. A state of emergency, and the President has a right to go to the nation and speak to the people without making it a political occasion."

"If Bush had given this speech last night I would agree with you," Jennings answered. But Bush had already taken his action as president, calling out the troops, the night before. Tonight, he is just making a campaign speech.

The argument was as heated as things ever got at ABC. But Wald did not force the anchor to change the program. It would be the beginning of what some at ABC, and certainly the White House, would see as a liberal bias by Jennings against the reelection of George Bush. And ironically, it would come at a time when others in the network were becoming convinced that the network management was cowed by friendships inside the White House. The question of ABC's fairness would linger for the remainder of the campaign.

The press had reserved its true investigative stare, however, for whomever emerged as the real challenger to Bush, be it Kerrey or Clinton or someone else. Two weeks after New Hampshire, Clinton won in Georgia and became that someone.

Five days later, the Sunday *New York Times* ran a front-page story by one of its top investigative reporters, Jeff Gerth. "Clintons Joined S&L Operator in Ozark Real-Estate Venture"

Gerth tried to detail that Bill and Hillary Clinton had been partners in a real estate venture during the 1980s with the owner of an Arkansas savings and loan association. Friedman recognized the piece for what it was, a jumbled mess. It wasn't clear whether the Clintons had done anything wrong. The only curious fact was that they were 50 percent partners in a deal in which they put up less than 50 percent of the finances. But since the deal went sour, they seemed to have lost money in the venture.

"I didn't know what the hell the story was trying to say," Friedman said, and the S&L story never surfaced anywhere else. But the story had another more powerful effect: it signaled to the rest of the press that the mighty *New York Times* had turned its investigative beam on Clinton's past. And that helped trigger an avalanche of press scrutiny.

The next week Clinton won in Super Tuesday, and the week after that in Michigan and Illinois. As he racked up victories, something strange began to happen, something that the press clumsily and arrogantly tried to deal with and badly botched.

Bill Clinton frightened people, especially the Democratic political professionals in Washington with whom the press corps mingled. Wooten heard it. So did Hal Bruno, and Jeff Greenfield. After Gennifer and the draft, Democrats wondered what the hell else was in Clinton's closet that might come rattling out.

One of Hal Bruno's key tasks during the primaries was to count superdelegates, members of Congress who could commit to any candidate they liked. The superdelegates had the power to tip the nomination at a certain point to a given candidate. As Bruno and his colleague in the political unit, Katherine Berger, went about their counting, they found that people were refusing to commit to Clinton—even after he had the nomination assured. "This guy scares them," Bruno told Friedman.

They heard another worry. Since the Democrats Clinton faced were so weak, no one had done adequate opposition research against him. "We don't know what is out there about this guy," a prominent Democratic senate investigator told a group of Capitol Hill colleagues at lunch in the spring, "and the Republicans do." Reporters heard doubts about Clinton from voters, too.

When David Broder and Dan Balz of the Washington *Post* conducted a focus group outside Chicago in March, they found undecided voters were sick of Bush, but even warier of Clinton. People started cussing. "Slick," "slimy," "cunning," "smooth, smile, and screw you."

And reporters had their own suspicions. Wooten still believed Clinton had lied to him about the draft that day in New Hampshire. He just didn't know how. And if he lied about this, what else? Was there a timebomb ticking out there?

Unfailingly reactive, the press set out to answer the doubts. In New Hampshire, the press had left the question of adultery and the draft unresolved because it felt uncertain about its role. Now, in Little Rock, it tried to get at what it perceived as the same character issues by looking at areas where the press felt more at home—money and corruption. The monster eye was not only unleashed, but had special sanction.

The problem was the execution of the search. Rather than look into Clinton's character, it looked for isolated incidents that might hint at something wrong, and it tended to see the worst.

Within days after the *New York Times* story, reporters from all over the country descended again on Little Rock. Soon there were so many that, in government offices, local Arkansas reporters took to requesting whatever documents the national reporters had just looked at. In the Capital Hotel, the unofficial press headquarters, reporters from the Washington *Post* and the Los Angeles *Times* kept running into each other in the lobby while waiting for faxes to arrive. Hotel waiters were soon able to tell anyone who inquired which newspapers had staff in town.

As the press horde crowded the Capital Hotel, Doe's Eat Place, The Blue Mesa, and Shug's rib joint, rumors began to spread throughout Washington of stories about to break. Clinton had an illegitimate child with a black TV anchorwoman in New England. Clinton once beat up his pollster for bringing him bad news. The Washington *Post* was about to publish that Clinton had once propositioned the daughter of Ron Brown, the chairman of

the Democratic National Committee. *Playboy* was about to publish that Clinton had an affair with Elizabeth Ward, the 1982 Miss
America from Arkansas. (Ward posed for Playboy and afterwards
denied any involvement with him.) The Los Angeles *Times* was
about to publish that Clinton was involved in cocaine. The Los
Angeles *Times* had affidavits, but it also had doubts about their
reliability.

The Republicans played off the rumors and tried to feed
them. The Los Angeles *Times* received two anonymous faxes in
Little Rock that, when traced, came from the Republican opposition research team at the Republican National Committee. The
paper also received letters from mothers who said they had heard
stories about young women in Arkansas defiled by Clinton. When
the letters were traced, they came from the mothers of Republican
workers. Chris Isham, head of the investigative unit for *World
News*, also received similar tips from Republicans. None of these
were published or broadcast.

The whole campaign became shrouded in an uncontrollable
psychology of revelation—a search to unmask the façade of candidates. It was fueled not only by Clinton's equivocating style and
record but also by the hysteria of a press corps grown too large, by
the cynicism of the day, and by a lack of standards over what
constitutes public character.

Friedman also sent a team to Little Rock, but he was not
looking for "another smoking gun story," he instructed. Investigative television was difficult and there was so much of investigative
work about Clinton going on, he felt his viewers would be better
served by some clarifying pieces. So he sent his team out with two
assignments. The first was to do a piece about what kind of governor Clinton was. Did he help the state or hurt it. The story was
overdue and, he thought, frankly obvious.

The other was more complicated. After all the investigative
pieces that had appeared elsewhere, take a single case and use it
to offer some context about what it is like to do business in
Arkansas.

The group worked under Chris Isham, the senior producer for investigative reporting at *World News*. Producer Rich Greenberg went down without cameras to dig up stories and sources and came back with a potential investigative case about a single bond issue and the potential conflicts of interests involved. It became the basis of the story about what it was like to do business in Arkansas. Correspondent John Martin and producer Kim Schiller were sent to follow Greenberg's research and produce the pieces for camera. But such stories took time, and by the time Martin and Schiller had finished them in April, Clinton had faded in interest behind Ross Perot. The pieces did not run until the Democratic convention in July. ABC was largely irrelevant amid the scrutiny of Clinton except as a vague echo.

In Little Rock, Clinton and his aides were becoming frantic. The goddamn press jackals were going to destroy him. Clinton called an old friend, someone he had long trusted to do the hard and sometimes dirtiest work for him, his former gubernatorial chief of staff Betsey Wright, who was teaching a seminar that semester at Harvard.

The monster eye's examination of Clinton was about to become even more bizarre. Wright organized an elaborate system, a high-technology counter-media program, to monitor, intimidate, and stymie press coverage of Clinton's background.

Within days, she had a staff of eight and a one-story office building behind Clinton's Little Rock campaign headquarters. She began removing Governor Clinton's records and his personal files from the state capitol building. She kept track of which files reporters were requesting there, what sources they had called from their hotel rooms in the Holiday Inn and the Excelsior, and who they had been seen talking with in the bar at the Capital Hotel.

She called reporters to tell them what they were working on. She told one reporter she had "sightings" of thirty-five reporters from the national press around the state. On one occasion, Wright, now a private citizen, called a state police officer who was engaged in an interview with a newspaper reporter and ordered him to stop talking.

Reporters were warned by their sources that local reporters were spying on them, that the Clinton campaign was taking photographs of them, that their phones were tapped and that the carbons of their hotel phone messages were delivered each night to the Clinton campaign staff. They did not know if the warnings were true.

One hour after Los Angeles *Times* reporter Ronald Ostrow arrived in Little Rock and before he had even checked into his hotel, the state police commissioner being interviewed by two of Ostrow's colleagues said to them ominously, "So, I understand now there are five of you."

Some reporters took to making sensitive calls from phone booths to avoid any taps. In late March, when Los Angeles *Times* reporter Richard E. Meyer tried to use a pay phone in downtown Little Rock, he became convinced he was being followed by a four-person surveillance team.

That night, a group of reporters from the Los Angeles *Times* and *New York Times* met at the Holiday Inn and plotted a crude sting operation hoping to finally ascertain whether they were being monitored. *New York Times* correspondent Michael Wines left an anonymous message for William Rempel of the Los Angeles *Times* about delivering documents the next day in a public park. The next morning, reporters from the two papers staged a phony exchange in open view in the park while other reporters trailing them patrolled the area writing down license plates and noting anyone they saw. The amateur sting team came up empty. But reporters would later discover that Betsey Wright knew about it anyway.

The Wright antimedia campaign was one of the oddest and most blatant attempts to intimidate and possibly impede reporters that many in the political press had ever seen. And it fell miserably on its face. By Illinois, March 17, Jerry Brown was attacking Clinton for "a scandal a week."

Wright's heavy-handed style probably made it worse. Her intimidation, even if all the stories of phone taps and surveillance were false, made national reporters suspicious Clinton had something to hide. That only added to the reporters' professional error of seeing the worst in the facts they had. Wright also argued that local reporters had already written all these stories, but that claim was specious, too. If Arkansas voters weighed these issues considering Clinton for governor, the rest of the country had the right to evaluate them, too. Yet this did not excuse some of the pieces done.

Investigative reporting is a form of argumentation, of pointing to wrongdoing and reasonably establishing it for the reader. It is not the same as simply reporting events. Two of the *New York Times* pieces, both by Gerth, were written in the form of exposés but failed to make their case. One, implicitly accusing Clinton of watering down an Arkansas state ethics law, was simply wrong. Clinton had championed it. Another, focusing on how Hillary Clinton's law firm did business with the Arkansas state government, said only late in the story that she declined her share of fees from those cases. And it failed to report that the firm's percentage of that business did not grow after Clinton became governor.

The Los Angeles *Times* produced two other pieces that failed to make their case. One focused on how Clinton lobbied for the state to pass a bond issue for a new police radio system, even after it was known that the company underwriting the bond issue was headed by a Clinton friend under investigation for cocaine. The wrongdoing Clinton was accused of was not established, and may not have existed. The other story suggested Clinton had protected a state medical examiner from firing because the doctor had protected Clinton's mother in a wrongful-death charge in her work as a nurse. Again, the facts presented did not establish the key assumptions of the story. One of the reporters involved had even lobbied against writing it in exposé form. In all cases the stories were legitimate, but all of them should have been explored as features, with neutrality, not in the necessarily accusatory tone of investigative exposés.

The problem, however, went further than these stories. The press had become victims of an uncontrollable search to unmask the façade of candidates. It was a new kind of pack journalism, something beyond the classic definition of reporters sitting on the press bus and agreeing on what would be the lead of their stories. And when the stories were unfair, the pack did not correct them, it made them worse. In the age of instant and constant communication, local television and radio would take the dramatic outlines of a story and repeat them endlessly on the news—at four, five, six, eleven, overnight, sunrise, and then morning shows. Against the avalanche, it became impossible for any newspaper or TV program to maintain for its audience a semblence of nuance or context.

Out on the stump, too, Clinton had to answer these charges not in a reasoned way, with four or five reporters and a fair length of time. The scale of the modern campaign press corps meant the gangbang nature of the Gennifer Flowers confrontation was now the norm, not the exception. A candidate in trouble faced forty cameras and two hundred reporters at a time. And in that environment any presumed scandal became a slaughter—even when the two hundred reporters considered the story unfair.

Television was not driving the process. None of the investigative work that forced Clinton's candidacy into this shadow was from the networks or local. Nor were they to blame for the stories' problems. Too many of the original print investigation stories were flawed or overheated on their own. The cruel reduction of television, however, magnified the errors.

In a stronger field, even Clinton strategist James Carville privately conceded, Clinton likely wouldn't have survived. As election returns rolled in the day of the Illinois primary, a young campaign aide exulted about how well the campaign had gone. "We ain't exactly running against giants," Carville growled.

Many at ABC were horrified by the process they were engaged in. "This is disgusting," said Mimi Gurbst, the assignment editor on the national desk. Gurbst was open with people about how she felt. She liked Clinton. But even others who were skeptical of him, like Chris Bury, largely agreed. Friedman, too, thought the process had swollen out of control, and among all the stories of the primary season Friedman was proudest of one that tried to describe its oppressive nature. It was a piece in which Bury tracked the effect of another Jeff Gerth story in the *New York Times* accusing Clinton, wrongly, of excluding himself from the reach of an Arkansas ethics law. The story revealed a lot about Friedman and ABC and the state of network news. The executive producer assumed people were hearing news from so many other sources that the networks' role was to somehow provide context. It had become an observer of the process, not the driver.

With some jealousy, Friedman also watched as Koppel and *Nightline* moved more quickly on an idea that Friedman himself was considering: to spend a day tracking the candidates, from the moment they rose till they went to bed, to reveal the "grueling inhuman nature" of the process. Like the draft program *Nightline* had done a few weeks earlier in New Hampshire, this show was watched by nearly the entire political press corps, and it helped to remind them that the objects of their attention were still people. After winning the New York primary the following day, Clinton would never again suffer the full glare of the monster eye of the press. He was the certain party nominee, and the pack had enough.

But there was one other factor that drove what happened, and it was most obvious to those closest to the race, people like Jim Wooten. The campaign that Bill Clinton waged to win his party's nomination was tough, and skillful, to be sure, but it had also reinforced the idea that he was a man who would say anything.

Clinton's campaign crew had left New Hampshire dazed and unprepared. When his advisers met in Manchester to plot post-primary strategy only days before the New Hampshire vote, none of them had read through Tsongas's famous 85-page manifesto, "A Call to Economic Arms," though Tsongas was now his main opponent. For more than a week afterward, Clinton's team kept waiting for Nebraska senator Bob Kerrey to deliver "the speech" that would turn things around, and floundered over where to campaign—Maine, South Dakota, Georgia? Feuds broke out between the professional campaign consultants and Clinton's friends, whom they dubbed the Semi-Pros.

As Clinton watched Brown challenge Tsongas in Maine, Kerrey win South Dakota, and Tsongas about to win the caucuses in Washington state, the candidate made a critical decision, one he would repeat again and again. He rejected plans to reintroduce his main ideas by waging a serious and substantive campaign, starting with a speech in Georgia detailing citizen responsibility. Instead, Clinton was persuaded by aides who argued he had to win something—anything—to get back into the race, and that to do it he had to run a rough, tactical, punch and counter punch campaign. It betrayed a man who called himself a new kind of Democrat but, for better and worse, was a thoroughly conventional politician.

So Clinton's aides crafted a strategy to counter Tsongas that positioned Clinton in a different place within the Democratic party from where he had been placing himself for nearly a decade: to paint the former Massachusetts senator as little more than a surrogate for Bush and run to the left of him.

A week after New Hampshire, Michael Kramer of *Time* wrote an analysis piece comparing Tsongas's and Clinton's economic plans, a piece that was as much essay as straight reporting. It fit Clinton's argument precisely, and Clinton media adviser Frank Greer seized on it for a TV commercial, which became the cornerstone of Clinton's attack.

Paul Tsongas or Bill Clinton? *Time* magazine says, "Much of what Tsongas proposes smacks of trickle-down economics." He even says he'll be "the best friend Wall Street has ever had." Another capital-gains tax cut for the rich, a cut in cost-of-living adjustments for older Americans, and a five-cent-a-year hike in the gas tax. But that's what

went wrong in the eighties. Bill Clinton wants change. No more tax
breaks for companies moving our jobs overseas, but new incentives to
create jobs at home. More education and job training, and making the
rich pay their fair share. Bill Clinton. He'll put people first.

Clinton was not changing his positions, but he was certainly
changing his image. Clinton the moderate, the new kind of Democrat, became Clinton the populist of Democratic tradition. And
the message "reinventing government" was replaced by "put people first." Wooten and other reporters saw a basic dishonesty:
"Tsongas is a lot closer to Clinton on economics than Bush," said
Walter Robinson of the Boston *Globe*. Clinton's campaign was
chameleon-like. It would be the first illustration of an ability to
adapt that would ultimately win Clinton the election, but would
also expose a prime weakness. He was a candidate who could learn,
but one whose ideological position could not always be trusted.

When Greer's ad quoting *Time* worked, and Clinton won
Georgia, it was recut to undermine Tsongas in every state the
campaign ran ads thereafter. Clinton also got his ads on the air
before Tsongas did, putting the ill-prepared Massachusetts senator
on the defensive. Clinton's team also knew where to buy time,
while Tsongas, who spent nearly as much as Clinton on TV, wasted
a fair amount of money. The ads were crucial. With voters less
than enthusiastic about their choices, local news stations in Florida
and elsewhere were giving the presidential race nominal coverage.

"We paid a price, but it was the cost of winning and made the
difference between winning and losing," George Stephanopoulos
said. "It's easy to say in hindsight that we could have done something else, but we went week after week literally not knowing if we
could make it through."

When things got bad enough, Tsongas made the same choice.
After the disaster on Super Tuesday, aides argued for him to
return to his message from New Hampshire: resist attacking Clinton, explain your real policies, position yourself as the truth-teller.

Gerald Austin, a rough-edged, Brooklyn-bred political operative, listened to the appeal for high-mindedness and replied curtly: "Not enough time. Not enough money."

It was a sad truth about modern presidential primaries that had nothing to do with the press or the candidates. Trying to run a substantive campaign was too expensive and required more time to communicate to voters than the system would allow.

Tsongas instead ran the slickest ad of the campaign, featuring two factory workers talking about Clinton being untrustworthy, an ad full of innuendo and suspicion, offering unsubstantiated charges, and nothing affirmative about Tsongas. Thus the unpackaged candidate's final act was to embrace the divisive and destructive tactics he hated. Two days later, Tsongas ended his campaign, privately bitter toward Clinton.

Most sadly, the system had become so strained, that Clinton was denounced for failing to rise above it—by the press that itself was driving it.

In the meantime, Friedman and ABC had failed in their hope of covering the race differently. NBC was at least trying. It had attempted to cover issues somewhat, and to sort through when candidates were dissembling. But NBC's success was uneven. Its ranks were too thin, and its coverage was suffering, because NBC's correspondents were rarely in the field with the candidates. When they did go, their lack of feel for the race showed. Lisa Myers had all but predicted Tsongas would win Florida—he didn't. And inside NBC, producers felt that Andrea Mitchell's coverage was both too superficial and too subjective. Half the time she was rendering opinions. "We're aware of it," said one NBC executive. But at least NBC was trying.

CBS, on the other hand, had all but stopped covering the race. Political editor Susan Zirinsky's team found it hard to sell most stories about the race. "For the six to eight weeks after New Hampshire, voter rage was the only thing a lot of executives around here were particularly interested in," one CBS veteran political journalist said. "Bash the institutions, bash the Congress, bash Clinton and Bush, and let's look at the interesting anger. And at the highest levels, people feel if you put a politician into a piece it diminishes it."

CBS correspondent Eric Engberg marveled about how, two days before the Pennsylvania primary, he was sent to do a story about a steamship called the USS *United States* being mothballed.

At ABC, the problem was different. For all that people had criticized Friedman, ABC ended up providing more coverage than the others, but it was coverage as usual. *World News* had covered the process, the horse race and the spectacle. Gralnick's election night specials were fine, but standard—though even that had taken effort. Arledge had to fight hard to win approval for prime time on the night of the New York primary. But network-wide, ABC had done little to explain who the candidates were or what they stood for—the stuff that might have helped voters choose. All through the primaries, *World News* did just four pieces examining what the Democratic candidates' positions were.

Friedman insisted it just wasn't possible to seriously compare the ideas of five presidential candidates on the nightly news, with twenty-two minutes a night. It also didn't matter that much, he argued. The policy differences between the Democrats were minimal at best, except for something startling like Jerry Brown's flat tax. No wonder voters didn't follow them. During the primaries voters cared about character.

Friedman was only partly right. The usual two-minute coverage of issues on television was not particularly edifying. The problem was that neither Friedman nor anyone else at ABC had explored whether there was a better way. And they had never seriously tried to cover character, either.

Friedman and Jennings had made one attempt at innovation. At an ABC-sponsored Democratic debate in Dallas, they had tried to come up with a format that would get beyond the canned answers and theatrics and approximate a spontaneous exchange of ideas. After the candidates refused to be given a hypothetical crisis to solve, Friedman and Jennings proposed at the last moment having the candidates question each other while Jennings sat back. But the Clinton and Tsongas campaigns became enraged and denounced Jennings for his arrogance at trying to trick them.

By April, the public seemed inured, even belligerent, toward both the campaign and the press's revelations about the candidates. When the Los Angeles *Times* and NBC ran a story in June accusing Clinton of protecting a state medical examiner who had exonerated his mother in a wrongful death, it made no dent whatsoever in his campaign's fortunes.

The spectacle reached its nadir in the New York primary, where the New York tabloids and local television, as usual, turned the candidates into characters from some familiar morality play— Clinton, the rube lost in the big city; Brown, the wisecracking tough guy. By the Pennsylvania primary in mid-April, it seemed as if voters had learned nothing. Wooten sat in his hotel room in Philadelphia and marveled at the fact that Clinton was running introductory biographical ads about himself. He assumed, correctly, that Clinton's research showed voters knew nothing about him.

It was worse than he knew. Clinton pollster Stan Greenberg had found voters were angry at the press for failing to provide them adequately with the information they needed—in this case Clinton's true life history. They were angry at what they perceived the press was doing to the process. Some people even trusted information less if it came from the media. The press wasn't covering character—only isolated incidents in candidates' lives mostly selected to reveal flaws. When ABC ventured into the revelation game, in mid-April, no one had the stomach for it.

John McWethy was the kind of guy who described himself as straight arrow, nothing flashy or flamboyant. He thought that was one of the reasons sources trusted him, one of the reasons he had done so well. He had come to journalism late, after a splendid career as an unpublished novelist, and then as a print reporter for *U.S. News and World Report.* One day in the early years of the Reagan administration, McWethy had asked a question at a presidential press conference. In New York, Roone Arledge was watching. That man should be in television, he thought, and McWethy was soon hired by ABC. Nearly ten years later, McWethy was a consensus choice as the best of the network correspondents at the state department, and still a rising star at ABC.

McWethy was in California working a story for *20-20*—about troubles with the Air Force's new C-17 transport aircraft—when one of his sources mentioned that in the 1970s he had seen drugs used at the home of then California governor Jerry Brown while the source was working as a state security officer guarding the governor.

McWethy let it pass, but the source, James Pashley, an investigator for McDonnell Douglas, brought it up again at dinner a few days later. Between 1975 and 1976, he had seen marijuana roaches in ashtrays, and evidence of cocaine. Pashley said he had even borrowed a narcotics kit from a buddy in the LAPD and run tests.

McWethy was not exactly enthusiastic—politics was not his specialty—but he knew this was potential dynamite. He asked if Pashley would repeat the allegation on camera back at the hotel in silhouette, his identity obscured. Then McWethy hoped to send it off to "the great ABC machine" in New York. "Give it to anybody you want on the campaign trail," he would tell them, and that would end his obligation.

In New York, Friedman and Jennings never stopped for a second to think it wasn't a story. Neither did Chris Isham, the senior producer for investigative reporting at *World News.* Nor, frankly, did McWethy, after Friedman ordered him to keep on the story.

If the story was true, Friedman thought it said a lot about Brown, who was wandering around talking about Bill Clinton suffering from "a scandal a week" and suggesting in "a not very veiled way" that Clinton was not fit to be president. "The issue was not whether he smoked pot but whether he as chief lawmaker at a time when they were arresting fifty thousand people a year for drugs was tolerating drug use in his home," Friedman explained. "It was not a close call at all."

"Under California law," Isham argued, "if Brown knew about this, it might actually constitute possession of cocaine."

Curiously, there was never any discussion that they needed someone on camera full face. They asked everyone—even Pashley eventually—but when no one said yes, no one at ABC argued they should hesitate. Anonymous sourcing was so common on television and in print, they all explained later, it never came up.

Over the next few weeks, Isham tried to track down any police he could find who guarded Brown's house between 1975 and 1980, eventually talking to fourteen people. In time, some of the story started to fall apart. Isham related in memos back to New York that early accounts of the parties at Brown's house as wild encounters featuring sex and wild drug use were unsubstantiated, and the sources backed away from them. But McWethy and Isham still felt the drug stories held up.

Three days after the New York primary, they had four sources confirming the story, two on camera in silhouette.

They relied heavily on instinct in accepting the story. Friedman, Isham, and McWethy thought the four sources' accounts varied enough that they did not sound concocted, and they had all been reluctant to talk. They knew Pashley's record as a reliable whistleblower. And they had other so far unsubstantiated sources, not police, giving them even more damaging information off the record about drug use at the house and around Brown. In their minds, they were being conservative.

Finally, no one told them they were on the wrong track.

The script went through sixteen drafts, vetted by attorneys, before being ready to go on the air. The piece ran more than four minutes long and led the broadcast.

And people hated the story, especially the silhouette sourcing. Inside ABC, one of McWethy's closest friends behind his back said, "This stinks." One of the top producers at *World News* said, "The sourcing was crap and we should have backed away as soon as our sources backed off the orgy stuff."

At CBS, political editor Susan Zirinsky asked political correspondent Eric Engberg if they should follow the story. "ABC is holding a pile of loose shit in their hands," Engberg said. "I don't want to touch it."

By early evening, Brown's attorney, former San Francisco mayor Joseph Alioto, was on the phone threatening libel and demanding a retraction.

One of the doubters was Ted Koppel, whose *Nightline* program that night focused on the allegations. Koppel wanted to interview one of McWethy's sources for the show, and before the interview began, Koppel came into the room where the cop was waiting, and started grilling him. What had he seen? What proof did he have that Brown knew about it?

"Why should I believe you? You don't know much," Koppel announced coolly.

The source fell apart. The interview that followed was so bad Isham had to beg Koppel to tape it again. Then during the show Brown stunned McWethy with how forceful his denials were. He denied ever even having a party in the house.

Rather than doubting the story, Friedman became furious at the public reaction. Newspapers used anonymous sources every day. "On television, you can actually see and hear the person." What hypocrisy.

McWethy felt disoriented. "We could bring down a president on the basis of two anonymous sources," he said, referring to the Washington *Post*'s legendary rule that it needed two corroborating anonymous sources for its Watergate stories. "And here we had four anonymous sources, two of whom were on camera, and we were getting nailed. It blew my mind." Perhaps the problem, he thought, was politics. "I don't understand the playing field."

Friedman ordered two followup pieces the next day—a second by McWethy airing more evidence and one by Ken Ka-shawahara from California quoting various people who knew Brown saying the story could not possibly be true. And he wanted them to keep going. He was damned if he was going to let this thing vanish and have everyone think he was wrong.

The calls came in by the hundreds, pro and con. Several came from entertainment people, some of them famous, backing the story, but none allowed Friedman to use their names. Another call came from one of Brown's former top political aides. Brown was lying, he said, and so were the people ABC had quoted defending him. B.T. Collins, Brown's former chief of staff, had said Brown despised people even using alcohol. Every reporter who had covered Brown knew that was a lie.

Finally that Friday a call came from a police supervisor confirming what their other sources had told them. His name was Robert Ford, and with coaxing, he agreed to say so on camera, full face over the weekend. In the meantime, ABC hired private investigators to do a background check on Ford.

Their final story ran the next Wednesday, quoting Ford, plus another supervisor calling him a liar. As McWethy, on his way to shoot his standup close, walked into the Bubble, the large open room one floor below the Rim where editors kept track of ABC's crews, Mimi Gurbst, the national desk assignment editor, told him, "You look like you're going to your execution."

It would be the last story ABC did on the subject, and the press remained mostly doubtful. But the principals involved in the story at ABC continued absolutely to believe its accuracy.

McWethy thought he had an obligation to investigate the story. "Maybe we take ourselves too seriously," he said. "Maybe we investigate too much."

Jennings, who was always so conscious of the audience, thought the problem was timing, not sourcing. A week earlier, *USA Today* had exposed Arthur Ashe had AIDS because, it said, he was a public figure. Even Jennings was outraged by that story.

After all the blasts against Clinton, maybe everyone was sick of exposés and dirty laundry.

No such doubts afflicted Friedman. "I have never seen such pious bullshit," he said of the press reaction.

But Nancy Gabriner, Jennings's political producer, believed their mistake went deeper than sourcing or timing. The problem was that Brown was not going to be president. After the New York primary, Brown's candidacy was all but dead, and Clinton's nomination all but certain. ABC was doing this to a nonfactor. "I trust McWethy, so I believe the story is true," she said. "But why are we doing it. I worry about what these kinds of stories are doing to the process."

There was something going on out there in the country. But the campaign somehow wasn't addressing it. Somehow they were covering the wrong things.

"I'm not embarrassed," Friedman said, but he wasn't pleased either. "We will just struggle through the primaries." That answer wasn't good enough. And when the process, the press, and candidates failed to make the race meaningful, something else did.

★

CHAPTER

7

PEROT AND
THE NEW MEDIA

Roone Arledge was the first person who suggested *World News* do something about Ross Perot.

It was at one of the exclusive weekly Tuesday editorial board meetings on the fifth floor. Around the news division, these meetings were shrouded in secrecy. Only executives were invited—show producers like Friedman, vice presidents like Gralnick, plus Arledge and his executive team from the fifth floor. To those who attended them, however, the meetings were often mundane. The talk of the campaign was the kind you heard at any cocktail party.

This meeting was in early May. Shouldn't we do something about Perot, Arledge asked. The president of News nudged. But rarely ordered.

Friedman said nothing. He tried to avoid saying much in meetings, generally, just like he avoided putting things in writing. But he didn't think much of Arledge's suggestion. By the time the year was over, he was perhaps the last man to understand Perot's appeal.

Maybe he suffered from a regional bias, Friedman would say later. Maybe he was isolated or just a snob. Or maybe other networks and newspapers had a lower standard of what to put on the air, he would joke. Whatever it was, he was ashamed they didn't understand the vein Perot was hitting, and how much frustration and anger there was out there. "That it could be so easily tapped by a man who is so obviously unqualified," he told Jennings, "is pretty fucking frightening."

Friedman missed something else, too. Perot's emergence was about more than people's alienation and anger. How he rose was equally significant. When the process and the press failed to connect with Americans' concerns, a new structure, and a new media, now existed to broach it instead.

Jeff Greenfield was only kidding when he said it, but it was true: "If Ross Perot had not existed, talk radio would have invented him." For Perot's rise was a positive reflection of the same change in communications as the brief emergence of Gennifer Flowers. And in the end, Perot may have been the most powerful argument for why the traditional press was so necessary.

The morning after Perot appeared on the *Larry King Show*, no one on the Rim noticed. "I never watch Larry King," Friedman said. It was Friday, three days after New Hampshire, and they had enough to worry about. Friedman had sent most everyone home for the weekend. Judy Muller, who had the dubious pleasure of covering the irrelevant Iowa caucuses, was sent to South Dakota for the next primary.

No one else in the press noticed much either. The Los Angeles *Times* ran a tiny item on page 18 two days after the King program about Perot's offer to run for president if voters in fifty states put him on the ballot. Two weeks after that, the United Press International ran a small item about Perot's phone banks out of Dallas. So did the *New York Times*. The Washington *Post* ran its first small item at the end of March, a month after the King show.

What was significant was who *did* notice.

The day after Perot's interview on the *Larry King Show*, radio talk show deejay Michael Harrison came to work like any other day to conduct the No. 1 talk show in Connecticut. His show was known for talking politics, and Harrison, a former rock-deejay in Los Angeles, even ran a trade newspaper in his spare time that tracked the favorite subjects on talk radio around the country. He didn't know about Larry King's show the night before. But his listeners that day wanted to talk about little else. Harrison also knew next to nothing about Perot. But he figured he better find out.

Carlotta Bradley, host of the No. 1 show in Wilmington, Delaware, had the same experience. So did talk show host Mike Siegel in Seattle and Mary Beal in Wichita, Kansas. In Los Angeles, the substitute host for the No. 1 rated Michael Jackson radio talk show was Susan Estrich, who had managed Michael Dukakis's hideous campaign in 1988. Over the next few days, a lot of callers asked Estrich to tell them about Perot. She didn't know much. "I could tell them about Bill Clinton or Paul Tsongas."

In the weeks that followed, invisible to the people on the Rim in New York, Perot's candidacy moved through the subterrain of American culture. In North Carolina, electronics-supply company executive Marty Henderson was listening to a radio talk show in Charlotte one Saturday when he heard there was a Perot meeting in a local park. He went, and since he had met Perot once at an electronics convention, he was elected by the volunteers as the state chairman of the Perot petition drive there. It was the first time he had been involved in politics, he told Joe Klein.

By the time the Washington *Post* and *New York Times* took serious notice of Ross Perot in late March, he was at 20 percent in the polls, and he had done it without benefit of party, elections, or even attention of the establishment press.

The power of the alternative media began to show itself in other ways, too, even before Friedman and Jennings had any interest in Ross Perot.

In late March, after a week of getting mauled by the New York press, Clinton's command team decided to react by doing more media—not less—and to do pop-culture media. In the course of a few days, Clinton appeared on drive-time shock jock

Don Imus, Phil Donahue, Discovery Channel talk show host Charlie Rose, and anyone else's program he could get his face on.

As Friedman watched on one of the twelve sets that hung from the ceiling on the Rim, he thought Clinton's first appearance on Donahue something of a revelation. The first thirty minutes Donahue pounded Clinton all over again for adultery and for a recent admission of smoking marijuana.

Clinton at one point threatened to sit in silence for the rest of the program. The audience started jeering Donahue. Angrily, a woman finally rose and denounced Donahue. Donahue! She denounced sensitive, caring Phil! "Given the pathetic state of most of the United States at this point . . . I can't believe you spent half an hour of air time attacking this man's character. I'm not even a Bill Clinton supporter, but I think this is ridiculous."

Friedman thought it one of those moments that he loved, a flashpoint that revealed something about the process, a moment when the public had broken though the wall. He made sure correspondent Chris Bury, who was covering Clinton, used the woman in his piece that night.

Two days later, Donahue staged a debate between Brown and Clinton—and the talk show host managed to get the candidates on his program to do what Jennings and Friedman had sought in Dallas and caught hell for. Donahue left the two men on stage and walked away. Friedman accurately guessed what had happened. Donahue had simply walked into the Green Room before the show and suggested it. Frank Greer, Clinton's media adviser, tensed. "I don't think it's a good idea, Bill," he told the candidate.

"Why not," Clinton shrugged. "Sure."

It was just Donahue. There were no layers of bureaucracy to go through, no vice presidents and correspondents and advance people. There were things these pop shows could do that mighty ABC could not.

Sitting in his Manhattan office with his Alaskan art and his mother's paintings, Jennings was feeling his own sense of isolation from the country.

Two nights after the riots in Los Angeles, when he and Gralnick put together their special around Bush's address to the nation, they wanted a black leader to react to Bush and settled on Benjamin Hooks, the head of the NAACP. The show was fairly dreadful. Hooks babbled on about things he had said a thousand times, that people had been hearing for thirty years.

The next day, at home on the Upper West Side of Manhattan, Jennings was fiddling with the radio and heard a local black talk radio show in New York discussing the riots and Bush's speech. The show was fascinating, and he thought his own paled badly.

They always seemed to be a step behind in "establishment TV land," he told Gralnick later. There was so much going on out there. "And we always reach for the traditional people."

This was Jennings being insecure and self-critical, Gralnick thought. But others at ABC saw it as one of those moments when Jennings's radar was out. For one thing, maybe *World News* needed shaking up. There was a sense of drift about the place. And one thing was certain. Something was going on this year, and neither the campaign nor the press had put their hands on it.

In fact, the appearances on Donahue, the rise of Ross Perot, were part of something that had been building for years. One of the first to see it had already been president. In 1975, shortly after he left the governor's office, Ronald Reagan had a choice of two offers to do commentaries in the media. One offer was to do a daily five-minute show on Mutual Radio. The other was to alternate two nights a week with Eric Severeid on the *CBS Evening News with Walter Cronkite*. Cronkite's show was then America's most popular news source, and Cronkite, according to one survey, "the most trusted man in America." He had dominated the evening news for a decade, and largely set the standards for the news that most Americans saw each night. Reagan already wanted to run for president. He chose radio. It was a better way to reach people, Reagan told his publicity man Michael Deaver. Talking through radio has more credibility than the evening news, he said, and when people listen to something rather than see it on TV, the message has more staying power.

Deaver came to believe that Reagan was elected president of the United States later because he was on the radio everyday for five years talking to fifty million people a week.

In the years that followed, the medium Reagan considered more credible than the nightly news would explode. Between 1982 and 1991, the number of radio stations devoted entirely to talk, much of it political, would triple to six hundred, according to statistics from the National Association of Radio Talk Show Hosts. All told, 1,450 of the country's 7,500 radio stations listed themselves as predominantly news, talk, or public affairs. And that did not account for the number of all news or music stations that now included some talk shows in their formats. By 1992, surveys by Times Mirror consistently found that forty percent of radio listeners said they use radio mostly for news and information. By 1991, with commuting times growing, and people compressing more activities into every day, a study by the brokerage firm Veronis Suhler found that the average American spent three hours a day listening to radio, second only to television. (Americans averaged four hours and nine minutes a day of television.)

In the early- to mid-1980s, the talk format that had been gaining strength on radio roughly began transferring to television—in the form of Sally Jessy Raphael in 1984, Oprah Winfrey in 1986, Geraldo Rivera in 1987, and, in the case of Larry King on CNN in 1985, literally from radio to television. In 1991, NBC started to imitate the success of these independent shows by launching a live audience show called *A Closer Look with Faith Daniels*.

They amounted to a new kind of media, a modern variant of the old afternoon blue collar tabloid, a hybrid of entertainment and journalism, public affairs and primal scream.

Only some of the reasons for the rise of the tabloid and talk media were obvious. The advent of cable television had expanded the dial in most cities from five channels to fifty. The Reagan administration allowed the number of radio stations to grow by 17 percent and the number of television stations by 36 percent. The baby boom generation, at whom most commercial culture was aimed, had reached a point in their lives where music was no longer so important to them.

But part of the explanation for the phenomenon, too, was that the press—like the rest of the political institutions—had become part of the elite establishment from which people felt alienated.

Over the last generation, newsrooms were no longer staffed by blue-collar high school graduates who apprenticed on the night shift tearing wire copy and lived in the old neighborhood. The newspaper people of the new generation often came from the Ivy League, inspired by the press's role uncovering Watergate, and they moved like tourists through local papers in Cincinnati and Wichita on their way to Washington and New York. As chain ownership and the logic of quarterly profits took over, the press became more professional, but also more detached from the communities it served. News became a product aimed at demographic sectors.

The sense of an Olympian elite press applied especially to network television, whose members were celebrities pictured in the society pages and profiled in magazines.

And in Washington, journalism had become infected by the culture of the TV talk show. Over the last fifteen years, journalists had become coequals sitting alongside the politicians they covered, not just asking questions but offering opinions—and getting rich and famous. In 1981, *This Week with David Brinkley* on Sunday mornings had done away with the big desk separating newsmaker from inquisitors. By 1990, CNN had taken this coziness to new extremes on a program called *Capitol Gang*, a political insider talk show that dispensed entirely with the distinctions between politicians and reporters. An official each week was invited to be a guest with the media types on the panel, everyone opining and calling each other by first names.

Regular people had even begun disappearing from traditional political coverage. When the press began using polling heavily after 1976, fewer everyday citizens showed up in political stories on network television, Daniel Hallin found at the University of California at San Diego. The public was measured more often as statistical percentiles, their opinions solicited in response to the political equations as framed by the media. In effect, polling had subtly shifted the agenda away from regular people and to the press, even while it presumed to give everyone a better sense of the electorate.

This was the environment in which talk radio and tabloid television evolved. One did not have to be elite to play, or even to shape the agenda about what got discussed. "Larry King and Donahue and talk radio and even Rush Limbaugh are interactive media," said Deaver. "There is a way to get in." On the networks, in contrast, like politics in general, "people were disenfranchised."

Phil Donahue, who had been doing talk TV since 1967, felt the first "crack in the exclusive club" controlling politics in 1984. He was asked that year to cohost one of the Democratic debates at Dartmouth, in Hanover, New Hampshire, with Ted Koppel. Afterwards, Donahue recalled, "I really took some flak from the stone heads like Jack Germond"—the "high priests" he called them—for being too informal, too familiar. "There was a lot of 'how did this creep get in here. He is not a boy on the bus.' " In 1984, he invited Walter Mondale to be on his program and was turned down. In 1988, Dukakis turned him down.

By 1992, however, Donahue had become what he called "this kind of hybrid bastard figure who interviews presidential candidates and does fashion shows." Jerry Brown was campaigning on talk radio before New Hampshire and doing Donahue by early spring.

Larry King saw it, too. "It is a different ballgame now," King said. "You can move past the Beltway pontificators and right to the public. In 1980, there were four TV channels. Now there are fifty."

The weekend of March 22, a month after he appeared on the King show, Perot finally made the front pages of the Washington *Post*, the Los Angeles *Times* and the Sunday *NBC Nightly News*. He had also appeared that morning on *This Week with David Brinkley* via satellite from Dallas.

Draped casually across his chair, head tilted in a wry smile, Brinkley began solicitously: "If you were elected what would you do?"

Step one, Perot said, was the deficit—and protecting the job base.

When George Will began trying to decode what Perot was getting at—did protecting the job base mean barriers to imports?—Perot quickly became testy. "No, no. See, you need an hour to explain these things. Everything has to be soundbitten on television." What he meant was the country needed to change from an adversarial to a cooperative relationship between government and business to rebuild key industries.

As he listened, Will thought Perot's argument confusing, nearly incoherent. "I detect what appears to be a contradiction in your political philosophy." How can you consider government in Washington gridlocked on one hand and on the other call for Japanese-style industrial policy?

Perot eyed Will suspiciously.

"Well first off, that is not my position," Perot shot back. "This is television at its worst. See, I've just stated my position. It got recast." Perot then tried to recast it back.

When Sam Donaldson asked whether Perot was helping fund the volunteer effort—something Federal Election Commission filings would later confirm—Perot lost his temper.

"Look, this is a volunteer effort," Perot snapped. "I am so sick and tired of having to answer all these questions."

Brinkley was appalled.

Now seventy-two, David Brinkley had been anchoring one program or another without interruption since 1956. Throughout that time, only a few people had earned Brinkley's full respect. Perot did not become one of them. "He was a damn fool. Very nasty. He would make such remarks as 'Well now that is a stupid question,' which is a judgment he is not equipped to make. So we had him on, didn't bruise him, didn't rough him up. Did not have him back."

It was sad, really, Brinkley thought, since some of what Perot advocated made sense. The country needed someone to test whether attacking the deficit was really political suicide, as nearly everyone in Washington assumed. The failure to confront problems was one reason Americans were turned off, one of the reasons this was such a dark time in American politics, he thought. "People have been lied to so much, and deceived so much, cheated, abused. Taken advantage of by politicians. It would be surprising if they weren't turned off. They deserve to be turned off."

Perot, however, would not be the man to change that, Brinkley thought. The billionaire would never appear on Brinkley again—even when he was the presidential front-runner.

Two days later Perot appeared with Phil Donahue: "The existing tax system is like an old inner tube with one hundred patches and every new patch is put on by a special interest." Seven days later, the last weekend in March, Perot made his maiden appearance on page one of the *New York Times* and on *60 Minutes*, where he appeared literally as the populist billionaire riding in on horseback. "My thought is, start with a blank sheet of paper, then . . . go to the American people on what I call the electronic town hall." Then David Frost. "You ever heard the incumbent president once mention the fact that during his tenure in Washington we've added three trillion dollars to the debt." Then on Larry King, again. "There is no excuse for every company not to make the best products."

On April 18, a poll of Texas voters showed Perot leading Bush 35 percent to 30 percent with Clinton at 20 percent.

Friedman thought the coverage was shameless, adoring, and he resented it. "He hasn't put himself on the line," Friedman told people on the Rim. "It is all polling data."

A lot of people Friedman knew were intrigued by Perot, nonetheless. One of them was Friedman's tennis partner, Clive Chajet, the U.S. head of the corporate image company Lippincott & Margulies. "This guy is going to fizz," Friedman told Chajet.

Friedman considered the billionaire a kind of political hologram, a creation of people's frustration projected through artificial polls that elevated Perot as an alternative to Bush and Clinton. Jennings thought Perot less interesting than the anger and alienation he was tapping.

Still, Friedman resisted covering him, even after his deputies, Dennis Dunleavy and Bob Roy, and investigative head Chris Isham, began arguing with him. He resisted even after NBC assigned reporter Lisa Myers to Perot fulltime and after Perot became a kind of darling of a press corps that was grateful to have him energize the race yet dismissive of a man they treated as thoroughly unqualified.

Three months after he first appeared with Larry King, April 20, *World News* finally aired its first piece on Perot, an introductory feature by Texas-based veteran Charles Murphy. "The cocksuckers commissioned the piece while I was on vacation," Friedman joked.

Friedman had no idea how out of touch he was. While he was resisting, the Bush administration was privately discovering that Perot posed a far greater threat to Bush than it ever acknowledged publicly. The same week ABC aired its first piece, Bush's team had conducted focus groups in California and North Carolina with Bush voters from 1988 who were now undecided. Three years after supporting Bush, these people were angrier than the Republicans had ever imagined. Bush neither cared nor understood the concerns of ordinary Americans, they told Bush's focus group coordinator Steve Lombardo. And when pushed to pick between Bush and Perot, they picked the unknown Perot overwhelmingly, a man about whom they had learned nearly everything from magazine shows, talk shows, features and word of mouth—and almost nothing from the establishment press.

The Clinton campaign, meanwhile, was trying to capitalize on the same popular culture media Perot was using merely to survive, even though he had all but won the nomination. In late April, media consultant Mandy Grunwald (with help from partner Frank Greer) had written a memo that, in addition to traditional campaigning, advocated a "parallel track of pop culture national and local media."

Grunwald's strategy was part of what the Clinton campaign called its Manhattan Project, an effort to reintroduce Clinton to voters—especially his middle-class biography—to rehabilitate his reputation. "We know that moments of passion, personal reflection and humor (available in these popular culture programs) do more for us than any six-second soundbite on the network news or for that matter any thirty-second television commercial."

Thus Grunwald called for inviting "a carefully selected TV journalist (Barbara Walters? Jane Pauley?) to tour his childhood haunts with Clinton; appearing on the last week of Johnny Carson (and if not that, Letterman? Arsenio? . . . Leno? All three?), plus a Larry King–style talk TV program (Who would allow a focus on his childhood/accomplishments etc. without one thousand Gennifer Flowers questions?)."

Radio was also key. There's a hip drive-time radio show like New York's Don Imus in every city, she wrote, and also a serious political show. They should commit to getting Clinton on one of them every day. Some people "say these kinds of things are 'unpresidential.' Bull. This is how people get information."

Nothing happened for weeks. Clinton's campaign had too many other problems. Finally in early June, in the basement of the governor's mansion in Little Rock, Grunwald presided over a key meeting to outline what she called her pop culture strategy. Clinton's full command team was at the meeting: Bill and Hillary Clinton, strategists James Carville and his partner Paul Begala, financier and friend Eli Siegal, the young political aide George Stephanopoulos, media consultant Frank Greer.

Among other advantages, Grunwald argued, this might be the only way to penetrate the news blackout the mainstream press had thrown over Clinton in favor of Perot. There was resistance. Clinton's problem already was that people did not see him as presidential. Finally Clinton spoke. "We have no option. We've got to do this."

In late May, ABC had had its own meeting to rethink the race and the impact of Perot. The gathering was at Arledge's house, where Roone was recovering from prostate cancer surgery. Jennings was there, with Friedman, Gralnick, Stephen Weiswasser, correspondent Jeff Greenfield, and a few others. Greenfield talked about how much anger he saw in the electorate, and Jennings talked about feeling out of step with the country. Why not do an hour special on Perot? Arledge suggested. It would be a way of catching up, and probing in more detail who he was.

Afterwards, Friedman began to make up for lost time covering Perot. It was the end of May. Only one primary remained, California. Greenfield did a piece summarizing how Perot's candidacy had evolved and another summarizing how the media polls were partly responsible for creating Perot's momentum. Wooten did a piece in California on Perot's supporters. This was late for such a piece—end of May—but Wooten summoned his formidable skills, and the piece, which contained only the barest narration, offered remarkable feel for the people involved.

Covering Perot presented special problems. The billionaire's campaign did not exist in a physical sense. It existed in the air, on television, on radio. It was an abstraction, vaguely defined, carefully controlled. There were no rallies, no platform, little or no record. Reporters assigned to Perot covered him by sitting in their hotel rooms in Dallas, calling the Perot petition office and asking on which radio shows Ross was appearing, and then arranging to listen to the interview. Perot might be anywhere. The reporter would be in his or her hotel. The radio show would be in Florida or Kansas.

Perot had a few simple rules for campaigning. He preferred television to print, because it afforded him more control. In print, he told aides, you might spend hours with a reporter and had no idea how it would come out in the paper. And he preferred live television to anything that could be edited. He also wouldn't do many rallies where you had to tailor your speech to your audience, he said. That smacked of traditional politics, of pandering.

By the time Perot dropped out July 17, his campaign would consist of two press conferences, and twelve or thirteen public appearances—plus hours of TV interviews. Most reporters had virtually no contact with him, and had rarely seen him interact with anyone in person.

The lack of contact made coming to any meaningful judgment of Perot difficult. Whatever the elitism and isolation of the mainstream press, it still functioned as a public surrogate to this extent: journalists met public figures in the flesh, and made some attempt to reflect their impressions. The role was important. Television was only the illusion of intimacy. Certain laws of decorum applied. There were questions one did not ask live on camera. There were situations a candidate would not face.

Yet as reporters gradually had more contact with Perot and people who knew him, the more convinced they became of his unsuitability to be president.

In late May, when Friedman finally assigned a reporter to cover Perot, he chose Morton Dean. Balding, friendly, talkative,

Jeff Gralnick (left) and Roger Goodman, executive producer and director of ABC's election specials and convention coverage, in TV Three, the newest multimillion-dollar control room at ABC headquarters in New York. They had the choice of 62 images at any one time of what to put on the air, but Gralnick was charged with cutting ABC's election costs nearly in half. (©1992 Steve Fenn/ABC)

Paul Friedman, executive producer of *World News Tonight with Peter Jennings*, was the man most responsible for deciding how the nation's most influential TV network covered the 1992 campaign. Friedman directed the No. 1–rated network newscast from the Rim, a drab open room on the second floor of ABC headquarters in New York, and quietly won the confidence of Capital Cities, ABC's corporate parent. (©1992 Capital Cities/ABC, Inc.)

Peter Jennings, then the 28-year-old anchor of ABC's nightly newscast *Peter Jennings with the News*, on election night 1966 in plaid pants, suede shoes, and a cigarette in his right hand. Jennings lasted two years in the job.

(©1993 Capital Cities/ABC, Inc.)

Jennings trying to settle down Ross Perot before the beginning of ABC's Town Hall in June. "I took your crap for an hour," Perot had fumed at Jennings moments before, following an ABC one-hour special that preceded the town hall. Perot had demanded ten minutes to rebut the ABC special, then proceeded to tell stories full of inaccuracies.

(©1992 Steve Fenn/ABC)

Peter Jennings and David Brinkley on election night. The two men had an uneasy chemistry on air—Brinkley felt underused, Jennings tried to be solicitous, but his staff thought Brinkley had an infuriating habit of stopping the show cold. (©1992 Steve Fenn/ABC)

One of ABC's few publicity photos of Roone Arledge. The legendary president of ABC News was a video savant, a man with an instinctive gift for what worked on the air, but by 1992 Cap Cities management considered him a difficult manager and a terrible procrastinator. As the year drew on, he seemed to his staff increasingly disengaged and under siege from a company that was unsure of him. (©1989 Capital Cities/ABC, Inc.)

National Political Correspondent Jim Wooten (left) at the podium at the Democratic Convention with his back to Bob Schieffer of CBS. Both are on the air but out of each other's camera shot. Wooten was the man who first questioned Bill Clinton on camera about Gennifer Flowers, after ABC got advance copies of the supermarket tabloid *Star* and shared it with the rest of the press corps. Wooten thought the allegations were not yet a story, but after asking the questions and sharing the *Star* with other reporters, ABC could not control it. (©*1992 Steve Fenn/ABC*)

Ted Koppel preparing to do *Nightline* at the Democratic Convention. Under Roone Arledge's hands-off management style, every show at ABC runs like a separate fiefdom. Koppel put Gennifer Flowers and Bill Clinton's draft letter on the air before *World News Tonight* was prepared to run the stories. Some at ABC thought Koppel difficult and aloof, "His Tedness," some called him, but many agreed he was perhaps the smartest on-air talent in television. (©*1992 Ida Mae Astute/ABC*)

Chris Bury, the boyish-looking correspondent who covered Clinton. Arledge wanted to replace him with a "heavyweight" who could cover the White House, but Friedman and Jennings wanted someone with Clinton whom they would not have to put on the air every night. Bury was the lone remaining correspondent in ABC's once vast Chicago bureau. (©1992 Steve Fenn/ABC)

Some of Roone Arledge's trophies (left to right): Sam Donaldson, Cokie Roberts, George Will, and Jeff Greenfield laughing as they work on their ad libs during rehearsal at the Democratic Convention. A key to why ABC prospered during network television's slow decline during the 1980s was Arledge's ability to woo gifted people to the network and then give them their own programs so they would stay. During and shortly after 1992, both Donaldson and Greenfield considered leaving ABC but chose not to. (©1992 Ida Mae Astute/ABC)

Brit Hume, ABC's contrarian and curmudgeonly chief White House correspondent. Hume was an outspoken conservative whose coverage of Bush outraged some of his colleagues. ABC News management, however, considered Hume uniquely thoughtful for television and thought his campaign coverage fair. Hume, in turn, had doubts about whether ABC's coverage was too liberal. (©1991 *Capital Cities/ABC, Inc.*)

Mark Halperin, the 27-year-old off-air reporter whom ABC assigned to cover Bill Clinton in January 1992, standing on airport tarmac somewhere along the campaign trail and talking on his cellular phone. Halperin traveled wherever Clinton was and knew more about him than almost any reporter on the campaign trail. (*Eric Wishnie*)

Nancy Gabriner (left), Peter Jennings's political producer—"She thinks, I talk," Jennings said—and Hal Bruno (right), the director of ABC's Political Unit in Washington, sitting in the pit just off camera below the anchor desk on election night. Gabriner was ABC's harshest critic. Bruno's two-person unit touched base with people in every state and compiled weekly reports to track how the race was going. His research was more accurate than the costly state-by-state polls that ABC commissioned on the eve of the election and that Friedman put on the air against his will.
(©1992 Steve Fenn/ABC)

Lee Kamlet, the field producer who worked with Chris Bury covering Clinton during the primaries and with Jack McWethy on features during the fall. (Eric Wishnie)

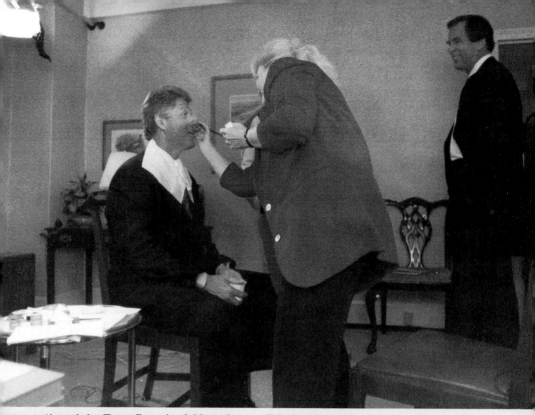

Above left—Terry Ray, the field producer on the White House beat, and correspondent Brit Hume in an edit room in
an ABC satellite trailer in Houston.
(*Douglass Obert*)

Bill Clinton being made up before being
interviewed by Jennings at Clinton's invitation during the Democratic Convention.
Jennings considered the interview mostly
pointless. (©*1992 Ida Mae Astute/ABC*)

Left—Bill Clinton in the back of his campaign plane holding a copy of the *Weekly
World News* supermarket tabloid. The
paper features the headline ALIEN BACKS
CLINTON! complete with a photo. Laughing are Michael Frisby of the Boston
Globe (left), correspondent Gene Randall
of CNN (center), and his producer Saul
Levine. (*David Peterkin*)

David Brinkley on the air. Brinkley has been on American screens in one role or another since he and Chet Huntley became a national sensation at the 1956 conventions for NBC. Most people in television imitated him without even being conscious of it. In private, Brinkley kept to himself, and thought American politics had reached such a low point that most Americans deserved to tune out. There were few people he had met in his career for whom he had genuine respect. He thought Clinton was afraid to come on his program. He thought Dan Quayle was smarter than people believed, and considered Ross Perot, who appeared on his show once, a "damn fool."
(©1992 Ida Mae Astute/ABC)

Jennings and Brinkley talking to Jeff Greenfield and Hal Bruno on the election-night broadcast. Brinkley said Greenfield and Bruno looked like two men bellying up to a bar. That self-mocking tone helped ABC destroy the competition that night in the ratings, leaving everyone at ABC euphoric. (©1992 Steve Fenn/ABC)

Cokie Roberts (left) and Lynn Sherr in makeup at the Republican Convention. Roberts, a rising star, kept Arledge's fascination in part by refusing to leave her job at National Public Radio and join ABC fulltime. Sherr was nearly dumped as a floor correspondent at the Republican Convention in an attempt by Arledge to cut costs. (©1992 Steve Fenn/ABC)

Correspondent Morton Dean, one of network television's veterans. Friedman assigned Dean to cover Ross Perot, with enviable results.
(©1993 Capital Cities/ABC, Inc.)

Correspondent
Jeff Greenfield (left),
in action (below)
at the Republican
Convention. (©1993
Capital Cities/ABC, Inc.,
left; ©1993 *Craig*
Sjodin/ABC, below)

Jennings reworks a script before going on the air at the Democratic Convention. When on live, Jennings ruled what ABC did on the air. His writing was often baroque, though it suited him, but when he edited his correspondents, he drove them crazy. (©1992 Ida Mae Astute/ABC)

A publicity shot taken by CNN for Ross Perot's second appearance on *Larry King Live*, this one in April. For Perot's first appearance with King, which launched his candidacy, CNN was not expecting enough public response to even have a photographer present. (*George Bennett*)

Young Republican volunteers who appeared on the floor of the Astrodome on cue with just the right chants and signs and stood in the front of the hall so that the Republican Convention appeared to be euphoric for the television cameras. (©1992 Michael Norcia/ABC)

Jeff Gralnick (center) with his arm around Roger Goodman on ABC's election-night set. Behind them are the technical staff at ABC in New York, a sign of how logistics generally drive television, before news or entertainment. To save money, Gralnick and Goodman used the same set they had left over from 1988, which was a copy from the 1983 movie *War Games*. Despite that, one TV critic called the set "postmodern" and predicted it would show the way for TV coverage into the next century. (©1992 Steve Fenn/ABC)

Jeff Greenfield interviews Pierre DuPont at the Republican Convention. ABC Field Producer Michael Bicks (far left) watches. Bicks was Jim Wooten's producer most of the year. (©1992 Craig Sjodin/ABC)

Local TV news crews do their standups in the freezing cold in Manchester, New Hampshire. There were so many local TV news crews in that state that voters were pushed off the sidewalks when candidates tried to meet them.
(Tom Rosenstiel)

In makeup and ready to go on the air, correspondents Chris Bury, Mort Dean, and Brit Hume sit on stools watching the second debate from the press room in Richmond, Virginia. Out of sight, the Clinton campaign had a series of radio and TV studios in the basement from which they produced hundreds of interviews with local stations that night, unbeknownst to the networks. (*David Peterkin*)

ABC correspondents Brit Hume, Sam Donaldson, and Jack McWethy. McWethy declined the White House beat for ABC because he thought the way television covered the president was more show business than journalism.
(*©1991 Capital Cities/ABC, Inc.*)

Dean was a veteran of twenty-five years in network news, most of them at CBS. Jennings sometimes made fun of Dean for seeming superficial, but Friedman respected his professionalism. The man anchored the morning news, covered politics, wars, did investigative work, all of it cleanly, unerringly.

Dean's first assignment was a Perot rally in Orlando, Florida, on May 29. It seemed more like an Amway sales meeting than a political rally. Volunteers sang and got up to offer testimonials. Crowds in Kansas, Alabama, Wyoming, and Idaho watched via satellite and cheered through the sound system. A man in a ponytail led the pledge of allegiance. Finally, Perot made his way to the stage. "I know you all want to see my wife, Margot," he said. "But I wouldn't let her come today. It was too dangerous."

What a strange remark, Dean thought.

The speech that followed was even stranger, one of the weirdest, least substantive, he had ever heard. At one point Perot left the stage, the rally apparently over, then just as suddenly returned to lead a singalong. After that, he started taking questions from the crowd. When the rambling event finally ended, Dean headed back to a small office behind the stage into which Perot had retreated.

When Perot emerged, Dean introduced himself. Most politicians Dean had ever met would have been happy to see a network correspondent. Many would have acted as if they knew him, even if they didn't. Perot just glared at him.

The businessman had "CEO eyes," the correspondent thought. Perot looked as if he were thinking, "Don't I pay for your child's education?"

Dean imagined it was a tactic, so he decided to stare back.

"Was your wife threatened?" the correspondent said. "Were you threatened?"

Perot tilted his chin. His look darkened. "You know better than to ask a question like that," Perot said. "You know what is going on out there."

Then the noncandidate turned in disgust and walked away.

"I had been called a dummy and an asshole by candidates before," Dean would recount, "but never the first time I met them."

Most encounters Dean had with Perot were as angry.

The next was in Perot's favorite restaurant, Dickies Barbeque in Dallas. Dean was having lunch with Jim Squires, Perot's communications adviser. Squires was regaling him with his theory about how the media had been taken over by corporate raiders and had lost its ethical moorings, its commitment to readers and to the truth. Squires struck Dean as the ultimate Perot volunteer, the former editor of the Chicago *Tribune*, now disaffected and living in angry retirement.

When Perot came over to the table to talk to Squires, the candidate treated Dean as if he were a servant.

The day after that, Perot arrived for brunch with the top people at ABC News, and it, too, evolved into a dark encounter that left people feeling uneasy about Perot, even a little threatened.

As the breakfast began, there were clearly two camps. Barbara Walters and Roone Arledge were in one, fascinated and flattering. Jennings seemed politely in the center. Gralnick, Stephen Weiswasser, and others seemed skeptical.

As the breakfast went on, Perot became increasingly testy. He seemed to see sinister implications in questions.

Finally, Weiswasser asked Perot to be more precise about something. Perot had been talking about how a root problem with government corruption was people leaving government to become lobbyists, though he made exception for the military. Weiswasser listened, stroking his chin. He thought Perot's proposed cure seemed vague and superficial and unlikely to solve the problem.

"Aren't you missing my point, Mr. Perot," Weiswasser asked again.

Perot gave one of his vague answers and Weiswasser pursued again. Then Perot seemed to snap.

"You've rephrased that question now three times," Perot said. "Are you going to do it again."

Perot pushed away from the table, as if he were about to walk out. His eyes turned cold. He gave Weiswasser the CEO eyes, what others called "the death stare."

"Is that why you brought me here?" Perot demanded. "I've just been through this for two hours at NBC. You gonna put me through this for another two hours? Is that what this is all about?" The room fell into a startled silence.

Chris Isham's investigative unit had already begun looking into Perot's background. In time, Isham would propose nine separate investigative projects into Perot's business and personal background. One of them concerned the relationship between Perot's daughter, Nancy, and one of her professors, who happened to be Jewish, at Vanderbilt University in Nashville. According to an anonymous source, Perot had become angry and persuaded his daughter to end the relationship. Allegedly, Perot even hired a private investigator to monitor the couple and purportedly the incident had damaged the Jewish professor's career. Isham confirmed the relationship existed and ended. The professor confirmed the relationship had existed and ended but declined to talk about it further. The professor also denied his career had been damaged. Isham's producer also found the man, now a sheriff, who supposedly had investigated the couple for Perot. He refused to deny or confirm his involvement. "Without confirmation from at least one of the principals, it is extremely unlikely that we will be able to confirm this story," Isham wrote in a memo to Friedman and Jennings. Given the shortage of resources, Isham proceeded with other stories instead.

One of those was Bradford National, a company that competed with Perot's Electronic Data Systems for the Texas Medicare contract. Dean was looking into claims by Bradford employees that they had been spied on and threatened by people employed by Perot.

People were afraid to talk, which wasn't unusual, but this seemed different. Dean met one man in New Jersey from Bradford who was simply terrified. "What are you afraid of," Dean asked him. "That if you go on ABC News and say something that Perot will be angry if he becomes president?"

"Oh, no, no, no," the man told him. "I'm not afraid of what would happen if he became president. I am afraid of what would happen if he didn't become president."

A Bradford secretary told Dean she was threatened by anonymous phone calls at home to keep from testifying in a lawsuit against EDS. "They never identified themselves," she said. But she wouldn't say anything on camera. "We don't want to look over our shoulders the rest of our lives."

Joseph Monge, the former chairman of the Bradford executive committee, told ABC producer Rich Greenberg and later Dean that he became convinced that he was being watched. As Monge traveled, often with only his closest associates knowing where he was, he received threatening anonymous phone calls indicating they had been monitoring his actions.

Monge traveled constantly, often overseas. He was chairman of California Life, a director of the Royal Bank of Canada, working with banks in Copenhagen and New York. The phone calls would follow him wherever he was. When Bradford finally lost the contract for Texas Medicare to Perot, the phone calls stopped.

Former EDS employees told Greenberg that they had their law firm hire private investigators, and on at least one occasion Greenberg confirmed it was to probe someone's sex life.

"I love Ross Perot," said one senior EDS official. "He's a great guy. I don't know if I'd vote for him for president. But he's crazy to tell you we didn't hire private investigators."

Producer Rich Greenberg marveled that the Bradford case

was more than a decade old and people were still afraid to talk. And these were major executives, top lawyers, people of accomplishment and power. They feared Perot.

Dean did not consider himself one of those guys who looked for the darker side of politicians. But he found these conversations chilling.

Another story detailed how Perot had tried to smear Richard Armitage, a Reagan administration employee who worked on POW-MIA matters. Some of what had come out publicly was wrong and unfair to Perot, and Isham had confirmed more that was damaging. Still another story, unreported but based on information provided to ABC from Perot biographer Todd Mason, alleged that four or six of the original "Sunshine boys" who launched Perot's famed Iran rescue mission were now estranged from the billionaire. Several had been fired, and one was denounced for failing to move with Perot to his new company.

Isham got none of the pieces on the air. Perot didn't stay in the race long enough. Investigative work on television is incredibly time-consuming. Getting people to go on camera was hard.

In the seven weeks it was seriously covering Perot, *World News* did twenty-four pieces. Many were pointedly positive, especially the ones that focused on supporters or politicians reacting to the Perot phenomenon.

The most critical were those that were following exposés in the print media about Perot's background. A Dean piece, playing off the *New York Times*, quoted a Vietnamese official alleging that Perot had sought business opportunities in Vietnam and Laos when purportedly seeking information about POW-MIAs. A Wooten piece quoted the publisher of the Fort Worth *Star*, which was owned by Cap Cities, saying that Perot threatened to embarrass a reporter to get the paper to ease off on their coverage of his Alliance Airport project near Fort Worth.

So the personal impressions that ABC's reporters were developing for the most part never aired. The closest Dean came was a story about a rare Perot rally in California June 18: "Perot is not listening to those who criticize him for not saying enough about the issues. Today there was less substance than usual."

Outside ABC, the press's relationship with Perot was similarly schizophrenic, though far harsher in print than on television. There were a few tough stories. But because he made the race more interesting, Perot enjoyed enormous coverage, which added to his credibility. By June, Perot averaged nearly sixty stories a week in the *New York Times* and Washington *Post* combined, a third of them on page one. That was more than double the number of stories about either Clinton or Bush. Clinton during that time secured the Democratic nomination. Bush had attended an environmental summit in Rio.

At CBS, Perot had convinced the network to become interested again in the campaign. "After months in which we couldn't sell anything political for the nightly news, they fell in love with him," said Dottie Lynch, the director of the network's political unit. "He was rage. He was alienation."

At the same time, CBS's populist approach was building ratings. For the first time in three years, Friedman saw his dominance of the nightly news being challenged. And it was by a news show modeled after local news—heavy on crime, health news, and tips on how to invest your money, less foreign news, and as little politics as possible. Anchor Dan Rather described his new program to the Los Angeles *Times* as "more contemporary and more relevant. . . . We are doing more lifestyle features." Executive producer Erik Sorenson was using a small cast of young people, drawn from local news, all of them remarkably good-looking, most of them under forty.

The CBS surge stirred intervention from the fifth floor and vague panic from Cap Cities. Ratings affected ad rates and ad rates affected quarterly profits. Studies were done and market research ordered. It found that CBS was stealing audience from NBC, a downmarket audience.

They should remain more serious in approach, Jennings and Friedman argued. CBS and NBC's battling for the populist audience created a niche for them. Yet Jennings also thought the panic was healthy. *World News*, he thought, was drifting. The worry suited his love of crisis. It would make them sharper.

During the 8:00 A.M. commercial break on the *Today Show* June 10, Bryant Gumbel marveled about the questions. His executive producer Jeff Zucker agreed. They had just spent an hour taking viewer-call-in questions with Bill Clinton, and none of the viewers had asked about polls or adultery or the draft.

Back on the air, Katie Couric brought it up again during the chatter that preceded the news. "We should probably take some cues from these questions when we are conducting our own interviews," she said.

"We really should," Bryant enthused. "Very much nuts and bolts."

"They wanted answers," weatherman Al Roker said.

"What you're going to do," Bryant added.

"Not polls," said Katie, "not reactions, but basic issue-oriented questions."

By June, the networks had reacted to Perot with the highest compliment of all. If the public was in love with the talk show candidate and tired of politics and journalism as usual, the networks would give them talk shows, too. The *Today Show*'s twenty-seven-year-old executive producer started the trend by inviting Clinton, who had been all but ignored by the press for a month. The rest of the networks—and candidates—quickly followed.

Clinton took twenty-seven questions that first day. The closest any viewer came to asking about polls, or character problems, or trying to provoke an attack on an opponent, was Sean from

Philadelphia: "I'd like to know your thoughts on Ross Perot?"

Pam from San Diego was more typical: "My question for Governor Clinton is [what is] his position on the continuation of U.S. nuclear weapons testing?"

The limit of this viewer call-in format was obvious. There was little chance for followup questions, which meant a politician could dissemble or lie freely. But these problems could be handled. NBC's Lisa Myers matched Perot's appearance on *Today*, for instance, with a *Nightly News* piece exposing some of Perot's deceptions. And contrary to what Couric and Bryant might have implied, the fact that voters didn't ask about them didn't mean people considered a candidate's character or veracity irrelevant. Voters just expected reporters to ask the rude questions for them.

But as a result of this, a good many in the press were quick to dismiss the call-in shows as silly and pointless. The Washington *Post* referred to them as "slow pitch softball."

That was a dangerous and irresponsible mistake. The call-in programs were revealing something important, if the press wasn't too threatened to see it. Too often, the questions journalists asked did betray how isolated the press had become from voters' concerns and how cynical reporters were about what was important about politics. Jennings began to sense that as he watched the talk show fad begin to happen. But he did not know the depth of the problem.

The truth was that most journalist interview programs had become so standard in form that good political consultants could now almost completely orchestrate the program, rendering them a mind-numbing and useless exercise.

Michael Sheehan, the most prominent Democratic television coach, for instance, told his clients that on any program on which they appeared they would be asked some variant of three basic questions. "Name two specific federal programs you would cut. Explain your flipflop on the following issue. How do you respond to the following poll, or allegation or opponent attack against you."

Sheehan could even anticipate what those questions would be in the case of each politician, prepare canned answers and advise his clients to spend as little time as possible answering them.

Rather than anything meaningful, most campaign interviews thus became so orchestrated they offered viewers little of value other than ritual combat. The interviews conducted in 1992 bore Sheehan out.

On May 22, for instance, ABC morning news anchor Mike Schneider asked Ross Perot ten questions on a *Good Morning America* segment. The first asked if Perot would declare his candidacy on the air right then, the second asked him to respond to polls, the third to respond to the charge he was unspecific on issues. For his fourth question, Schneider asked Perot "how you plan to deal with the federal deficit, how you plan to pay for national health care, how you plan to reduce the Pentagon budget." Perot said the question would take an hour. Schneider's next two questions asked Perot to respond to Republican attacks, one that he was "a monster," the other that he was "a dangerous and destructive personality."

The show that adhered closest to Sheehan's ritual formula was *Meet the Press* under NBC Washington bureau chief Tim Russert. On June 8, for instance, Russert and his panel put Jerry Brown through exactly the paces Sheehan predicted. Russert began by asking what programs he would cut to reduce the deficit. When Brown said defense, Russert asked, "So how many service people would be unemployed with your cuts?"

Brown did not have an exact number. "You don't know?" Russert accused.

On March 22, Russert had Clinton on. "Can you assure the Democrats across the country this morning that there is nothing in your background that might emerge which would doom your candidacy and the Democratic Party?" he asked. Put in the position of denying something for which there was no evidence, Clinton, not surprisingly, answered in the negative.

"How do you deal, then, with the Washington *Post* survey

the other day that 46 percent of the people said you didn't have the honesty and integrity to be president?"

How could a candidate be expected to reasonably answer such things?

NBC correspondent Andrea Mitchell then pressed, "Governor, let me explore a few examples with you of how you've changed your record over this campaign, which is perhaps why you've attracted the name over the years of Slick Willie." The conversation on issues that ensued was so arcane, on both sides, that few voters could have followed it.

In isolation, some of these questions may have been fair. The bigger problem was that they were light years ahead of what citizens wanted or needed to know. To Sheehan, the journalist panel shows had devolved into a political version of the TV show *American Gladiator,* in which the guest contestants try to run an obstacle course while the show's muscle-toned cast members pummel them along the way.

The problem was cynicism. Journalists didn't ask politicians basic questions about what they believed in because they doubted the sincerity of policy positions anyway. So they probed instead to expose the inconsistencies that confirmed their view. Implicitly, the press was saying the broad philosophical outlines of a candidate's ideas were unimportant.

The journalists also had their own agenda—to make news. That would get their program into the newspaper the next day. And they wanted to appear tough, informed, scoring points with their colleagues.

Greenfield, like Jennings, was one of those journalists who thought broadening the media spectrum was great. First it allowed viewers a way in. Next it was a way around the 9.5-second sound-bite. The first time any candidate in 1992 appeared on national television for one hour was with Larry King. Perhaps most important of all, it allowed politicians to give a more human, more rounded sense of themselves. Greenfield thought this human dimension was what was missing from modern media-driven politics.

The great political communicators, like Reagan or his speechwriter Peggy Noonan, understood how limited the nomenclature of politics had become, Greenfield thought. Part of what separated these politicians is they spoke the same language most Americans spoke, using phrases from popular culture, pop music, and television. Larry King saw this too. As much as anything else, King said, the important thing about his show were the subtle cues, watching a guy as he listens to your question, or keeping the camera on him as they played the music and went into a commercial.

Friedman watched the phenomenon with more suspicion. "It doesn't say anything about the elite media," he told people. "It is the old thing. The audience has alternate sources. They use some sources for some things, some sources for other things."

In May, as Perot surged, the national print press began publishing investigative pieces about the Texas billionaire. The *New York Times* culled memoranda from Nixon aides in the federal archives to suggest Perot was a Nixon insider, a supposed revelation meant to suggest hypocrisy because Perot described himself as an outsider. Stories in the Washington *Post* and Los Angeles *Times* questioned his business record. The psychology of revelation and cynicism that dogged Clinton was dogging Perot.

But these did little to damage Perot's support. In one of the most intriguing comments of the year, Perot even told Michael Kelly of the *New York Times*, "It doesn't matter" if newspapers write damaging things about him. "I think you could print any story you want on the front page of the *New York Times*, and there is no reaction. It just blows away."

People, Perot said, just didn't read any more.

The quote struck Friedman as absurd, a sign of Perot's

naivete. Wait till the stories reached a critical mass.

Greenfield thought Perot was missing something else. The early press probes of Perot bounced off him not because the press had become irrelevant but because it was writing about questions that at the moment were not what the audience wanted or needed to know. The stories suggested he was not perfect, or that some of what he said might be exaggerated. So what? In isolation, the stories amounted to "gotcha" journalism. Who cared whether he was an outsider or insider?

What mattered was what would happen if people actually elected him. What did he believe in? What might he do? How, for instance, did a guy flirt with the conservative MIA movement and the leftwing Christic Institute at the same time? How could a man be attracted to Reagan's supply-side economics and the leftwing economic analysis of Jesse Jackson at the same time?

The early press probes of Perot also fell flat because they were carried by the press alone, not echoed by any of the combatants in the race. In mid-June that finally began to happen. Over the course of ten days, Vice President Dan Quayle on June 12 called Perot "a temperamental tycoon who has contempt for the constitution;" Campaign chairman Robert Teeter said Perot lacked "the judgment or temperament or respect for our laws to be president;" the Washington *Post* reported, possibly erroneously, that Perot had once investigated Bush's children. Drug czar Robert Martinez said Perot had a "penchant for skulduggery" and was "not fit to be president," and White House press secretary Marlin Fitzwater suggested Perot harbored paranoid delusions.

By June 23, the *New York Times* had found the number of Americans who viewed Perot negatively had doubled over the last six weeks. By June 28, an ABC poll had Perot dropping eight points in three weeks. The race for president was now a dead heat, the poll suggested. Six days later, Perot had dropped another ten points.

* *

At ABC, Jennings, executive producer Tom Yellin, and a few of the frontline correspondents and producers were already at work on the hour-long Perot special, and a ninety-minute town hall meeting with Perot that would air the same night in the *Nightline* time-slot.

Friedman had suggested to Jennings they examine case studies of Perot's life. He was impressed by various pieces from the *New York Times*. Jeff Greenfield was assigned to look at Perot's experience with General Motors. John Martin looked at the Alliance Airport. John McWethy looked at his MIA-POW record. Cokie Roberts looked at his forays into reforming education in Texas.

As they worked, Jennings later became convinced, Perot infiltrated ABC with what in effect was a spy. Jennings began getting helpful phone calls from a man named Murphy Martin, a Texas newscaster with whom Jennings had worked in the early days at ABC. Murphy had heard ABC was doing the special, he told Jennings. He had once worked for Perot, he said. He wanted to see if he could help his old friends at ABC as a kind of adviser. Martin would check in and ask if Jennings wanted any help about Perot, to see how it was going.

Murphy would surface months later as Perot's media adviser and admaker.

Three days before the program, the calls from Murphy stopped, the same day that Perot called Tom Yellin, the executive producer of the Perot special, threatening to pull out of the town hall session that was to follow the hour special. Perot had heard about what ABC was planning, he said. Wasn't it true that ABC hoped the hour special would whip the live audience into a frenzy so they could destroy him during the live town hall afterwards. Why, for instance, had the special left out "the guts of my life, the building of Electronic Data Systems?"

Yellin used a favorite line of Jennings. "With all due respect, Mr. Perot, our reputation is more important to us than yours, and it is not in our interest to make you look bad at the expense of our own credibility."

Then Perot said something curious. He knew what he was talking about, he said, because, "All the beautiful people in New York had called him and warned him that this was a setup job."

"Who are the beautiful people in New York?" Yellin asked. The call was so weird, Yellin had begun taking notes.

"You know who they are. And I don't call them. They call me."

He assured Perot they weren't setting him up.

Then why are these people calling him, Perot asked. Maybe it was the Republican dirty-tricksters. Maybe they were trying to plant this idea in his mind. "You know what they try to do, don't you," Perot told Yellin. "They try to occupy my mind." They were trying to get him thinking defensively. And they were doing a pretty good job.

Before this encounter, Yellin had felt drawn to the freshness of Perot's candidacy. Now he thought Perot sounded unstable. He looked at his watch. The call had lasted forty-five minutes.

An hour later, Perot's attorney Tom Luce and his press aide James Squires called with the same message. They were going to recommend Perot not appear on the program, they said, because they had heard from people inside ABC the show was a hit job.

When Yellin told him about the threats, Arledge was unfazed. If Perot pulled out, the president of News said, the message that left would be worse than anything ABC could say about him. He'll appear.

The next day, Jennings began getting the calls. First Perot's attorney Tom Luce threatened to cancel. He heard it was going to be a hatchet job. The audience had been stacked. Then Jim Squires called. Then Luce again.

Jennings was driving home from picking his son up at summer camp in New England, taking the calls on his car phone. By the late afternoon he lost his temper. He imagined himself, above all, a fair man. He had surpassing self-confidence in the idea that he was sensitive to the forgotten side of a story. And for better or worse, he was never known as an investigative reporter per se, or for hatchet jobs. "You have been treating me as if I am not an honorable person and I am tired of this," he said in his laconic, upperclass way. "At this point, I frankly couldn't care less if Perot appears or not."

In every encounter they had with Perot he behaved appallingly, Jennings was thinking. It was gamesmanship and intimidation. But it was also a sign of amateurism and a shocking lack of understanding of the media.

The next morning Luce called back at 7 A.M. He had spoken to Mr. Perot, he told Jennings. And Perot would appear.

Monday night, June 29, Perot arrived with Teddy Roosevelt's great-grandson, and the billionaire was still not happy. As Yellin and Jennings escorted him to a Green Room where Perot could watch the hour-long program, Perot kept peppering him with questions. What are you going to have on the program? Why are you doing a segment on Alliance Airport?

"I don't have a reputation for hatchet jobs," Jennings said. Wait, and you will be surprised.

Watching the Perot special from his home in Bronxville, a suburb of Manhattan, Paul Friedman was not impressed. "I thought it was a wet kiss," he said later.

When Jennings called for his critique, Friedman told him as much. "Maybe it was a little soft," Jennings agreed. Watching from the Rim, Nancy Gabriner thought they had pulled their punches. Yellin himself admitted it was "benign." The show closed with a quote from former Texas congresswoman Barbara Jordan that certified the tone of the piece. "If Ross Perot were elected president, would it be the end of Democracy in America? No it would not."

Perot certainly had nothing to complain about, Jennings thought.

The anchor headed over to the room where Perot had been watching, to greet the guest and escort him to the set of the Town Meeting that would begin at 11:30. The businessman was standing eerily still in front of the TV monitor.

"You see, we did a fair job," Jennings said smiling.

Perot turned and glared at Jennings with a look of utter derision.

"I took your crap for an hour," the CEO said. Jennings was startled. "And now I want a chance to respond."

Jennings was raised in a family where manners mattered. Certainly, he answered quickly. "That's one advantage of the town meeting," he said, trying to put Perot at ease. "It gives you a chance to respond. Which is rather unusual."

When the Town Meeting began, Perot spent the first fifteen minutes denouncing ABC's preceding program. Among other things, Perot denied ever lobbying for Alliance Airport in Fort Worth. "I never once came to Fort Worth to lobby. Rest my case. Call the mayor tomorrow and check it out. . . . I'll love you to call the mayor. He'll love it too."

Watching in the audience, correspondent John Martin was incredulous. He had Perot's son on tape saying his father had done fully half the lobbying for the airport himself.

Mort Dean had the same experience when Perot denied to an audience member that he knew anything about an EDS employee, an Orthodox Jew, being fired for having a beard. Perot claimed he was out of EDS by the time that case occurred. Dean knew that was not the case.

The cumulative effect of Perot's distortions was corrosive. It persuaded people that something about Perot was not to be trusted. The next day, Friedman decided to have Dean do a story pointing out the inconsistencies in Perot's account.

First, an ABC News producer in Texas had asked the mayor on camera whether Perot had lobbied him. "I met with Junior all the time—Ross Jr.—and I met with Senior frequently," Robert Bolen had answered. Dean had that on video.

Next he wanted to treat Perot's claim about knowing nothing about the case of the beard. In fact, the man had sued Perot's company, and in a widely publicized case, EDS had fought back. A federal judge had even ordered the man reinstated. The idea that Perot didn't know, or wasn't involved with EDS at the time, was patently absurd. Dean wove all this into a script, and Friedman and Jennings approved it.

As Dean sat with his producer in the Slant Track, the editing department at ABC, cutting the piece for the next day's program, Mort Myerson, EDS's former chairman and Perot's confidant called. Ross isn't an anti-Semite, Myerson said.

"This story isn't about anything like that," Dean told him. "This is about whether the man was fired for having a beard."

"I have been talking to people who know about that case," Myerson said. "We sent people out to talk to that fella's rabbi. The rabbi said you didn't have to grow a beard to be in his Temple. We found out how many beards there were in the congregation."

Dean thought Myerson must be kidding. Why would they do that?

An hour later Myerson called again. "I have some gratuitous information," Myerson said. "You mind? That guy tried to grow a beard before he converted to Judaism. Back then he told us the reason was that he had skin problems." That reason wasn't adequate for EDS. Then the man converted.

"Are you suggesting this guy became a Jew so he could have a beard?"

"Well it sort of speaks for itself," Myerson said.

Dean thought this whole conversation seemed weird.

Meanwhile, things were going downhill for Perot's campaign in general. Dean and others were hearing more and more accounts that the volunteers around the country were angry because they were being pushed out of their state petition movements by professionals hired by political consultant Ed Rollins. Perot was dropping in the polls. He was having continuing problems with gays, too, who were still furious over the comments he had made to Barbara Walters on *20-20*.

The first week in July Perot had to publish a clarifying statement on his position on homosexuality.

July 10, as the campaign dissolved, Perot campaign management persuaded the candidate to agree to a press conference to answer reporters' questions, something he had done just once before, this time at the airport after a rally in Lansing, Michigan.

From the moment he walked over the masking-tape X on the floor of the hangar, it was clear Perot was doing this against his will.

"Good to see all of you," he feigned. "I just wanted to stop by."

Could he be specific about his stance on gays? The new statement was confusing.

"No." Perot bristled.

What did you talk to your volunteers about?

"Jobs," Perot answered curtly. When pressed, he added, "They are concerned about retooling, reindustrializing America."

"Can you be a little more specific about gays in the military?" Dean asked.

"No," Perot snapped before Dean had finished his sentence. Several reporters shouted, trying to follow up.

"I released a statement," Perot said, his anger rising visibly. "Spent a great deal of time on it," but it was really more important that with his limited time he focus on jobs and the tax base, "issues that concern all the American people."

John Broder of the Los Angeles *Times* began to lose his temper, too. "Mr. Perot," he said, "we've heard those slogans about jobs and the economy. When are you going to give us some more specific guidance on what you think we ought to do."

Perot stared at him with what Broder thought was pure contempt. When he was ready, Perot answered, he would release his plan. "I will do it once. We will do it right."

And now, after four questions, Perot was finished with the

second press conference of his presidential campaign.

"Mr. Perot . . . Mr. Perot . . . Did these volunteers . . . Will you talk about the Willow Run plant."

"How are you going to deal with the friction among your volunteers, Mr. Perot," John Mashek of the Boston *Globe* asked. "That does seem to be growing. Do you have friction?"

Perot turned, angrily. "Only in America," he said with disgust, "when you look at the miracle that the volunteers have created in the last few months, would you focus on the tiny little problem in these people who self-selected themselves." It was an insignificant problem, three or four people. "So I assume that's about the level you guys want today. So I am on my way to Texas."

The truth was Perot's campaign was tearing apart at the seams from the transition from a volunteer petition drive to a professional campaign. Reporters were seeing it in every state. At the rally just ended in Lansing, two different people had identified themselves as Perot's state coordinator.

"If it's an insignificant problem," said Broder of the Los Angeles *Times,* "why are you devoting four days to bringing them to Dallas?"

Perot stopped in his tracks a second time. "What was that question? Why did I?" His composure gone, Perot was shouting, then storming back toward the reporters while screaming at them to hush. "Ho, ho, ho, ho, ho!" He came up next to Broder. He brought the volunteers back to Dallas, he said, but "that meeting had nothing to do with friction. That had everything to do with planning ahead."

Perot was covering up. His own press secretary had told reporters the meeting was partly to confront the problem of friction.

"But there were two more sessions," Broder said, "for the leaders to come down. What was the purpose of that?"

Perot, challenged, began to back off. "If they are there, I don't know anything about it," he said. And he turned to leave again. "You guys as usual," he began to say, sounding as if he was about to hurl an insult. Then he stopped himself. "There are a lot of myths out there," he said softening. "That one may be true, and I just don't know it."

Reporters would see Perot in public again just one more time—at a speech to the NAACP the next day—before he dropped out of the race. Perot clumsily referred to his black audience as "you people" and retold old stories about how his daddy had played protector over black employees with an almost plantation style benevolence. After being jeered by the crowd, Perot escaped to his limousine. As Perot made that horrible dash to his car, he looked utterly frustrated, Dean thought, as if every time he opened his mouth trouble bit him in the tongue.

Perot had exposed the press's failings and its strengths. He had given Clinton a month of cover to rebuild his campaign. And he had given voice to the electorate's anger, and consequently George Bush's weakness. By early June, the Clinton campaign's dial groups, where voters watched videotapes of speeches and ads and registered their reactions with hand-held meters, showed that everytime Bush's face appeared, the needles dropped.

July 13, a few days before Perot dropped out, Bush advertising consultant Mike Murphy wrote an internal memo for campaign chairman Teeter: "The President is heading toward defeat in his reelection effort," he began, unless the Republicans drastically changed course. But their problem was not Perot. The Texas billionaire was "a man with an appealing twenty-minute act now beginning a three-hour performance," he said. "The question is not how to defeat Perot, but how to keep Perot's disaffected voters from defeating us with Bill Clinton. On election day, Perot will not carry a single state."

If Clinton "uses Perot to redefine himself," Murphy's memo went on, "and we continue thrashing about in the trap of trying to win while on defense," Clinton would probably get 41 percent, "quite formidable in a three-way race. This is the real primary

Clinton must win—the race to become the anti-Bush candidate."

Murphy's prophecies were eerily correct: Clinton would get 43 percent and Perot would not win a single state.

But Murphy was advocating that Bush adopt a far-rightwing stance, built on divisive wedge issues to make his opponents seem unacceptable and dangerous. Both for its rightwing fanaticism and its cynicism about Bush, Murphy's critique was rejected out of hand. Murphy was all but banished from Bush's campaign.

Four days later Perot's campaign was over. Bruno had been calling Ed Rollins each night, getting status reports on how it was going. But they had no idea that Thursday Perot would drop out.

Rich Greenberg and Karen Burnes were finally ready with one of their investigative pieces. This one detailed that Perot had fired employees at EDS who became ill because they were considered financial liabilities. They had several cases, including internal memos and on-camera interviews. They were in the early rundown for that night's show.

Friedman was on the Rim when the word came that Perot would be holding a press conference at 11 A.M. Jennings rushed to the Bubble to do a special report, with Gabriner and Bruno beside him.

Friedman picked up the phone and called his tennis partner Clive Chajet who had been so intrigued by Perot.

"I assume," he told him, "you will be throwing rose petals at my feet Sunday."

★

CHAPTER

8

THE CONVENTIONS

In the big control room called TV Three, Roger Goodman was watching Al Gore divided into 110 discrete images on the wall of TV monitors in front of him.

Gore was in Madison Square Garden accepting the Democratic party's nomination for vice president and helping transform American politics into a new kind of public family therapy.

Back in TV Three, ABC's state of the art control room, Roger Goodman was directing how this would look to the thirteen million or so people who watched it on ABC.

Staging a political convention is a little like setting explosives. Once the fuse is lit, things happen pretty fast. The party professionals can do a lot in advance. They can angle the klieg lights for the proper corona. They can try to spin the way reporters will view the story. They can even teach southpaw George Bush to gesture with his right hand. But for the thirty to forty million Americans who watch a convention on television, what is seen is largely a matter of hundreds of decisions made by those who direct and produce the broadcasts at the television networks. And the most important element of politics on television—what pictures go on the air—is decided literally with the snap of a finger and beamed from camera to consciousness.

There is no time for review, just a cut to the next shot every three or four seconds, image upon image, creating a sense of political reality in electronic pentimento.

"I'm proud my father and mother could be here tonight to see me join a ticket that will make good on the best advice they ever gave me, to tell the truth and always love my country," Gore was saying.

Goodman, a short man with wavy brown hair, was ready. "Give me mommy and daddy, give me mommy and daddy," he shouted. "Give me mommy and daddy. Slow dissolve."

To his left, the technical director pushed a button on the console at his fingertips, and the picture of Gore's elderly parents moved from one of the 110 screens onto the center monitor in the middle of the wall.

"My mother, born in a time when women weren't even allowed to vote, became one of the first women to graduate from Vanderbilt law school."

"Give me his mother. Give me his mother," Goodman yelled. The image of Gore's mother moved to the center monitor and out over the air.

"Everybody stay," Goodman said.

Next to Goodman sat Jeff Gralnick, the executive producer in charge of live political programming. He was talking to Jennings and the correspondents. Goodman talked to the camera operators. At other networks, the executive producer sits apart from the director, a sign of TV's hierarchy. But at ABC the technical side has always had a special status. Goodman was a vice president, an Arledge protégé. He insisted his executive producer sit next to him, where they could interact with a half phrase and a whisper, "like two Jewish tailors," was how Goodman put it. In the row behind them, just over Gralnick's right shoulder, sat Roone Arledge, the ABC News president.

"Martha is here," Gralnick had said quietly into his mouthpiece so that Peter Jennings and others listening would know that the president was now in the control room. Jennings was sitting thirty blocks away in Madison Square Garden, connected to Gralnick by an audio receiver in his left ear. The anchor was the other person who had control over the proceedings. As convention coverage had become shorter over the years and budgets shrank, the shows, like much in television news, were increasingly driven by the allure and whim of the star. Jennings and Gralnick decided the editorial content, the words. But the pictures were Goodman's.

After every show he directed, Goodman took home the tape and reviewed his work. And he always did it with the sound turned off. He didn't want to be distracted by the words.

"My father was a teacher in a one-room school who made his way to the United States Senate," Gore told the audience.

"Give me the father, give me the father, give me the father," Goodman was shouting. "Now lose it."

The operator of camera eight was shooting the whole family and was about to pull back for a wider shot. Goodman saw the movement among the dozens of monitors. "Eight stay," he yelled to the camera operator in the Garden. He liked the shot as it was. "Take eight," Goodman said, and a shot of the family moved into the center monitor.

The images were there only an instant—a man in a funny hat, a businessman, a child.

As the summer drew on, the Republicans increasingly would charge the media with bias toward the Democrats, and they would cite the network coverage of the conventions as their prime example.

The charge was ironic.

The paradox of politics in the television age was that the medium and the politicians were uneasy partners. Both were interested in creating a compelling TV show, one for political reasons, the other for commercial.

And that symbiosis was clearest of all inside the control room, the place where the director matched the images one against another into the collage of television. It was the unspoken truth:

what Goodman tried to do as director was "amplify what the speaker on the podium was saying," he would explain later. Anything else would have made the program incoherent. If the pictures had contradicted the words, the convention would not have made sense. Even fewer Americans would watch. And the same was true at all networks.

Goodman's own reference point was sports, where he had started at ABC in 1964 and learned his trade fulfilling Arledge's visions. If Arledge was one of the chief strategic generals of the visual age, Goodman was his cavalry leader, the man he looked to to make his imaginings possible, the Jeb Stuart to Arledge's Robert E. Lee. The two were once so close that some at ABC described the relationship as father and son, and though Goodman in recent years had distanced himself slightly from his mentor, his office was still next to Arledge's on the executive fifth floor.

"Ready six, take six." Three seconds elapsed. "Take four. Next thing would be his son, three paragraphs down," Goodman said.

Gore was now describing how his son, Albert III, was struck by a car outside a Baltimore Orioles game.

"Stand by take on the son," Goodman was saying. "Dissolve to ten," Goodman said, and the picture of Gore's son slowly dissolved over the picture of his father talking about him.

"Give me the kids," Goodman said, and a picture of the rest of the children appeared. "Stay right there. Take six. Pull back six. Ready ten. Ten."

At any given time, Goodman could choose among sixty-five different images to put on the air. ABC itself had twenty-five camera positions, plus the shared network pool cameras, and those of the Democratic party cameras. There were several cameras on Gore, another on his kids, one on his parents, his wife, Hillary Clinton, and still others scanning the hall for conventioneers to help illustrate Gore's speech. Democrats with kids like Gore's. Democrats weeping as Gore spoke of his family and his son's near fatal car accident. Democratic parents.

*   *

The partnership of television and politicians was clearest at the conventions. The parties and the networks worked together for months planning and organizing these affairs in tandem, setting camera angles for mutual benefit, coordinating logistics, all of it off the record.

The coordination was sometimes secret, sometimes not. And sometimes the network news was even temporarily allied with the party to gain leverage inside their own network. Once the Republicans decided they would have Patrick Buchanan speak on the Monday of their Houston convention in prime time and sent ABC a schedule with Buchanan going on shortly after 10 P.M., ABC vice president Jeff Gralnick would quietly call Republican convention chairman Craig Fuller.

Put Buchanan on at 9:50, Gralnick would tell the party official, not 10:05. Then I can convince my network to let me go on at 9:30, not 10:00 and we can both get thirty minutes more airtime.

Gralnick's ploy would also be designed to give ABC more control over its broadcast. If Buchanan went on twenty minutes into ABC's program, Gralnick would have more time for Peter Jennings, David Brinkley, and the rest of the team to introduce for the country what this convention would be about. This was also a way of screwing NBC, which would not go on the air until 10 P.M. that night.

Lane Vernardos, Gralnick's counterpart at CBS, would put in a similar call to Republican organizers.

Fuller would quickly agree, and Gralnick used the schedule change to get an extra thirty minutes of airtime out of ABC. On the last day of the convention, when Craig Fuller, Charles Black, and James Lake completed the last of their daily off-the-record briefings for ABC officials about what to expect that night, Fuller even said to the group, "You guys have been great. You made this a pleasure." If the party officials really believed that the networks had been unfair or ideologically motivated, they showed no signs of it.

It was no different at the Democratic convention. In a trailer outside Madison Square Garden, chieftains of the convention had told Gore to pause fifteen minutes before coming out to make his speech. They wanted to wait for NBC's situation comedy *Cheers*, then the top-rated television program in America, to end. Then NBC would begin its convention coverage at 9:30 P.M. eastern time, and the audience would grow by ten million people.

"Stay right there," Goodman was saying. "Take six. Pull back six. Ready ten. Ten."

"I need the three girls," Goodman yelled. He wanted a picture of the three daughters and didn't have it. Three camera operators suddenly provided it. Goodman wanted a quick collage of the family. "Take six. Take seven. Take eight."

Gore was talking about changing the world.

"Dissolve to eight. Go get 'em eight."

The parents of Al Gore were heading to the stage to join their son. "Here comes Mommy and Daddy. Ready nine. Take six. Take nine."

This strange symbiotic complicity between television and the politicians at conventions had been there from the beginning, ever since a contingent led by CBS first begged the parties to allow the networks to sell commercials during the conventions in 1952. Politics was so important to television that the companies who sponsored those first 1952 conventions on each of the three networks were makers of TV sets: Westinghouse at CBS, Philco at NBC, and Admiral at ABC. CBS that first year even conducted classes to teach politicians how to look good on screen: "As a result of her tutoring, Mrs. [Georgia Neese] Clark [the United States Treasurer] has decided to wear a gray shantung dress with pastel collars and cuffs," read the CBS press release.

The conventions became the place where the fledgling news

divisions could win viewer loyalties and where the new masters of the great light could make their reputations. A steady young man with a knack for ad libbing to pictures emerged anchoring CBS convention coverage in 1952, named Walter Cronkite. Four years later an older more serious man and his younger sardonic partner became the sensation at the conventions on NBC. Chet Huntley and David Brinkley were so successful that a few months later they replaced John Cameron Swayze as the network's anchors.

This fundamental dependence had never really changed, even after the conventions were stripped of their nominating power following 1968 and became four-day commercials, their every detail scripted down to the minute.

Even if the networks sought out and magnified conflicts at conventions—fights over the platform or who would speak in prime time—these seemed trivial diversions compared with the more essential business of conventions: If the party could stage the right scenes and the candidate and others could deliver key speeches effectively, the networks, drawn like a moth to light, would supply Americans with supporting pictures.

When a true master held the floor at a convention, the partnership between the networks and the politicians was clearest of all. When President Ronald Reagan came to the crescendo of his convention address in 1988, amid weeping delegates and falling balloons, then NBC director George Paul rose up from his chair, did a little shimmy with his more than 200-pound frame and shouted with glee, "Start pumpin', baby! I'm buying, he's selling."

The question was: Did the partnership between the networks and politicians overwhelm everything else? Did their essential common need for a compelling TV show render the words unimportant? Who, in other words, was in control of the broadcast, the parties or the networks?

If the critics only knew. The first problem, rather than bias, was that not very many Americans wanted to watch this stuff anymore. Since 1960, the percentage of households watching TV tuned to the conventions had dropped steadily from 82 percent to 37 percent.

And the costs were astronomical. ABC had spent close to $30 million covering the two conventions in 1980, and about $20 million in 1984. Even with major cutbacks, they had still spent about half that, $10 million, in 1988. Considering the ratings were about a quarter of what a decent prime time show would be, the losses were heavy.

Even if high ratings were in the interest of both the parties and the networks, the battle for gavel-to-gavel coverage of conventions was long lost. The order at ABC had come nearly a year before that they could not afford either the time or the money. Now they were fighting over whether Jennings would even get to go to the Republican convention in Houston or be allowed to broadcast inside the hall at the Democratic convention in New York.

As 1992 began, Arledge had told Gralnick and Goodman they had to produce both conventions for about $2 million each, less than half of the scaled down version of 1988, a quarter of what they had spent in 1984.

The most obvious way to cut back was not to bring the anchors. If Jennings and Brinkley stayed in New York on the regular *World News* set, they wouldn't have to build a skybox, or bring the producers of the nightly news, or need the technical support to do the show from Houston, or build a control room.

To maximize how much they could do, Gralnick developed three budgets. The first would be a classic convention, with two anchors, a skybox, and the full retinue of aides, technicians, and hangers-on.

The second budget would be for bringing the anchors on the cheap.

The third would meet Arledge's dream number, no anchors, a skeletal crew, $2 million per convention.

By spring, Arledge seemed resigned to the third budget, even though the Democrats were holding their convention just thirty blocks away. Gralnick thought Arledge was trying to impress Cap Cities that he could save money. Many thought that Arledge was fighting to keep his job.

But Jennings wasn't pleased, and in late May he asked for a rare formal meeting to make his case. He was probably fighting a rear-guard action doomed to fail, but he thought he should try. Jennings, Friedman, Gralnick, Weiswasser, the lawyer installed at news to look over Arledge's shoulder, and others were there. "If we won't go down the street to cover a story anymore," Jennings argued, "where will we go?"

Arledge sounded sympathetic. So did Weiswasser. But they did not relent.

A week later CBS announced that Dan Rather would anchor from the Garden. Suddenly ABC reversed its policy. NBC already was going, because they were engaged in a joint production of convention coverage with the PBS *MacNeil/Lehrer Newshour*. CNN was going of course, too, with their parade of nameless anchors. Jennings's appeal to editorial conscience hadn't done it. Fear of publicity had. ABC wasn't going to be the odd network out. The TV critics would pound them.

Arledge called Gralnick and Goodman almost immediately. What's the cheapest you can get an anchor skybox into the Garden? It would have cost ABC $400,000 to convert a luxury box into a usable skybox. The boxes, which were just the luxury boxes refitted, were too small, and the camera angles were horrible. To get the podium and an anchor in the same shot, you had to shoot down the top of the anchor's head.

Then Goodman had one of his technical brainstorms that Arledge loved. At the National Association of Broadcasters annual convention, he saw a new kind of chromakey machine for projecting images behind an anchorman. The new device could link two cameras via computer to move in tandem. If they put Jennings and Brinkley in an enclosed room in the Garden, they could project the picture of the convention hall behind them, the camera shot of the anchor and the camera shot of the background would move in synchronization.

The only way viewers will know it's not a real skybox is when we tell them, Goodman explained, which we will have to do for ethical reasons. In effect, they were getting the anchors into the hall for only about $200,000 more than they had budgeted to do it without the anchors. The biggest problem was Jennings and Brinkley, sitting in an enclosed plywood room, would be isolated from the energy in the hall. So someone came up with the gimmick of having Jennings open the show from out on the floor of the convention hall amid the delegates. After the first commercial, he would run to the little plywood room and Brinkley.

Everyone was excited. It would be their big surprise, a break with tradition—open with the anchor on the floor, something no one had done before. But then they lost their exclusive. The weekend before the convention started, Dan Rather toured his CBS skybox, and as crews from the other networks watched through their cameras they could see Rather going ballistic at what his work conditions would be. Thereafter, Rather decided he would anchor the whole damn show from the floor. At ABC, people hoped the idea bombed.

Even with the cutbacks, the parties knew that the networks were still the key. The private planning document the Democratic party wrote to produce its convention was a book filled with charts and tables about television—what days of the week had the highest viewership and how many households were wired for cable. "We all know that network coverage is declining both in terms of hours aired and ratings, but the convention (as broadcast on the networks) still has a dramatic influence on the polls," the document read.

Later, the Republicans would charge the networks rolled over for the Democrats. In fairness, however, the press was not kind to the Democrats during the most critical moment of the convention—Clinton's speech. "Clinton did not give the speech that excited this convention tonight, Gore did," Cokie Roberts said on the air. "People were getting a little bored. They were fidgeting," Lynn Sherr announced.

For the most part, though, the Democrats did enjoy a huge ride in the coverage. "The Party has changed the course this week," the *Today Show*'s Bryant Gumbel declared; "Clinton and his team have managed to keep this convention right where they want it—in the middle of the road with no major crackups," Tom Brokaw said; "New York governor Mario Cuomo, a reluctant convert, sounded like a true believer," said CBS's Richard Threlkeld.

At ABC, one of the strongest voices to argue the Democrats' success was Greenfield, who was also viewed by Republicans as one of the fairer correspondents in network television. Greenfield saw merit to Republican criticism during the 1980s that the Democratic party was dominated by the left. And he thought that, had Reagan been more attentive to the poor, more engaged as president, paid more attention late in his term to the deficit, he had the power and vision to have gone down as one of the greatest presidents. But Greenfield saw real change at the Democratic convention, and he based that assessment on who had been selected to speak, what they had said, and how Clinton had changed the platform. "In essence, the platform, like this convention, is beckoning the disaffected Democrats home," he said in one piece for *World News*.

The criteria was justified, and Friedman had his correspondents use the same one at the Republican convention. Wooten dissected Pat Buchanan's speech to point out that Bush has long had problems persuading conservatives of his trustworthiness. Cokie Roberts dissected the Republican platform and noted it might pose difficulties for Bush politically. If Clinton kept liberals like Jesse Jackson out of prime time, while Bush highlighted conservatives like Buchanan, it said something real about each nominee's ability to control the party to his advantage.

The other factor influencing the press, one that was less

legitimate but even more persuasive, was the polls. And the extraordinary thing about the polls was that the Democrats enjoyed their huge bounce after only one night of their convention. On Tuesday, the second day of the Democratic convention, Jeff Alderman's ABC poll showed Clinton surging to first with 45 percent to Bush's 28 percent. Perot, who would drop out the next day, was at 20 percent.

The next week, Clinton got even more of a free ride in the coverage of his bus tour. That Monday, as the bus tour hit high gear, Friedman led the broadcast with a poll, only the second time he had done it all year. The coverage seemed a discouraging preview of what the fall might be like. For all their brave talk, the networks still could not resist the pretty pictures. Jennings, vacationing in Canada, thought it a poor display. Friedman thought it was another example of the press stampede, a form of hysteria in which balance and context were lost, the same group think that had declared Clinton dead, Perot fabulous, Bush inevitable, and, later, Bush incompetent. But to call this stampede liberal was too simple.

Rather than ideological, most of the evaluation inside ABC and elsewhere about the Democratic convention concerned form. Arledge thought they had spent too much damn time bouncing between floor correspondents.

The last night of the convention was one example. After Clinton finished his acceptance speech, culminating the convention, Jennings wanted to go to each of his six correspondents one last time for reaction—Jeff Greenfield, Cokie Roberts, and Lynn Sherr on the floor, Jim Wooten on the podium, then Sam Donaldson and George Will in the sky booth.

It was a big crowd, and as they moved to Jeff Greenfield first, Gralnick warned them collectively how long to talk—twenty seconds.

Jeff Greenfield went a minute, Cokie Roberts a minute twenty.

When Jennings got it back from her, she interrupted him and

kept talking. Her point was well made—that Al Gore rather than Clinton had riveted the hall—but christ, we've got four more correspondents, Gralnick was thinking.

"Thank you, Cokie," Jennings said when he got the microphone back a second time. "Let's go up to Jim Wooten on the podium. Jim, your impressions?"

"Well, I think what Governor Clinton needed to do tonight"—Wooten began.

"Say goodnight," Gralnick said in his IFB earpiece.

—"one of the things he needed to do was present the possibility of—well, to present the possibility that he can be seen as a president, to cross that threshold in the minds of the American people. That was one of his tasks."

"Peter, Peter, Peter," Gralnick was saying in Wooten's ear.

"I suppose he did that," Wooten said.

Live television was hell like no one knew. Mastering it was a mind-stretching task that involved being able to listen to the control room, think of what you are going to say next, and simultaneously speak to several million people while looking good.

Jennings was a freaking genius at it. He had to assimilate Gralnick in one ear and interact with Brinkley through the other. Behind him, sitting out of camera sight, Nancy Gabriner and Hal Bruno would hand him notes, which he would read while still on the air, and sometimes while still talking. For all intents and purposes Jennings was the one in control of the program. If he wanted to go to the archbishop of the Greek Orthodox Church and listen to the invocation for sixty seconds of time worth about $500,000, he could do it, and no one could stop him without making the broadcast look silly.

But they were cramming here. Wooten went on a few more seconds and managed one other interesting point. After Clinton's speech, the Democrats had filled the podium with every political notable in the party, a made-for-TV picture of unity. It also cleverly kept the podium reporters from trying to run up to Clinton for an interview.

Jennings still wanted to hear from George Will and Sam Donaldson and Lynn Sherr and then go to Brinkley for one more comment.

No one had ever tried to cover a convention in an hour a night. Should it be a highlight show? Should they cover the speeches straight through? How much analysis should they do? What was the purpose of this?

"They need to come up with a new way of covering these," one of the network's most important correspondents said later that night in New York.

"On Tuesday, we did not go live to the podium even once," said Gabriner.

Friedman was not involved directly other than advising Jennings informally, but he thought they should seriously consider producing taped packages to show people what they weren't seeing live. Otherwise, he thought, they were falling into the trap of only seeing what the party programmed into prime time. "By truncating the coverage, you never got to see all the diverse elements of the Democratic party which would scare the shit out of the electorate."

Jennings thought their analysis had been all right, but they hadn't reported much on what was going on. If they had, he thought, they would not have given the Democrats such an easy ride. In fact, there was more dissension down there than people saw. It was hardly better on the other networks. At NBC, they had given six minutes on Wednesday to Cuomo's nominating speech. The result of the cutbacks, ironically, was that the news accounts of the conventions on programs like Friedman's *World News* had become more important. They would need to do better, everyone felt, for the Republicans in Houston.

For the second convention, Gralnick and Goodman had figured out a way to produce a long-distance convention on the cheap. Back when Goodman directed golf tournaments for a living, he used to shoot the entire eighteen-hole course, fifty camera locations, with just twenty cameras. When the action moved off the first tee, that camera crew would race over to the sixth tee and shoot there, then run back to the first tee again when needed.

In Houston they used the same principle. For the anchor booth and other closeup shots they still used the traditional high-quality "studio-field" cameras the way the networks always had. But for most of the other camera positions they used lightweight lower-quality portable cameras, which they could plug into one camera location, then unplug and run to another.

Altogether, Goodman and Gralnick brought fourteen cameras and crews for twenty-five camera locations, fewer trailers, and a portable control room that was one-third the size of what they used in Atlanta for the Democrats four years earlier. In the end, Gralnick took 155 people to Houston, 133 fewer than to the Republican convention of 1988. He thus cut his costs in half, to around $2.5 million, the same price as New York. From his perspective, if they could improve the program and keep the ratings up, this convention would have been a smashing success.

Roone Arledge, however, wanted some other changes too. For one thing, he wanted Jennings to go to fewer people for those "whip arounds" of analysis. Maybe, in fact, they didn't need to bring so many correspondents to Houston in the first place. Arledge didn't say it but the message was clear. This would make him look like he was saving money.

He picked two people to be cut, Jim Wooten, the chief political correspondent, and Lynn Sherr, the longtime floor correspondent.

When word leaked out around ABC, people were shocked. What the hell was Arledge thinking? Wooten was the network's senior political correspondent and he wasn't going to cover the convention? If he wanted fewer whip arounds, why not just tell Jennings to do fewer whip arounds? How much money was this going to save?

Arledge left it to Gralnick to tell them. Wooten was up at his house in Cape Cod preparing, doing research, and writing his ad libs.

"I'm just the messenger," Gralnick said when he called. "But you're not part of the convention team."

Lynn Sherr had already been told and had become depressed and upset. Everybody felt lousy about it.

Wooten didn't blame Gralnick. Jeff and Roone hadn't been close for years. He really was just the messenger. But quietly, Wooten was deeply hurt.

When Friedman heard about it, he solved at least part of the problem by telling Arledge, "I'm bringing Wooten down to Houston on my budget for *World News* because I need him as a reporter." But Wooten would still not be on the prime time show.

When Jennings heard, he told Arledge of another problem. It didn't look good cutting Sherr, one of only two women floor correspondents. Privately, he also thought she didn't deserve it.

Things became even more confused the week before the convention when Sam Donaldson and David Kaplan, his longtime producer, headed to Yugoslavia to cover the civil war in Bosnia. On the road from the airport into the city, a sniper fired a single shot into the rear of their transport vehicle. The bullet penetrated the back door, went through the rear seat, and struck Kaplan in the back. Doctors labored for two hours but the bullet was too close to Kaplan's heart.

The killing draped the network in black. On the air that night Donaldson, distraught, shaken, narrated a story about his own friend's murder. When they came back with the body, Donaldson was too upset to come to Houston and sit in the box with George Will and pontificate about balloon drops and bombast.

There was now an empty chair in Houston. Maybe they would put Cokie Roberts in the booth with Will. Or maybe Wooten. In any case, they could correct one screwup. They could at least get their chief political correspondent into the political convention coverage. But before anyone called Wooten to tell him this might happen, Arledge called Lynn Sherr instead and told her to get on a plane and come down.

Meanwhile, Arledge was in New York and badly distracted. He was either becoming self-destructive, or in his own inimitable way he was trying to arrange a showdown with Cap Cities management to resolve his uneasy relationship with the company and Weiswasser. The man who had built ABC News—and who to a large degree still had kept it on a high level while CBS dove downmarket and NBC careened in several directions at once—was engaged in a series of incidents that fueled talk he would not be ABC News president much longer. The weirdest of which was the saga of the Gulf Stream jet.

All of the top ABC executives have the right to use the company's fourteen-seat Gulf Stream by booking it and charging the cost to their department's account. Arledge was scheduled to come down to Houston on Monday the seventeenth with Tom Murphy, the company chairman. Murphy had arranged his schedule to fit Arledge's, but by the week before Arledge started calling and changing it, over and over. Finally, Murphy in exasperation told Arledge, "Roone, you take the plane. I'll fly commercial."

Then, to further accommodate his schedule, Arledge asked the Kaplan family to postpone until later in the day their son's memorial service that Sunday at which he was to speak. Finally, Weiswasser had requested that Arledge and the Gulf Stream stop in Atlantic City to pick him up on the way to the memorial service in Washington. Arledge refused that as well. If he was trying to ingratiate himself with Cap Cities, this was not going to do it.

Late Sunday night, an angry Wooten was having a drink in the bar at the Marriott Medical Center where the correspondents and executives were staying when Gralnick found him.

"You're back on the podium," Gralnick said. Arledge had changed his mind.

Greenfield and Sherr would be on the floor. Cokie Roberts

would be in the analysts' booth with George Will. Wooten would be on the podium.

What happened? Wooten asked.

Ask Arledge, Gralnick said, motioning to the back of the bar. Wooten went over to talk to the president. They talked for more than a half hour. The subject never came up.

"Basically, the president was persuaded that if he didn't allow his chief political correspondent to cover the political conventions, the chief political correspondent would probably punch him in the nose," Gralnick said.

Such were the psychodramas that constituted putting together a network's convention program. When it came to the editorial content, basically, you assembled whom you considered the brightest people and you gave them microphones and they talked, and you hoped they were insightful. And ABC had nearly stumbled over that. But there was no coordination of the words. Most of the planning involved money and machines and production. As the week progressed, indeed, management was more worried about "making good TV" than refining the political analysis of the event.

The program began a little roughly Monday. Jennings was going to start on the floor talking to delegates, the gimmick they had tried in New York. But this time he started with a delegate from Indiana. The guy froze on camera.

"What do you think the big challenge is here this week," Jennings asked him.

"I—I—I really don't know."

Oh christ, Gralnick thought.

The look of white fear was sweeping across the poor bastard's face. "Uhh. Uhhhh. Uhhhhhhhhhhhh. Abortion mostly, and the tax," the guy tried.

And that was as good as it got.

"Uhhh. Whatever he's going to do. You know. I—I don't know."

A wonderful beginning.

"Okay, thanks very much. Hope you have a good week," Jennings said.

Things got better from there. The Republicans were running uncharacteristically late. When Reagan made it on stage, at 11:20, Gralnick noticed the Gipper glanced at his watch and seemed angry.

Brinkley had already told them that Reagan wasn't too fond of Bush. "Reagan feels that since Bush was elected he has been rude to him, standoffish."

But the sliding Republican schedule gave them an hour to fill, like the old gavel-to-gavel days, and they had been pretty good. Greenfield summarized how the Republicans were unaccustomed to being behind and blamed the press. Lynn Sherr described how delegates had told her they wanted Bush to lay out a plan for the second term—any plan. Brit Hume, at the President's hotel, described how up Bush was when he arrived in Houston that day. Jennings interviewed the keynote speaker, Texas senator Phil Gramm, and George Will talked about the upcoming Reagan speech.

Watching in his hotel room, Paul Friedman thought this a happily intelligent introduction to what was at stake this week for a party in trouble. The only strange moment, though, was lost on viewers when Jennings introduced Wooten, given that Wooten had been squeezed in at the last moment. "Also joining us this evening . . . is our chief political reporter Jim Wooten, to whom we have given a lofty position for lofty views, James."

The next morning, Arledge made it clear he was not pleased with the show's opening and the frozen bozo from Indiana. From now on, he said, whoever Jennings interviewed on the floor to open the show had to be preinterviewed. So Gralnick and Jennings decided to open with two governors, George Mickelson of South Dakota, and Jim Edgar of Illinois.

In other words, to keep the show moving, they had gone to

more polished and less spontaneous interviews. The tyranny of making seamless television further tipped the scale of power to the party.

Things were more complicated that night, too, because Arledge seemed in an odd mood. The weird political pressures of the executive level seemed to be weighing heavily of late. Arledge walked into the booth with about two minutes to air and asked, "Who is the opening guest? You going back to that guy from Indiana?"

"How about two governors," Gralnick said.

Arledge didn't respond. But a moment later, Arledge was unhappy that Gralnick and Jennings were interviewing former education secretary Bill Bennett, a possible presidential contender in 1996. Arledge thought Bennett still lacked star quality, at least the kind that would mean anything to ten million viewers in 1992. "Who the hell is Bill Bennett," he was saying to Gralnick.

Sitting behind Gralnick in the tiny trailer they had converted into a control room, Arledge smoked a long cigar and said little the rest of the night until the end. How and when the networks got off the air had become an important issue. At NBC and CBS, they now tended to go off the air without saying goodbye so that local affiliates could go to their own news shows as soon as the speech was done. This pattern left no time for any summation or interpretation. Perhaps Arledge wanted something similar to please affiliates. But Gralnick liked to push the envelope, to stay on several minutes longer for the sake of the show—and thus a struggle played out live in the booth.

ABC this night was scheduled to have four commercials between the time the speeches ended and the signoff.

"Why do we have so many commercials?" Arledge asked.

This was Arledge's style. He was like a Jewish mother. He never said things directly. It was all guilt. Gralnick didn't answer him.

"Why do we have so many commercials? The other guys have so many commercials?"

"I don't know," Gralnick said.

"Let's find out," Arledge answered from behind him.

"Roone," Gralnick said, "here's what I plan to do. When the speech is over, Peter says, we'll be right back. Then two minutes of commercials. We'll go to Cokie [Roberts], and Jim [Wooten] and Greenfield briefly. About a minute fifteen total. Then in fifteen seconds Peter says we'll be right back. Then two minutes of commercials. Then come back for a goodnight from Peter and Brinkley."

"Why do we have so many commercials?" Arledge said again.

"Do you want me to drop the commercials?" Gralnick asked, his sarcasm only slightly hidden.

"Why do we *have* so many commercials?"

At this point they were into the last set of whip arounds with the floor correspondents. Cokie Roberts was running long, and Gralnick was telling her to give it back to Jennings, saying "Peter, Peter, Peter," in her ear. George Will then issued twenty crisp seconds and they were into commercials.

As the break continued, Jennings began thinking to himself out loud from the sky booth about whether to read from a Clinton fax that had been sent in reaction to Phil Gramm's keynote speech.

Gralnick and Arledge were still sparring in the control room.

"Shut up, Jeff," Jennings told him, "I'm trying to think."

"Fuck you, Peter," Gralnick answered.

The profanity was meaningless, and no one cared. This was live television, no teleprompters, no scripts, just wires and personalities who have a strange mix of talents, the right voice, the right looks, the ability to think while listening to someone in one ear, and also talking, and one hundred television critics from every dumb shit newspaper in the country ready for someone to lose their cool on the air and give them a column to write and maybe a career to end. No one cared about cursing. No one cared about Arledge the Jewish mother. It was just the weirdness of making it up as you go along in front of twelve million people. The tension was something no print reporter or any sane human being could imagine, no one who hadn't breathed in the red light and taken into their mind the idea that their image was in every living room in America, so that from then on, whenever they went into a restaurant or a dry cleaner or bought a red-hot Polish sausage the guy lit up because he was selling the dog to someone famous. Someone on TV.

Arledge now told Gralnick, "You've got to handle him," meaning Jennings.

A moment later they were off the air, and assembling outside the control room trailer when up walked Tom Murphy, the chairman of Cap Cities, with his son. The weird tensions Arledge was facing seemed even weirder.

"Son, I want you to meet this guy," Murphy said, pointing to Gralnick. "There are a lot of people around here who say they work and run things. This is the only one who does."

Off the air, the Republicans' efforts in Houston to control their impression on television were reaching new levels. They began the night before, around 11 P.M., when the Bush convention team met to analyze what had come out in the day's network coverage, what they had wanted to come out, and what the principal news items and images would be for the next day.

Those were then typed up as "talking points" and slid under the doors in the middle of the night of all the Republican officials who might speak to the media that morning.

So Treasury Secretary Nicholas Brady on Wednesday could go on CBS *This Morning* and say "It's been hard for the President because he's had a big filter, the Democratic party." And on Fox morning news: "George Bush gets his chance to express himself directly." And on CNN's *Daybreak:* "without a lot of filtering by Congress."

For local stations, the Republican party had arranged about

six hundred interviews that day—from local delegates to cabinet members.

And, on the Republican satellite channel, the party had a full schedule of broadcasting available free to anyone who was interested—aimed particularly at key swing state audiences.

On Tuesday morning:

6:00–6:30 A.M. Senator Mitch McConnell of Kentucky

6:30–6:40 A.M. Alternate delegate Ed Gochenour of Georgia

6:45–7:05 A.M. State Senator Posthumus Jeff Hartgen of Michigan

7:10–7:30 A.M. Campaign adviser Clayton Yeutter

7:40–8:00 A.M. Lt. Gov. Mike DeWine of Ohio

8:00–8:25 A.M. Sen. John McCain of Arizona

8:35–8:40 A.M. State Sen. Robert Jubelier of Pennsylvania

8:40–9:00 A.M. U.S. congresswoman Barbara Vucanovich of Nevada

9:00–9:30 A.M. State GOP chairman David Doyle of Michigan

The party also produced a fifteen-minute "news" package each day, complete with reporting from party correspondents, that it made available free to any local station that wanted. All were available on satellite Galaxy 6; transponder 12V, Channel 12, audio 6,2 and 6,8.

By 9:30, the GOP was holding a press conference for the print press.

The Republicans also assigned "minders" to each network during the conventions to help them secure guests and provide other help as well as to keep an eye on them. And every day the top party officials also offered the networks daily briefings about what was to occur each night, spin sessions designed to further influence the network coverage.

"This is our night to essentially raise the crowd in the dome and at home to the point where they are ready to listen to the President's message," Craig Fuller told a group of about ten producers in Hal Bruno's trailer the last night of the convention.

Over the years the networks had become more cynical about these sessions. Jennings and his correspondents generally skipped them. But those who went, like Gralnick, Bettag of *Nightline*, and Bruno, head of the political unit, insisted they were not manipulated by them. The party thought the journalists were fooling themselves.

Then there was the control the party exercised over the images the networks could photograph on the convention floor. Delegates in both parties were forbidden from bringing their own placards on the floor. All signs, even those carefully painted to look handmade, were produced by the party. There were supposedly 10,000 for the week, one signmaker told a *Nightline* crew.

The Astrodome was massive. To make sure that the images the network cameras saw were exciting, the party arranged that, at key moments, troops of rehearsed young people flooded onto the floor and filled the first fifty feet in front of the podium and in the aisles. They knew what to chant when, and they were standing in front of most of the delegates so they couldn't be missed by the cameras.

From the high ground on the podium, just to the right hand of the speaker, the managers of the convention, convention chairman Craig Fuller and Republican party chairman Rich Bond, had banks of television sets built into consoles in front of them so they could measure precisely how the convention looked as it went out to America.

As Jim Wooten saw Fuller and Bond with their sets, he noticed something slightly depressing about his own role. The convention managers kept the sound on all these television sets off. "They really don't care what we say, only how it looks."

Metaphorically, that was the Republicans' problem. For all of their skill (and they still far outdistanced the Democrats in production savvy and organization) the Republicans could not really control the words this week. And they knew it.

The fissures within the party were too great. And even the

inherent symbiosis between television and the party could not mask it. Real things still mattered most in politics.

Even though the Republicans had an elaborate system for all speeches to be submitted to a team of Bush speechwriters to ensure they hit the right themes, several people refused to comply, including Buchanan, and Bush simply lacked the power or the will to make them. Fuller, Teeter, and Bond had arranged a delicate strategy to compensate. They would allow the party to send out mixed messages, and hope that the harshest ones were delivered early in the week. The hardliners could own the platform, and they would get their men on TV in prime time Monday and Tuesday nights.

By Wednesday night, the tone of the convention was supposed to moderate. They would have Mary Fisher speak, the beautiful and articulate former White House aide now a victim of AIDS. Then Barbara Bush would speak, bring out her kids, and then the President would come on stage for the picture, the President and his family of twenty-three kids and grandkids.

Since most people would see the convention only in newscasts, creating the right picture to epitomize the rhetorical message was critical. Bush's message was that he could be trusted and Clinton could not, that he had the right values and Clinton did not, that a good man would make a good president, and George Bush was a good man. The picture of the big loving family, the Republicans hoped, said that exactly.

But the words that gave the picture meaning had been spoken two days earlier by Patrick Buchanan, not by Barbara Bush or anyone else. "We let others define family values for us," a senior aide to Dan Quayle said.

When the picture came Wednesday, George Will neatly seized on its subtext. "Peter, what we saw tonight is symptomatic of a very strange transformation of American politics. Time was, not long ago, when we talked about what were recognizably public goods and government actions: Social Security, rural electrification, defense. Tonight, we talked about hugging your children and it's all right to cry. This was a prolonged sensitivity session, but it had a very hard political edge to it. Tonight was a sustained innuendo against the Democratic Party that they don't like marriages, families, women in the kitchen, or children. This is the heart of that question, 'Can you be one kind of man and another kind of president?' They're saying Bill Clinton—and generically Democrats—are bad people."

"And given all your travel around the country, George, do you think it plays?" Jennings asked him.

"I don't think so," Will said. "I think there are an awful lot of Democrats who are going to be profoundly offended by the innuendo."

Marilyn Quayle's speech preceding Barbara Bush's hadn't helped. The vice president's wife echoed the same exclusionary tone as Buchanan's. "Not everyone joined the counterculture," she scolded. "Not everyone demonstrated, dropped out, took drugs, joined the sexual revolution, or dodged the draft." Moments later, she added, "Women's lives are different from men's lives. We make different trade-offs, we make different sacrifices, and we get different rewards. Helping my children as they grow into good and loving teenagers is a daily source of joy for me. There aren't many women who would have it any other way."

Examined closely, Marilyn Quayle's statements were ambiguous, but her tone and delivery were unmistakably harsh.

Republicans would accuse the press of seizing on a few moments from the convention unfairly, such as Pat Buchanan's speech and Marilyn Quayle's and Pat Robertson's, ignoring the more moderate moments. The criticism doesn't hold up. On the air, actually, ABC did not emphasize Marilyn Quayle's speech. Gralnick reprised about three minutes of it, including these harshest moments. Jennings called it "uncompromising" and "tough." But Friedman used none of it the next night on *World News*. And neither on the prime time broadcast nor the news the next night did they use any of Pat Robertson's even harsher speech earlier that evening.

The strain also seemed to be showing on Bush. Wednesday afternoon, the day Barbara Bush and Marilyn Quayle were supposed to moderate the convention's tone, Jennings taped an interview with Bush at the White House's request. It would be the only time the two men would speak during the entire campaign. Friedman and Jennings had decided beforehand to focus on politics—tactics, polls, strategy, and the convention—not policy.

Jennings opened with the polls. ABC's poll suggested Bush wasn't getting a bounce from the convention yet. Did it have anything to do with "what some people think is a fairly negative tone" at the convention, the anchor asked.

The convention had been "very upbeat," Bush contended.

Jennings kept at it. The Republican party chairman had said Democrats are "not America." Buchanan had said there was "a religious war for the soul of America." Did the president "buy that stuff?"

Bush said he wanted people to believe what he said, not others.

Fine, Jennings pressed, but his question was did Bush agree with those statements?

"I can't agree with all the rhetoric," Bush acknowledged, after some evasive sentence fragments. "This is a free speech country."

But Jennings pushed further. Bush was the President who had spoken of a kinder and gentler America, he reminded. Was Buchanan's speech kinder and gentler. Bush again evaded.

For all the familiarity, all the speeches, all the minutes on the tube, presidents are largely hidden from the press. Brit Hume saw Bush usually from the distance of the camera stand, a few minutes a day, or a few times a month at a group press conference. Rarely do American presidents sit like this for lengthy interviews with a single interrogator, and even more rarely were they pressed on a subject with multiple followup questions. Bush was becoming visibly angry.

Did you ask these kinds of questions of Clinton, Bush demanded.

"I'm sure we did," Jennings told the President. But he did not stop. "Do you want to put any distance between yourself and some of Mr. Buchanan's gay-bashing?"

Bush's voice was beginning to crack. His throat sounded dry and his smile was now crooked. "I want to stand with what I told you, Peter," he managed.

In all, Jennings asked seventeen of forty-two questions about how Bush felt about the tone and substance of the convention.

He asked about Bush's unfulfilled promise that he would fire anyone who engaged in "the sleaze business." He asked about Clinton's allegation that the Republicans were turning Hillary into "a Willie Horton-like issue," a reference to a black criminal who Bush used as a symbol of Democratic softness on crime in 1988.

Bush bristled. I don't see a connection, he said.

"I don't either. I am just asking," Jennings said.

"Well how the heck can I explain it if you can't," Bush shot back.

It ended with Jennings pressing Bush on what he meant when he promised a hard hitting campaign. "Anything it takes?"

"What does anything mean," Bush asked. "Break the law?"

"You're the one who has to define it, sir," Jennings said.

"Well, I don't think I have to define it at all," Bush snapped.

"Well, you're the one who can much better define it than I can, is my point."

"Well, if you could define what you mean by anything," Bush answered angrily.

As Bush rose when the interview ended, he demanded, "Are the mikes off."

He's going to curse us, Nancy Gabriner thought. The President of the United States was about to refer to America's favorite anchorman with reference to either the sex act or the bathroom.

Suddenly Marlin Fitzwater, the presidential press secretary, rushed over, grabbed the President, and pulled him out of the room.

Within minutes, Dorrance Smith, the former ABC executive producer and now senior counsel to the President, was on the phone with Friedman.

"Jennings was posturing," he said, being argumentative. "The President is really angry."

Dorrance Smith was a former Arledge protégé, head of *Nightline*, the *Brinkley Show* and *Weekend News*, and once a possible successor to the presidency of News and a Friedman rival.

The President, Smith said, wanted to see the interview Jennings had with Clinton at the Democratic convention. He wanted to see if similar questions were asked.

Friedman, with that quiet unflappable confidence in his voice, said he'd be delighted to give him a transcript of what he put on the air.

"But don't go on the attack on this issue that Peter didn't raise any substantive issues," Friedman countered. "This is a political convention. And if the President wants to turn the conversation to issues he is certainly capable of it. I mean come on. What issues did you want us to cover?"

Well, what the President is going to speak about, Dorrance said. What Mrs. Bush is going to speak about.

"Dorrance, you mean to say if we had asked him that he wouldn't have said, wait and see," Friedman said.

"Perhaps," Smith said.

"Oh come on."

But the call may have had some effect. When Friedman, Jennings, and Stew Schutzman put the interview together for *World News*, they made it about as benign as possible. Bush came off cool, never angry. They told themselves that the rest of the show was fairly hard on the White House so this shouldn't be. The interview, however, would mark a turn in Jennings's relations with the White House, particularly with people who only heard about it secondhand.

On Thursday afternoon, the architects of the convention, Craig Fuller, Charlie Black, and James Lake, came by for their last spin session.

"They were really forcing it," Bruno said. "You could see the unhappiness in their faces." Tom Bettag, the executive producer of *Nightline*, agreed.

Bush top aides did not even know what the President would say in his speech. "We don't know what's in it, but I am sure that he will talk about where he thinks the country is, where he wants to take it," Bush strategist Black admitted. That was an ominous sign that it was being done at the last minute.

That last night, Quayle spoke first. "Stern, strong, unsmiling," Brinkley announced when it was over. Privately, Brinkley rather liked Quayle. He considered him not nearly as stupid as his reputation, but still appearing immature.

"Pushed all the right buttons," Lynn Sherr said.

"Probably the best speech of the Vice President's life," said Wooten.

Greenfield was the most probing of all. "I think this argument about the cultural elite, in part, serves him very well. If he is a joke . . . he is saying to these delegates in particular, 'When they are laughing at me, they're really laughing at you and at what you believe in.' "

The nub, however, was still to come, Bush. Everyone had said all week it had to be a home run, which of course it didn't really have to be at all. But it certainly mattered. Hume had discovered that new chief of staff Jim Baker's aides had toughened the speech significantly at the last minute.

As Bush finished speaking, Brinkley began the post mortems.

"Well, I thought it was a very good speech, bearing in mind it was a political speech. That's a separate art from any other kind of endeavor."

Jennings couldn't believe it. He thought Bush's speech was absolutely dreadful. The anchor thought it best to keep his opinions to himself, to leave the others to opine. So he was relieved other cast members differed. Cokie Roberts called it "the President deciding instead of being presidential to be a fighter."

George Will was the most cutting of all: "a first-rate, crackerjack vice presidential speech." Jennings regretted not having pointed out on air at some point that Will was one of the country's most renowned Bush-bashers.

Greenfield ran long but was interesting, as usual. Bush on foreign affairs was strong, but on domestic, "a little long, a little diffuse and you could see—clearly see—the impact of this speech that was worked on by a committee. . . . when you compare the mesmerizing speech of four years ago, I don't think this was in the same league."

In a minute, they were off. It was over. There was no party. Arledge had canceled it because of Kaplan's death, which was fitting. But there was a sense that this had been a more interesting convention, and that they had done a better job of it.

Were they being unfair to the White House? Was there bias in the press?

Gralnick, the man in charge of ABC's convention coverage, was elated with the conventions, especially Houston. But his reasons had nothing to do with politics, and they said everything about what motivated television. They had done this for less money than anyone had ever dreamed they could, Gralnick thought. They learned things that would save ABC money in the future. They had not missed major speeches like the competition. They had stayed on the air longer after the speeches ended, and they had won the ratings. Especially Thursday, the key night, when their ratings swelled every half hour they were on the air.

That meant people were turning from other networks to them.

"We got on. We got off. We made a little money," Gralnick liked to say.

The grand conspirators who saw ideological bias were talking about something that was scarcely on his radar screen.

The Republicans had also been far more successful than the Democrats on the most important tactical issue of all: They had forced the networks to carry their speakers live and unfiltered— Buchanan, Reagan, Gramm, Kemp, Mrs. Bush, Lynn Martin, Quayle, and Bush. If the Republicans hadn't been off schedule on Monday, forcing the networks to vamp, the speeches would have accounted for roughly 80 percent of air time all week. The Republicans also managed far more exposure for Barbara and George Bush, plus other surrogates, than the Democrats had for Clinton and his family.

The problem was the party. It was divided, and that couldn't be masked. When they were interviewed, Jack Kemp or Bill Bennett could scarcely conceal their disapproval with fellow Republicans like Buchanan and evangelist Pat Robertson and even Phil Gramm. Off camera, Republicans were even angrier with each other than on. "We're going to get the conservatives for this," a New York delegate told one producer. "We've got the music, but not the words," Bennett complained to Greenfield.

The divisions within the Republican party overwhelmed the managerial skill of its planners. Bush was afraid or unwilling to treat Buchanan as harshly as Clinton treated Brown. The convention had not moderated because Bush was not clearly moderate. Even one of Quayle's top aides would come to call it a disaster.

All of that might have been erased if Bush's speech had laid out a compelling positive vision. And this is the irony about the prevailing view that conventions have become unimportant because they no longer really nominate candidates.

Far from being irrelevant, conventions have become the most important events in modern campaigns. George Bush's speech in 1988 was the critical moment of his political career, just as 1992 was perhaps the last chance he had at winning reelection, and he squandered it. The reason that conventions—and particularly these speeches—are crucial is precisely because they are unfiltered by the press. They stand as the only time Americans see a candidate offer his vision undiluted for an extended period, not chopped up into bits by the media or leavened through the theatrical confrontational format of debates. The conventions allowed George Bush to win the election in 1988. They may have cost him reelection four years later.

This is why the Republican criticism of the coverage of the convention is misguided. And why the prospect that the networks will stop airing the conventions is so irresponsible.

★

CHAPTER

9

THE FALL

"Now for the political news," Peter Jennings said coming out of the first commercial. He always looked so casual on the air, as if he were waiting for a friend to come back from the fridge so he could finish his sentence.

It was September 9, the Wednesday after Labor Day weekend. The fall campaign had finally begun. Friedman had put the political segment into the second block of *World News*. "First, an explanation," Jennings began.

Friedman and Jennings had labored over what the anchor was about to say. Friedman would come to think the wording was one of the things ABC News did right this campaign. The executive producer of *World News Tonight* finally knew how he wanted to cover the race.

"We're aware that a lot of you are turned off by the political process and that many of you put at least some of the blame on us," Jennings said. So for the next couple of months, Jennings went on, they were going to do this differently. "We'll give you the day's headlines," but "we'll only devote more time to a candidate's daily routine if it is more than routine. There will be less attention to staged appearances and soundbites designed exclusively for television."

Watching in the "war room" of Clinton campaign headquarters in Little Rock, Clinton's chief strategist James Carville muttered out loud that ABC was going to make their job harder.

In Washington, James Lake, the communications director for the Bush-Quayle reelection committee, shook his head angrily. This was the press taking its arrogance to new heights. Who the hell did they think they were?

In New York, Roone Arledge was not happy either.

The plan Jennings was about to unveil had begun to form in Friedman's carefully calculating mind in mid-June—based on the conversations with Jennings about what was wrong with fall campaigns and the press's coverage of them.

Boiled down, they had realized traditional political journalism was numbingly simple. One assigned smart correspondents to travel with candidates and trusted them to bring back the story. The problem was the candidates had mastered this approach. Their advance men arranged the camera angles, set the backdrops, and even dictated where the press could stand. The candidate was only visible to the public and the press for short, controlled periods of time, and otherwise kept out of sight. In 1988, the traveling press corps usually saw George Bush just three times a day, at speeches where he spoke for about fifteen minutes each, a cumulative forty-five minutes. Reporters, especially television, weren't covering the campaign, only the fraction of it the candidates allowed.

No wonder the coverage degenerated into horse race, polls, tactics, and a focus on the attack soundbite of the day. That at least the press had access to.

To reach beyond that, they had to remember the simple truth about television the politicians had already learned: that too often logistics drove coverage, not the other way around.

In effect, the networks decided what the news was when they chose where to place their cameras and correspondents. If they put their star reporters on the bus with candidates, daily photo ops are what went on the air. The first step to change was keeping key correspondents off the planes.

The second was to figure out what to report on instead. If they didn't focus on the daily photo op, what would they cover? This, it would turn out, was the challenge they only partly solved.

Finally, there was the question of how to cover issues.

Television's usual treatment of what candidates stood for was often obligatory boilerplate, Friedman thought, a couple of interviews and a handful of accomplishments flashed on screen for seconds—like bumper stickers on a passing car. Could they do better? And could they stick to their good intentions?

When Arledge returned from colon cancer surgery in June, Friedman's thinking took on new urgency. Arledge had begun asking questions about the fall and about *World News*. Where was Jack McWethy? Ever since McWethy left the state department beat, he had disappeared. He should be on the air.

And who should cover Clinton? The Arkansas governor had spent much of June repairing his reputation. Perot was beginning to drop. The race was actually beginning to look even. They should decide whether to keep Chris Bury on Clinton or replace him with someone with a higher profile, Arledge said, more of a star, a heavyweight. If Clinton did win, Arledge wanted someone covering him who could cover the White House in the fall.

This traditional thinking was exactly what Friedman and Jennings wanted to avoid. If Arledge prevailed in assigning someone big to Clinton, Friedman thought it would lock them into traditional coverage.

Bury was doing a fine job, the executive producer told his boss. He should stay. Arledge backed down, for now.

Friedman had already had the same thoughts as Arledge, too. In May, Friedman had asked McWethy to fly up from Washington for lunch to talk about the White House, and McWethy hadn't been terribly interested. He had covered the White House for *U.S. News & World Report* and had watched how television did it, and he didn't think much of it.

TV White House coverage puts show business over journalism, McWethy had told Friedman. It is predicated on getting a famous correspondent on the air each night, not on finding out what is going on inside the White House. The correspondent is pinned to his workspace, waiting to see if the show wants a piece and then churning it out. In the process, TV had surrendered itself to being manipulated by wherever the president wanted to go in front of cameras. TV wasn't so much covering the White House as using it as a soundstage. And that was what Ronald Reagan had understood and used so well.

To break the cycle, McWethy argued, ABC should have two chief White House correspondents who worked as equal partners. While one took a turn covering the daily events, the other would do the off-camera work, learning how the place worked. Then they would swap.

It's an interesting idea, Friedman said, but Roone would never go for it. He wants a star on the White House lawn.

Friedman was being disingenuous. He also wanted a star. But McWethy's ideas—and his lack of interest in the White House—had influenced how Friedman thought about covering the campaign.

When Arledge began pressing for McWethy to cover Clinton in July, Friedman decided he better move swiftly to outflank anyone who wanted to resist change. By the end of July, Friedman had put his ideas on paper, something the usually careful office politician was loathe to do. "Memos like this one are always risky (which is one reason I hardly ever write them)," the memo began, layered with meanings.

"And this one is going to ramble (because no one is going to edit me the way we edit you)," Friedman continued.

"We intend to do the best job of covering a political campaign that any network news broadcast has ever done. Although we will cover the daily events aggressively, we will emphasize the kinds of stories that help viewers understand the issues and the process."

To stick to their intentions, Friedman developed an elaborate format, with graphics and special titles. The daily political report would begin by noting the candidate's day—what used to comprise TV political coverage—but now Jennings would usually dispatch with it with just a voice-over narration of pictures and maybe a quick candidate soundbite. Only if the candidate made "real" news would they run a full story.

Thus, the memo failed to mention, Bury would stay on Clinton. Hume on Bush.

Next would come what television usually did least well—broader analysis of the election. This is where Friedman would use the correspondents he was holding back—Jim Wooten for overall political theme stories, Jeff Greenfield on image making, media, commercials, and analysis, Cokie Roberts on the House, Senate races, and women in politics, John McWethy on analysis and investigative pieces. It would be the largest cast of correspondents any network had ever assembled to do analysis.

They would then deal with the miscellany of the day in something called campaign notes that Jennings would narrate—funny gaffes, odd moments on the trail—and the polls. This also created a slot to minimize the polls.

They would handle policy in American Agenda, four to five minutes each, three days a week, for seven weeks. The pieces would take weeks to prepare, and the key, Friedman thought, was that the Agenda correspondents were already specialists on these issues. So the stories might be more than bumper-sticker TV.

Finally, Friedman decided to ask the polling unit to organize focus groups of undecided voters whom Jennings could follow through the fall. If this was the year the press should listen to voters, this would be a way of doing it at a time when it made sense.

Over the eight weeks from September 8 to November 4, they would also take the broadcast on the road at least three times, perhaps four, to talk to voters.

Without saying so, the plan also made Jennings more of the

centerpiece. This was TV, and the research was plain: the only thing most viewers consciously noticed was the anchor. " 'Twas always thus," Friedman would say. When Walter Cronkite was still at CBS, producers for the evening news identified Cronkite's opening and closing statements by writing "magic" in the scripts, a reference to the anchorman's mysterious hold over viewers. With all its cutbacks, NBC News had exploited the sway of the anchor to a degree that was perilously irresponsible. Brokaw was holding up that network like Atlas. On occasion people at NBC referred to Brokaw as simply T.V. NBC News president Michael Gartner called him the franchise, and "the man with the affidavit face." The miracle at CBS was the schizophrenic power of Rather, who drove some viewers away and held the loyalty of so many others. But that was television. You spend all day thinking about content, and America watches or doesn't because they like your sweater, or your tie, or your voice, or they don't. If they were going to do a lot of politics at ABC, they had to get Jennings's mug into it.

Much of what Friedman was proposing also was not new. He and Jennings were crystallizing what the press was doing in general. But Friedman and Jennings's plan took it further, and made it more systematic. Implicitly, they were also acknowledging the press's power. If the press's influenced events as well as observed them, it had a responsibility to do more than simply record what the candidates gave them.

Reactions varied. But Arledge's was the most ominous. "You're a brave memo writer," he told Friedman. In the end, *World News* would fall back to covering the race as it always did, Arledge predicted. And it sounded like Friedman was going to put on too much politics.

Arledge was a complex man, easily misunderstood. What some people saw as his appalling detachment others respected as an ability to delegate. What some dismissed as lack of intellectual sophistication others knew to be his reliance on a genius gut instinct. And say what you will, other networks had cut more and suffered. Under Arledge, ABC had held the line on quality and flourished. He was inscrutable, certainly. That was part of his power. "He is a much smarter man than I am, and I don't say that about many people," Koppel said. "And he doesn't know how smart he is."

Contemplative, perhaps arrogant, Friedman had developed his own ties to Cap Cities management, but he respected Arledge, and he did not discount his boss's instincts. He was proposing devoting half of the program to politics for two months. That was more than enough time to kill the audience.

ABC's reign as No. 1 had lasted three years, a streak exceeded only three times in television—by Huntley-Brinkley, Cronkite, and then briefly by Dan Rather. Friedman might be staking his future on this plan. And if ABC News fell from No. 1 because it covered politics, chances are it would be the end of serious political coverage on network television for years.

In September, the week before *World News* was to launch the format, pressure on Friedman increased markedly. The morning of August 24, Hurricane Andrew lashed across the southern tip of Dade County, Florida and whipped Louisiana the next day. At CBS's new downscale *Evening News* program, Erik Sorenson summoned Dan Rather from vacation and rushed him to the scene. That week, the *CBS Evening News* passed Friedman and Jennings's *World News* in ratings—for the first time in eighty-seven consecutive weeks. The streak had ended.

CBS. "News for the fucking brain dead," fumed Jack White, *World News*'s producer for national news. CBS's show borrowed heavily from local news. Correspondents did their standup closes walking toward the camera, a gimmick that generated a sense of visual movement and made correspondents the stars of their stories. It also, Friedman believed, gave viewers a chance to see female correspondents' legs. Correspondents appeared live via satellite hookup so they could then answer rehearsed followup questions from Rather—another local trick to create the sensation of being up-to-the-minute, even if nothing was happening at that minute. Mixed in with a diminishing number of the leathery-faced

veterans like Bob Schieffer and Eric Engberg were a new generation of prettier faces like Scott Pelley, Edie Magnuson, and Bill
Lagatutta.

"Everybody's young, everybody walks, everybody's got nice
hair," Friedman sneered of CBS's broadcast. "A lot of us couldn't
get hired there. But don't think it doesn't add to the pressure over
here."

Cap Cities management had been increasingly fearful of
CBS's rise in the first six months of the year. The market research
ABC had conducted in the early summer had been depressing. It
confirmed that CBS was positioning itself to hold the audience for
the tabloid show *Inside Edition* that led into local news in so many
CBS markets. In short, network news wasn't driving the future of
TV journalism. The syndicated tabloid shows were. The research
also showed that most viewers discerned no difference between the
reporting of Jack McWethy and that of Gizelle Fernandez, a beautiful dark-haired woman whose appeal, some of her colleagues
alleged, owed more to her cheekbones than her grasp of the First
Amendment. People saw CBS as more biased, less fair, less objective—mostly because of Dan Rather—and they didn't care. "It
made you want to quit the business," Friedman said sourly.

Inside ABC, some were also worried because they thought
Friedman was overrated. "*World News Tonight* is pretty goddamn dull, to tell you the truth," said one of the most respected
talents at the network. "The pacing, the stories. It's Number One
because Peter is the best anchor on television." Objectively, Jennings was at his best, however, because the judicious Friedman
brought it out of him.

Whatever the reason for *World News*'s success, Friedman
and Jennings were feeling pressure to make some changes because
of CBS. Friedman had already agreed to add more of what he
called R&P stories—rape and pillage. He had also agreed to
change the graphics and music on the show after the first of the
year.

Now, if CBS's ratings continued surging and *World News*

dropped to No. 2 for a sustained period, the financial consequences were enormous. The difference between being first and
second in nightly news ratings was about $15,000 for a 30-second
commercial or close to $30 million in revenues a year. The compe-
tition to be No. 1 in evening news was a ruthless pursuit. Friedman
would doubtless be forced to change the broadcast, most likely in
some way imitative of CBS's downscale style. Jennings, the roman-
tic idealist, might become so irritable he would just catch on fire
one day and they would walk into his office and there would be
nothing left but a pile of ashes, a kerchief and an Armani blazer
hung over a chair. Maybe it would be Arledge's undoing, too. A
good number of people inside ABC News were convinced by then
that Cap Cities seemed to want an excuse to be rid of him, or at
least marginalize him.

"If this is the beginning of the end, what should we do?"
Jennings asked Arnot Walker, his public relations aide. Should
they start saying publicly what they thought of CBS?

"No," Walker answered. "We will die with dignity."

The day before *World News* launched the new political format, Arledge began the Tuesday editorial meeting with an edict:

"I want to tell my executive producers here, you're going to
do politics at your own peril and the peril of your own broadcasts."

Nothing in television remains exclusive for long. Two days after
Jennings launched the new format, CBS issued a press release
announcing that it, too, had a new plan for political coverage. The
evening news would travel each Friday to a new place and do focus
groups and spend less time on the daily stump. And the network
had instituted Campaign Reality Check, a daily analysis piece that
sounded exactly like Friedman's dry-sounding Campaign Focus.

With its limited resources, NBC had moved in this same
direction already. NBC's Washington bureau chief Tim Russert,
political coverage head Bill Wheatley, and news president Michael
Gartner had helped shape the early thinking about keeping corre-

spondents off the campaign buses and focusing more on voters' concerns. But the results had been mixed. NBC didn't put more junior correspondents on the buses instead. It had no one on the campaigns regularly. Usually, NBC had camera crews on the campaign buses only every fourth day, just enough to remain members of the network pool for the sharing video. The system had worked fine for Lisa Myers covering Perot, who didn't have a campaign bus anyway. But the results were shaky at best for Andrea Mitchell covering Clinton. Her pieces lacked the texture of being there. And too often she had to cover the day's events and also analyze them in each piece—too much to do in two minutes. NBC executives publicly denied it, but their intention was to save money as well as to change their journalism, and it showed.

Whatever their motive or depth of commitment, however, all three networks were moving away from airing what they deemed empty photo opportunities. They were trying instead to police campaign rhetoric for truthfulness, and cover voters and issues. It could now be tested whether changing television changed politics.

The day after ABC launched its new format, George Bush traveled to Detroit for one of the most important events of his campaign. Bush's vaguely defined fall election strategy had three parts. He had to establish that he had a credible economic plan of his own to neutralize Clinton's advantage on the economy; he had to raise doubts about Clinton—by challenging the Democrat's math and his habit of dissembling about his past and his positions; then he had to break the tie by reminding voters of his own command of foreign policy.

It was a difficult task, obviously. Not only did the Republicans have to control the dialogue of the campaign as it played out through the media, they had to shift it from being a referendum about Bush's record to a challenge of Clinton's vision. But Bush's team soon discovered that the new conventional wisdom of the media only made their task harder.

In the last week of August and the first week of September, George Bush's strategy had already suffered a heavy blow even before it began. The networks seized on the allegation from local Florida officials that Bush was late in responding to the hurricane and made up for it only when it became a political issue. In response, Bush spent the next week traveling across the midwest and south doling out federal pork barrel.

Clinton's internal polling saw an ironic but significant result. Voters began to see Bush as too political, not politically maladroit. That change in perception partially neutralized one of Clinton's greatest weaknesses, that he had never been anything but a politician. And the nightly news had created that story, Clinton aides thought. The race had also developed a basic stability. Bush had dropped from about five points back on the eve of his acceptance speech in Houston to ten points the week after. And he had stayed there. Now, the Thursday after Labor Day weekend, Bush was heading to Detroit to build the first leg of his fall strategy—to reestablish his credibility on the economy.

He called his plan the Agenda for Economic Renewal, and it gathered together Bush's existing economic proposals, plus some new ones, and linked them with a serious philosophical defense of minimalist government.

The night Bush delivered the Agenda in Detroit, Bush's aides had little to complain about from television. All three networks led with the plan. (CBS and NBC described it in fairly political terms, and both also did features about Clinton's economic plan. ABC gave more time to Bush's ideas alone—a straight account by Hume followed by a fairly critical analysis by economics correspondent Stephen Aug.)

The Bush campaign also worked local news. It held press conferences on the plan in all fifty states, did satellite interviews with local business people, and made a special satellite interview with Bush available just for local stations. The usage, word was, was heavy.

And Bush aired a five-minute TV commercial that evening

reprising the Agenda, which included an 800 number for people to call for a copy of the plan. In Clinton's focus groups, the ad would prove to be Bush's most effective of the campaign. The speech, Clinton aides had to admit, had been a good one.

But within a few days it became clear to both campaigns that Bush's Agenda for Economic Renewal had failed politically. Bush's private polls showed the Agenda speech and advertising boosted his credibility to steward the economy by just three points. Clinton campaign aides found that most people did not know that Bush had prepared a plan.

Professionals on both sides would argue at length afterwards over why Bush failed to convince voters his Agenda even existed. The subject bears a moment's reflection, though, for it goes to the heart of what drove the election and whether the press's new approach played a role in changing the nature of the campaign debate.

Some in Bush's camp blame his campaign team for not selling the Agenda hard enough—and they blame James Baker and his aides in particular. The weekend after the Agenda was introduced, the media plan called for Baker and the Agenda author Bob Zoellick to do the Sunday talk shows. As Baker had been dodging the press since leaving the state department to run the campaign, this appearance would have sent a message to the press that he was serious about the Agenda, Bush aides hoped. It also would have meant the Monday morning papers would have featured another discussion of the Agenda on their front pages. Newspapers, starved for news on the deserted sands of Sunday afternoon, usually feed on the Sunday talk shows.

Baker, however, refused to do the shows, and Labor Secretary Lynn Martin, Senator Bob Dole, and Vice President Quayle went out instead. The only stories in the Monday papers concerned Quayle's softening position against abortion.

In the focus groups testing the Agenda, Bush's campaign also found that voters were unwilling to listen to Bush on the economy. "They agreed with everything the President said in his economic speech," pollster Fred Steeper would explain, "but it just reminded them that he hadn't done anything a year earlier." The campaign never made a formal decision to change tactics, but it seemed to waver about how hard to keep pounding away at the Agenda. It was a critical error. Bush may never have succeeded in selling his Agenda, but without trying he was doomed.

Still other Bush aides blame the press. "We ended up giving a separate speech on each of the [Agenda] issues," one aide close to Baker said. But the press on those days often ignored the speeches and wrote about tactics or attacks. "They were not presenting the positive message, only focusing on the attack side." And it was not only the networks. "It was hard even with the print guys."

Other Bush aides went even further. Jim Lake, Bush's communications adviser, felt the networks' new approach was the height of network impudence—and ABC had taken it to a new extreme. The candidates running for president decide what the issues are, not the networks, he believed. The networks' job is to cover what the candidates are saying to the public—thoroughly and fairly. Dismissing the daily stump appearances was irresponsible.

Lake's arguments have some legitimacy. Taken too far, the new approach of the press did threaten to impose the press's agenda too much on the race. Hume worried about this, too. The one virtue of journalism, he thought, was that reporters could agree on what was news. The problem with this argument is that covering what the candidates say on the stump is not enough. The press also needs to evaluate it. And it needs to explore the candidates' record, and examine their advertising and what their surrogates are saying. The press erred at times by ignoring the stump appearances, but that did not harm Bush markedly. And it was a small price to pay for the gains the press did make.

A week after the Detroit speech, Bush went to Enid, Oklahoma, to deliver what Bush aides were telling reporters was another part of his economic Agenda, a critique of Clinton's economic plan. The Democrat, Bush would charge, believed in using government for European-style social engineering.

Hume lobbied hard for Friedman and Jennings to do a piece. But *World News* was on the road in Charlotte, North Carolina, for three days, part of the overall plan of listening to voters, so Hume lost the argument. Neither CBS nor NBC did stories about the speech either. Whatever the merits of Bush's accusations, he was laying out real differences between himself and Clinton—not just conducting a redundant photo op.

Five days later, Bush pulled a campaign stunt that in days gone by would have guaranteed network coverage. In one day, he touched down in the six states that surrounded Arkansas to attack Clinton's record as governor on the economy and on the environment. It was the beginning of the second leg of the Bush triad, undermining Clinton's credibility.

Not one network that day did a full story about it. Hume and producer Terry Ray again lobbied hard, and again they were probably right. But on the Rim they were trying to figure out whether to do a story about Clinton's draft record or about Perot getting back in. Trying to be analytical made it hard to be flexible. The old way was a lot easier. (CBS's fine veteran Eric Engberg the following day critiqued Bush's charges and found them technically accurate but often distorted and misleading—a critique that was the press at its best, especially television.) But the networks' failure to cover these two speeches affected Bush far less than his own erratic campaign plan.

In the seven days after Bush unveiled his economic Agenda, nearly each day he diverted his campaign message onto other topics—handing out military contracts, a speech to Christian Coalition, an attack on Clinton and the draft to the National Guard in Utah. The President was also making news ineptly by refusing to debate. Then, after all this, came the Enid speech.

However turned off voters were to Bush—and however difficult the press's new approach made his task—the President

could never have convinced Americans his Agenda was meaningful if he was so ambivalent about selling it.

Day to day, actually, the Republicans weren't bad at directing the media's focus. In the seven weeks between Labor Day and
Election Day, Bush's daily campaign events became the basis for
twice as many stories on *World News* as did Clinton's—twenty
stories out of those thirty-five week nights versus just ten stories
for Clinton. The Bush campaign knew tactically how to get on the
nightly news. But the Republicans lacked a coherent larger strategic argument about why Bush deserved to be reelected. The lesson
was obvious but too often forgotten: smart handlers and clever
advertising techniques don't win elections. Having the skill to
manipulate the media doesn't win elections. Those tactics only
work in the service of having something coherent to say, amid
economic and world conditions that make the public receptive to
hearing it.

The press had drawn some mistaken lessons from the Reagan
era, too. There was more to getting elected than dominating the
images on the network news. The content of the stories, the words
coming out of Reagan's mouth, really mattered.

When the Agenda introduction failed, a group of Bush aides sat
down to reevaluate their media strategy. The group wanted to
target the one voter group now deemed essential for Republican
victory—suburban women.

The popular culture media had always made the Bush campaign jittery. In the summer, after announcing that Bush thought
shows like Arsenio Hall were unpresidential, the White House did
dabble at a few more mainstream programs. But when Bush aides
decided to do the *CBS Morning News* in June, the prospect of
facing a live audience so unnerved them that they insisted on
picking it themselves from people outside waiting in line for the
White House tour. A plan to make a surprise appearance on the

Tonight Show during Johnny Carson's last week foundered over the logistics of how the President would be back in time to weekend in Maine.

Now, in September, the Bush campaign was effectively trapped. In the summer, it had misread the mood of the country by skipping the alternative media. Now, in the fall, it was failing to use the traditional press effectively to convey its message. If the White House changed direction and moved into the popular culture media in a big way, Bush aides feared people would think it was acting out of desperation.

After two days of meetings, Bush's high command agreed on a modest plan to reintroduce Bush's economic agenda in a way that bypassed the mainstream press and tailored the agenda specifically to suburban women. The plan was to blanket the morning television news shows starting with ABC's *Good Morning America.*

The Bush campaign would offer the president to *GMA* live for ten minutes every day for a week on the condition that he could discuss whatever he wanted for the first three minutes. Bush aides intended the President to use those minutes to reintroduce his economic message.

This should be only the beginning, James Lake and Fred Steeper urged. From this point on, Bush should do some popular culture show every day, they argued, guaranteeing his message of the day got out. Larry King would be next in line. Campaign chairman Bob Teeter and chief of staff James Baker were more hesitant. Let's see how the ABC show goes, they said, and then decide.

Bush appeared on *Good Morning America* six times starting the last week in September.

It did nothing for him.

After various arguments about why, the Bush campaign the second week in October again dropped its popular culture strategy—with the exception of Larry King—until the last moments of the race.

*   *

Ten days before the election, Ted Koppel got a call at home from Dorrance Smith, the former ABC producer who now worked at the White House. The two men knew each other well. Smith had been executive producer of *Nightline* for two years.

If George Bush agreed to appear on *Nightline*, Smith asked, was there a way to stay away from talking about Bush's role in the IranContra scandal and the Bush administration's pre–Gulf War arming of Iraq?

The subtext of such a call was unmistakable. Koppel figured *Nightline* was among the last programs on which Bush would ever consider appearing. Over the last two years, Koppel had made a special crusade out of exploring Bush's IranContra role and the arming of Iraq. And he knew that the White House had considered the coverage biased and irresponsible. The formal calls of outrage to Arledge had started more than a year earlier, presumably from Dorrance Smith himself. "Ted and the show are becoming the laughingstock of Washington," was the way Koppel heard the complaints. "He is making a fool of himself."

Now the White House needed *Nightline*. If the President were to come on, he would not consider it right to be subjected to an hour on IranContra and Iraqgate, Smith told Koppel.

That was fair, Koppel answered. Nor would that be his intention. But he wouldn't avoid those subjects. If they did an hour or maybe ninety minutes, he would expect to spend about ten minutes on those issues, Koppel said.

When he hung up, Koppel turned to his wife, Grace. The White House must think they haven't got a snowball's chance in hell of winning, he said.

There was a second call from Smith that sounded encouraging, but a week before election day the White House aide called back to say the plan was dead. The only conclusion, Koppel thought, was the President believed he simply could not afford to be asked questions on those two subjects a week before election day.

The last week of the campaign Bush took virtually every chance—except *Nightline*. He did an hour on *Good Morning America*, two half hours on the *Today Show*, two with Larry King, and even MTV.

He was also campaigning better. And by most accounts gaining some ground.

Clinton's plan after Labor Day was far simpler than Bush's. He wanted to talk for two months about the same three subjects over and over—the economy, change, and his concern for the middle class. The other thing he wanted to talk about was George Bush's record.

Stanley Greenberg's survey and focus group research also showed something basic. What was driving the election was people's desire to remove George Bush from the White House. It had been true in New Hampshire and it was still true. "We have to make it possible for them to do that," Greenberg would say over and over. Clinton also had an ace card. People wanted the Democrat to succeed. They wanted to disbelieve bad information about Clinton and believe the good. That had been clear by the way public opinion flipped after the Democratic convention. "It was not an even playing field," Greenberg would say later. And Clinton aides thought the media's new approach away from the daily stump speech and toward policy and voters made that task even easier.

To help it plot a media strategy, the Clinton campaign had developed a model of what moved public opinion. Despite the fact that local news was now the dominant source of information in the United States and the reality that the presidency was won state by state, presidential races were still national, the research suggested. Greenberg had done a regression analysis of all the polls from the last two elections and found that 75 percent of what one needed to know to predict the vote in any state came from national information. Only 25 percent of the information was state specific. "People are all watching the same news on the networks. And that is what drives elections. You cannot overstate the power of news."

In the week after Labor Day, Clinton and his team thought they could get on the nightly news by delivering a series of substantive speeches. They decided to take his economic plan and break out a speech a day on each aspect of it—industrial policy Tuesday, welfare Wednesday, the family on Friday, then a week later job training.

In large part, the campaign was wrong. In the seven weeks of the fall, *World News* did stories about only two of Clinton's speeches—a talk about the family at Notre Dame and his lukewarm endorsement of the controversial North American Free Trade Agreement. Both dealt with things deemed politically controversial. As for the others, welfare reform, job training, health care, industrial policy, small business, there always seemed to be a reason for skipping them. American Agenda was covering them. They had done them before. The show preferred to have Hume on more than Bury.

The larger trend in coverage, however, benefited Clinton. The networks' move away from daily stunts suited Clinton's cautious campaign plan by easing the pressure on him to do something new and bold each day. The emphasis on voters rather than candidates, in turn, kept reinforcing how unhappy people were. And when reporters talked to people, they got the impression Bush's chances were even slimmer than the polls indicated. One day in North Carolina, for instance, Jennings, Gabriner, and Stew Schutzman picked the suburb of Morgantown to interview people about the campaign. Over the course of four hours, much of it made worse by the daredevil driving of the Canadian anchorman, the three of them and their camera crew did not encounter a single voter willing to admit support for George Bush.

That night, White House aide Dorrance Smith called Arledge in New York. Since the Bush interview in Houston, the White

House had become convinced that ABC was hostile territory. John Ellis, a former network producer and the President's cousin, had taken to calling Chris Isham, the head of Friedman's investigative unit, to label ABC News Clinton North. James Walker, the President's nephew and an ABC correspondent, was also angry about what they perceived as *World News*'s bias, and so were others at ABC. The word in the White House, ABC reporters were told, was that Jennings was anti-Bush and pro-Clinton.

But others in the press were getting similar signs to those Jennings, Gabriner, and Schutzman had found in Morgantown. Bush was too unpopular to win. When PBS's *MacNeil/Lehrer* called to interview a list of potential southern swing voters about the election, it found that none of them were likely to vote for Bush under any circumstances. The program had to scrap the show and start calling another list.

Then there was American Agenda. Taken together, the Agenda series amounted to more than eighty minutes of TV time from September 15 to election day—an unprecedented commitment to serious coverage of policy. It didn't matter that Clinton's serious speeches weren't being covered as campaign events. His policy positions were being covered in the Agenda pieces on ABC, and usually at greater length and less attack oriented approach.

The structure of the Agenda series—indeed the grammar of journalism about public policy in general—also created a natural advantage for Clinton. All of the pieces concerned domestic policy, Clinton's strength. Clinton always had more policy proposals on the table than Bush—a function of his progovernment rather than promarketplace approach. Finally, while Bush's rhetoric could always be balanced against his record, Clinton's could not.

"Clinton proposes to give more federal support to local law enforcement," Beth Nissen reported in a look at crime. "The Bush Administration has talked about supporting local law enforcement," too. "But the President's 1993 budget request for law enforcement is almost all for federal agencies."

Finally, the Agenda pieces were always comparative so Clinton's ideas never were examined on their own merit—and Bush's minimal and often halfhearted domestic agenda usually paled. The worst that was said of Clinton's promises compared with Bush's is that he avoided being honest about how much they would cost.

For all that, Agenda was a remarkable achievement, probably the most thoughtful and sustained delineation of what presidential candidates stood for ever produced by network television. It was Friedman's best accomplishment of the campaign.

Taken together, the echo effect of covering the voters' mood, comparing policy proposals, and deemphasizing the daily campaign events worked like a chorus in harmony against Bush. Voters were rejecting Bush's arguments on the draft and family values. People thought the economy was in structural decline. Bush was campaigning in places Republicans normally didn't have to. Losing bred losing.

Then, too, the Clinton campaign just worked harder.

Tim Russert, the political aide turned NBC Washington bureau chief, had a favorite saying. "At least half of what a politician does every day is talk to the media, prepare to talk to the media, or read or watch the media."

In a campaign, those percentages go up, and Clinton's was as pure a demonstration of the phenomenon as possible. Under strategist James Carville, Clinton's campaign organization was a surprisingly lean and simple animal. Its central nervous system functioned to massage and manipulate the media. From a 20 × 40 foot office called the War Room in a former newspaper office in downtown Little Rock, the process began at sunset, when three men sat down to begin their electronic nocturnal ritual. Over the next twelve hours, the Nightwatch team set about reading every newspaper and wire service story they could assemble, gathering all the intelligence about the Bush campaign's schedule, monitoring the overnight network news programs.

Around midnight, the state reports began to arrive. Clinton's team required every state office to compile a report each night on the local TV and newspapers in their state.

When Clinton arrived at his hotel for the night, strategist Paul Begala would call the Nightwatch team for a last report.

At 2 A.M., the network overnight news programs came on. Nightwatch leader Ken Segal thought they gave the campaign a strong idea of what the morning news cycle would be on local and network television. Television, he had found, was incredibly poll-driven.

At 4:30 A.M., volunteers began calling in with the morning late editions, the Washington *Post*, *New York Times*, L.A. *Times*. By 5:30 A.M., the Burrells News service was faxing additional stories from local papers, and by 6:30 A.M. Central time, another aide from Washington had a summary of the three network morning shows, which were already on on the East Coast.

By 7 A.M., in addition to his one-hundred-page compilation of stories organized by topic and listed with table of contents, Segal had written a fifteen to twenty page briefing paper summarizing everything—intelligence on Bush's day, on Perot's, a summary of all the coverage, reviews of the latest TV and radio ads, the state by state reports, the vice presidential candidates, their wives, and any key surrogate spokesmen. A copy was faxed to Clinton's entourage on the road.

The morning meeting began then, at 7 A.M. Chief strategist Carville and communications director Stephanopoulos began with Segal reading the summary of the news. Someone would outline the campaign's "media hit" of the day—what message the candidate, his running mate, their wives, and surrogate spokespersons were to make. Stephanopoulos or Carville would remind staff of what Bush was doing, and what they wanted to force him to respond to. They would consider what attack they expected from Bush and what response they wanted to have ready.

Around midday Stephanopoulos got a report on how the flanking operation was working and made any adjustments by 1 P.M. At 7 P.M., the "day news flow" team, Segal's daylight counterpart, began the evening staff meeting with an account of the network evening newscasts.

A key objective of all this was to try whenever possible to get inside the opponent's story every day with your own positive story. Hence if Bush talked about foreign policy and leveled a charge, Clinton's team hoped the press would include Clinton's answer inside that story—separate from the Clinton story of the day.

The examples were myriad. One day in August, Clinton responded to a criticism of his health care plan before Bush had leveled it. When Bush went to Ypsilanti, Michigan, a few days after the Republican convention and attacked Al Gore on the environment, *New York Times* reporter Rick Berke was sitting in the Bush campaign filing center with twenty minutes to write the story when his beeper went off. The call was from Gore's press secretary, Marla Romash. If you would like to talk to Gore, she told him, call him at this number. It was a reporter's dream, Berke thought. He got a personal interview with Gore in response to Bush, even while he was trapped on deadline in a filing center in the middle of nowhere. And it was all because Clinton's campaign had tracked Bush's speech as he gave it, prepared a response, tracked down who was covering the speech for the *New York Times* and got his beeper number, all within a few minutes.

It was politics as the art of track and counterattack. And the canvas on which the art was painted was the media. There were other components. Overnight, the campaign faxed the message of the day to Democrats, including members of Congress, who might be speaking for the campaign. "If a Bush surrogate comes to your state attacking Clinton, be ready to strike him down," read a Clinton "National Talking Point" from August. "And if a Bush surrogate from your state goes somewhere else, make him pay the price at home."

The art of the daily message and the coordinated attack had been perfected by Republicans in the 1980s, and the Bush-Quayle camp still tried. The "Daily Line for Republican Newsmakers," for instance, went out by fax with talking points as similar and pithy as the Democrats'. Both sides were developing daily a national hymnbook, from which its partisans were to sing to their local media. But the Democrats had surpassed the Republicans.

As the technology changed, so did the means of response. The Clinton campaign tried to track where Bush was each day and book satellite time for vice presidential candidate Al Gore into those markets. In June, when Ross Perot would appear on talk shows like Larry King's, the Bush campaign began making a practice of calling the program to spar with Perot. The news accounts the next day invariably focused on the confrontation, effectively turning a Perot appearance into a potential Bush victory. In time, the Clinton campaign would use the same trick on Bush.

Down in "satellite land," where Clinton's team controlled the satellite atop its Little Rock headquarters, deputy press secretary Jeff Eller in his sparetime would troll outerspace on the satellite hoping to intercept network feeds or Republican satellite feeds to get a sense of what might be on the news later.

The guiding principle of this modern political defense is that a charge left unanswered for even a day might as well go unanswered altogether.

Finally, Clinton's campaign benefited, too, from the rising influence of the popular-culture media. Clinton was good at it. And Bush was not. All campaign techniques are candidate specific. Perot could get drafted for president on Larry King by force of his personality when probably no one else could. Clinton was good at town halls and shopping malls and talk shows.

But the popular-culture media also made politics more open to manipulation and abuse.

Larry King and Phil Donahue do not operate by the same standards or ethics as journalists—however loose those standards might be. Nor does C-Span cable network filter out by any journalistic norms of editing what it airs. And those realities, as much as anything else, explained how the episode of Bill Clinton's trip to

Moscow and the charges of McCarthyism that tarred Bush were ferried into the campaign.

The episode began when Representative Robert K. Dornan, the sly conservative Orange County congressman, decided to seize on a student trip Clinton had taken in Christmas 1969, which had included a week in the Soviet Union.

One of the curious customs of the House of Representatives is a period called Special Order. This is the time, at the end of the day, when House members can talk about anything they want for an hour. They do so, however, to an empty chamber. Without a shred of evidence that Clinton's Moscow visit was anything more than innocent, Dornan began using Special Order day after day to demand that Clinton explain traveling to the capital of communism during the Vietnam war.

In the age of cable television, however, Dornan wasn't talking to an empty chamber. He was being broadcast over the C-Span public affairs cable channel into potentially sixty million homes, and that changed everything. After C-Span began in 1980, the number of members who spoke in Special Order doubled. In one speech, Dornan called on outraged citizens to call the media about Clinton's trip. The next day, the Los Angeles *Times* among others received numerous calls. It did not take long for Dornan's daily diatribes to become the buzz of political Washington.

The traditional press held the line against reporting them. It fell instead to Larry King and Phil Donahue. On Oct. 5, King asked Clinton about the Moscow trip citing Dornan as his source. The next day Donahue did, too.

Dornan, in the meantime, had arranged a meeting with Bush and Baker at the White House to press his crusade. Anything like that had to be handled out of the campaign, not the White House, he was told. (Privately the White House and campaign were eagerly trying to find any information they could about the trip for themselves, an effort that led to one of the season's scandals. Political appointees at the State Department, in consort with

White House aides, rifled Clinton's private passport files. But the White House did not find the silver bullet Bush's desperate minions were hoping for, and then even more foolishly leaked the search to the press to raise more suspicions about the case, which ultimately only embarrassed the campaign.)

Then on October 7 Bush appeared on Larry King. "What do you make of the Clinton Moscow trip thing?" King asked.

"Moscow?"

"He says it was just a student trip."

"Larry, I don't want to tell you what I really think, because I don't have the facts. . . . But to go to Moscow one year after Russia crushed Czechoslovakia, not remember who you saw, I think—I think the answer is: Level with the American people. I've made a mistake. . . . You can remember who you saw in the airport in Oslo, but you can't remember who you saw in Moscow?"

Bush sounded as if he were reading Dornan's notes.

The next day Chris Bury sensed a Clinton campaign barely able to contain its delight. It arranged a small formal press conference for Clinton to respond, which was rare. Clinton lately had been hiding. Stan Greenberg's research found that for the first time since the days after the Republican convention, Clinton's remarkably stable lead was widening. Fewer than one in five voters considered Clinton's draft experience important, and those who did weren't going to vote for him anyway.

The press speculated that Bush's move was calculated. The Los Angeles *Times* discovered the meeting with Dornan. Hume had become convinced Bush's move was a gaffe, that King's question had caught them unprepared and Bush had blown it with his answer.

But the greater concern is the press. The case showed how the rise of Donahue and King and other quasi-journalists leaves the process more open to manipulation, innuendo, and rumor. The masters of talk have clout, but they operate by different standards.

There was also, really, nothing new about talk shows or popular culture media. Ted Koppel could still recall working as a young page at NBC in 1960 and seeing Vice President Richard Nixon in an effort to humanize himself appear on the *Tonight Show* with Jack Paar to play the piano. The same thing was considered revolutionary thirty-two years later, when Clinton did it on Arsenio Hall. Rather than something new, popular culture shows were just back in fashion. What was different, perhaps, was that more Americans had turned away from traditional press and took their political cues from more diverse sources.

It was also a mistake to think that one could ignore the traditional press. Since all the candidates were avoiding *Nightline*, for instance, "We sent our investigative unit to work instead," Koppel smiled. In time, doubtless, politicians will get that message, too. It may be more dangerous to ignore the aggressive press than to feed it.

At ABC, meanwhile, Friedman and Jennings's team were finding the hardest part of their plan was not covering issues but producing the analysis stories. Jim Wooten's hope back in January was that the campaign would reveal something about the country and its mood. What he managed to find, however, was a dull homogeneity. Traveling the country talking to voters, he kept returning with the same story, that people were tired of Bush. There were so many other reporters covering this campaign that Wooten and everyone else already knew this, and Wooten never succeeded fully in getting beyond it. McWethy's attempts to keep coming up with interesting pieces, too, were bedeviled by the stable simplicity of the race. Cokie Roberts also did fewer pieces than Friedman had envisioned.

Then in the third week of September, something else happened. Having never really gone away, Ross Perot appeared on the *Today Show* and said network policy required that he would have to be a candidate for office if he wanted to buy time to talk about his political ideas. Mort Dean checked with the advertising division. That was network policy, but Perot could have easily bought time on local stations or independent stations or cable. He didn't need to become a candidate, really.

Dean had dismissed earlier signs that Perot might return. While vacationing in Cape Cod during the Republican convention, he ran into a Perot activist who told him that Ross had just sent sixteen people to New York to make sure he got on the ballot there. The guy never intended to drop out, he was told. Dean called Friedman in Houston. "Go back to your vacation," Friedman said. Koppel had dismissed it, too, when Perot on the eve of the Republican convention told him that if the two parties did not address the issues he might reenter the race.

Then, a few days after the *Today Show* appearance, Perot told *CBS This Morning* he should never have pulled out. And if his volunteers told him to, he'd get back in. What a screaming joke, Friedman thought. Are the candidates and the press all going to fall for Perot's manipulations? Perot's return was an obvious fait accompli, and he had Dean put a story together.

To make things more bizarre, correspondent James Walker, who covered the POW-MIA issue for *World News*, discovered that, three days earlier, Perot had held a secret session with the Senate POW-MIA committee. If the committee encouraged him, Perot had told them, he could obtain the release of thirty American POWs. The story was ludicrous—and Walker had it exclusively. If Perot could get them out, why tell the committee in secret? And why the hell not just get them out? Friedman decided to lead the broadcast with it.

Perot's reentry saw the press's schizophrenic and predatory fascination with him begin all over again. For more than a week, he dominated the coverage. He coerced blue chip delegations from both Bush's and Clinton's campaigns to drag themselves to Texas and present their economic plans to his volunteers. Then, when they weren't satisfied, of course, he announced he was getting in anyway. For the midday press conference, the networks went into live special reports.

They were being had, suckered, Brit Hume thought. Perot

was at 7 percent in the polls, a nonfactor. Perot was having it both ways—using the press for publicity and denouncing it at the same time for being irresponsible. And for the sake of ratings, the press was playing along. They were being cowards. Panderers.

Actually, Hume was only half right. After a few days, the press attitude toward Perot shifted, and the coverage turned venomous. HE'S BACK, shouted the cover of *Time*, echoing a phrase from a horror movie. "Ego Trip" said *Newsweek*. "A pathetic figure, and I think that's the way he'll go down, as an asterisk in political history," Sam Donaldson said on Brinkley.

In the year of the new media, Perot was the ultimate challenge to the relevance of the old media and its traditional role as watchdog. He had dropped out in July—when the press's scrutiny of his life and the attacks from the White House were driving his popularity down. He then skipped the summer—when the press would have continued to probe his background. Now, just when the debates and the horse race all but precluded press exploration of his claims or his character, he had reentered. And he was certain to campaign mostly over popular-culture television and TV advertising so the press could not have access to him.

Chris Isham, the head of Friedman's investigative unit, went back to the list of stories he had prepared in June. He managed to produce one story a few days after Perot reentered—about how Perot Systems in order to save money fired employees who had become sick or in another case the managers who tried to help them. Then the debates were on them and the story sank like a stone.

Dean, meanwhile, went back through his notes and, among other things, decided to reread *On the Wings of Eagles*, the mythic account of Perot's life and rescue of employees from Iran. One point in the book struck Dean as particularly odd. The book claimed that the North Vietnam government hired assassins in 1970 or 1971 to try and kill Perot's family at home in Dallas. That would be a major event, Dean thought. Why had he not heard more about it? As far as he knew, no foreign government had ever contracted with Americans to assassinate an American on U.S. soil.

Dean began asking about the story when he did other Perot interviews. He asked reporters he knew in Dallas. He checked with police. No one knew anything about it. No police report was called in about it. In the years 1970 and 1971, three complaints were filed from the Perot house to police, one for a brick thrown at a mailbox and two for people kissing in a car in front of his house. According to Perot's account, the Vietnamese had hired the Black Panthers to kill him. An associate at ABC checked with the Panthers. They confirmed that they were at a conference in Canada once with the North Vietnamese but there was no plot against Perot.

When Dean brought it to the Rim, Friedman's team wasn't interested. "How can you prove a negative," someone told Dean. "Why would we want to do this anyway?" someone else asked. It was just Perot.

"Just let me follow this," Dean said. "It goes to the heart of who he says he is, a heroic man who takes risks."

Dean got the head of Dallas police operations on tape from the relevant period. "Listen to me—it didn't happen," Paul McCaghren said. "It did not happen. . . . There were only about eight people here that belonged to the Black Panther party. Two of those people worked for us and they told us every day what was happening."

Perot said the assassins were chased away by one of his dog handlers—a former marine—though he never identified the man. Dean talked to the only Perot employee who worked as a dog handler and fit that description. "As far as somebody coming aboard the property with ill intent, I neither saw it on my watch or even heard about it on somebody else's watch," Harold Birkhead told him. Perot didn't even keep dogs in 1970 and 1971, Birkhead said.

No one could pin down a date when Perot claimed it had happened. Finally, October 12, Dean was in his office in New York when Perot called. It was obvious, Perot said, that ABC was out to destroy him. And by raising this subject, Dean and Jennings would have it on their consciences that all kooks in the country like John Hinckley would get it in their head to try and get Perot.

Dean reminded Perot that the candidate had been talking about this for twenty years. He had put it in his book. He had mentioned it in congressional testimony. Perot became increasingly angry. When Dean asked for a specific date, Perot snapped at him. "I don't have to do your work for you. I'm not working for you."

It is an important story, Dean said.

"People try to kill me every year," Perot said. Every year Iranians drive up outside my house trying to get me, he said. "Crazy Iranian taxi drivers," Dean jotted down in his notes.

Then Perot insisted that Dean talk to three people who could confirm the story, former ABC newsman Murphy Martin, now a Perot employee working on his campaign, Tom Muir, a Perot associate and oil executive, and Perot's son. Dean talked to all three. But all they knew was what Perot had told them. No one could confirm the story. Muir in particular seemed almost apologetic.

Dean compiled the story slowly in the three weeks after Perot reentered the race. When it finally ran, it would drive the Texan into yet one last angry public meltdown. But that was still in the future.

CHAPTER

10

ADVERTISING

The phone call came just after Jeff Greenfield arrived at the office. George Stephanopoulos, Clinton's young communications director, was calling from Little Rock.

You know there was a new Bush ad, Stephanopoulos asked.

Despite some early grand intentions, Greenfield had not been paying attention to advertisements much, and he particularly wasn't worrying about them today. Ross Perot was expected to reenter the race that afternoon. Greenfield was thinking about the long piece he had to produce about Perot for *Nightline*. It was October 1, a month before election day.

No, he knew nothing about it, he told Stephanopoulos. Why the big crisis? The call was curious. Stephanopoulos had never contacted him before. Because this new Bush ad crosses over the line—even for Republicans—Stephanopoulos argued. He read Greenfield the ad over the phone. It is an outright lie, Stephanopoulos contended. Greenfield should do a story about it crying foul. Stephanopoulos would fax him the script.

Is the ad so effective? Greenfield pressed.

Not effective, dishonest, Stephanopoulos said. And Clinton was incensed. The night before, the governor called home to Little Rock from the plane, and his daughter, Chelsea, had already seen it twice while watching *Doogie Howser M.D.* on TV. So they were into a full-court press.

Stephanopoulos's true motive was more complex. Although Greenfield did not know it, the Clinton team was embarked on an intricate plan to undermine what it feared would have been Bush's most devastating commercial—and to use the press to do it. In the process, Clinton's team helped damage the credibility of the Bush advertising effort in general and exploit the newest innovation in media coverage, the so-called truth squads. The plot amounted to the most sophisticated use of the press perhaps ever in presidential campaign advertising.

Two years earlier the American press had taken an important step in how it covered the 1990 interim elections. Newspapers began systematically examining the candidates' television commercials for distortions and half truths. Often papers set these critiques apart graphically in boxes, which came to be called truth boxes.

Covering TV commercials might strike most people as hardly revolutionary. TV spots had been one of the centerpieces of public discourse, especially in politics, for three decades. But until 1990 political reporters tended to ignore TV commercials. The simplistic appeals and thirty-second logic of commercials seemed beneath the dignity of such professionals. These tough journalists were engaged in something more serious, following men of power around as they interacted with the people, supposedly parsing their arguments, measuring the chemistry between candidates and crowds, pinning these politicians to the wall, trying to find out the inner workings of strategy and polling data and congressional district targeting—the model of political reporting developed thirty years earlier by Theodore White. Because most political reporters were out on the road they rarely even saw the commercials that swayed actual voters.

After watching a California senate race in which candidates

raised $25 million to spend mainly on TV commercials, Keith Love, a political reporter with the Los Angeles *Times*, advocated something like truth boxes in 1986. Two years later, feeling revulsion with the distortions and vitriol of the 1988 presidential campaign, Washington *Post* reporter David Broder independently began advocating the same idea. "We need to treat every ad as if it were a speech" and not "be squeamish about saying in plain language when we catch a candidate lying," he wrote. Then, after seeing a particularly distorted ad early in the California governor's race in March 1990, the Los Angeles *Times* began analyzing ads in the gubernatorial primary contest. The idea instantly spread to papers in San Francisco and Sacramento, and then elsewhere to Texas, Florida, Kansas, Kentucky, Georgia, Minnesota, and Alaska.

The significance went beyond advertising. Policing what candidates said changed the relationship between reporter and politician. By labeling a candidate's statement as distorted or false, the press went from being a color commentator up in the booth to being a referee down on the field. Implicitly, this role acknowledged that the press not only reflected political events, it shaped them. That fact may be obvious to outsiders, but it is strangely difficult for reporters to accept. Journalists are trained to ignore the consequences of what they do. Worrying about consequences, journalists fear, will lead to self-censorship or bias. So they rationalize that their impact is minimal. Truth boxes conceded the press's power exceeded that.

As soon as the press began producing truth boxes, politicians began exploiting them. In California, gubernatorial candidate Pete Wilson quoted them in defense against an attack commercial by Democrat Dianne Feinstein. In Texas, Republican gubernatorial candidate Clayton W. Williams, Jr., had to redo one of his commercials because he used faulty statistics. Before long, quoting truth boxes by candidates to defend against faulty charges was standard part of the campaign dialogue.

This year, however, would be the first presidential campaign waged with the press truth squads on watch. As a general rule, advertising's role in presidential races is exaggerated. Contrary to what had become popular to believe, and unlike most statewide races, presidents are not elected because they make better commercials. News coverage drives presidential politics, not advertising. The sheer volume of news—and that means mostly television—overwhelms every other source. Ads are accents, visual metaphors of the key campaign themes. They work best when they refine and reinforce what people have already heard on the news. If the ads' images differ from those on the news, indeed, the consequences can be fatal, as Ohio senator John Glenn learned in his failed 1984 presidential campaign. The heroic astronaut in his TV ads seemed like a phony compared with the disappointingly mild-mannered monotoned politician seen campaigning on the nightly news.

The Democrats had especially exaggerated the importance of advertising after the 1988 campaign. With misty hindsight, Dukakis and his aides claimed George Bush was elected president because his adman Roger Ailes made dishonest TV spots on Bush's behalf, and because they had not fought back quickly enough with ads of their own. It isn't true. When Bush overtook Dukakis in the polls in 1988, in late August, neither side had ads on the air. By mid-September, when both sides began running ads, Bush's lead had already stabilized at between six and nine points—his margin of victory. And one study, which correlated advertising expenditures and polling data, found that Dukakis actually rose in the polls when Bush had more commercials airing. The study, by Michael Robinson, Clyde Wilcox, and Paul Marshall found that, "In the end, the correlations say that Bush's ad campaign was not the major factor in his victory and that money isn't everything in [presidential] politics, or even close." Neither is advertising.

The reason advertising is important is that it reveals what a candidate thinks his best arguments are. Ads are a window into a campaign but not the engine that drives elections.

* *

What one saw through the window in Bush's case was how difficult a task the Republicans had. In the summer, the Bush team took a pile of data, ran it through computers and came up with a "satisfaction index" for Clinton and Bush. Then it linked how satisfied people were with each candidate to how likely they were to vote for either one. This regression analysis revealed something prescient. If the Bush campaign could raise voter satisfaction with the President by one point, he would move up two points in popular vote. But if satisfaction with Clinton moved down one point, that dropped support for Clinton by only one quarter point. For those Republicans who understood politics, this was damning news. In the current political climate, political professionals were persuaded that attacking an opponent is a surer way to win elections than making positive promises. But the Republicans could see they were unlikely to win by destroying Clinton. The race was driven by dissatisfaction with Bush. "Everything else was irrelevant, but the President," one of Bush's ad team said. "Clinton was irrelevant. Quayle was irrelevant." The only way to win was to convince people to like Bush more, and that was not going to be easy.

The Republicans had failed to make that happen all year. At one particularly strained meeting to plot advertising strategy during the primaries, Mike Murphy, a staunchly conservative young adman linked to Quayle, had made the point with Robert Teeter. Do you remember the movie *Forbidden Planet* and the monster they called the Krell? Murphy asked the button-down campaign chairman. Murphy was referring to the 1956 science fiction classic based on Shakespeare's *The Tempest*. Teeter did not know it.

Well, these guys on a spaceship land on a planet, Murphy said. And this big monster attacks their force shield every night. And they shoot their guns at it, but it is invisible. And the more scared they get and the more weapons they fire, the stronger it becomes. Finally, they go underground and they find this big machine that magnified the evil and fear and negative emotions in man's spirit, and then projected it. So they were creating the monster themselves, and the more scared they got the stronger they made the monster. Our opponent is the Krell, Murphy said. We can't kill him because Bush created him. He is the anti-Bush. That's the problem. Until we fix the President, Bush's opposition is invincible.

Teeter looked at the young adman in disbelief. Murphy at the time had been talking about Buchanan. But by summer Clinton had become the Krell, the monster that could only be defeated by making people stop fearing Bush.

As the summer went on, the Republican team found they were clueless how to do that. It seemed as if nothing changed how people felt about the President. In late July and August, Bush's ad team, called the November Company, began testing scripts and storyboards for ads in focus groups and found two daunting results. First, there was great resistance to all the negative messages they tried against Clinton. People didn't want to believe bad things about him. One of the first ads tested was the last ad of the campaign, a dark attack on Clinton's record in Arkansas. Voters had grown so suspicious of Republican attack ads that they doubted the statistics cited in the ad.

The second discovery was that people resisted hearing that Bush had a domestic agenda. Fred Steeper had seen the same result in January in his New Hampshire polls, and it had not changed all year—not after the State of the Union address in January, the speech on economic policy in March, a prime time address to the nation after the Los Angeles riots in April, or the convention speech in August. People felt Bush didn't care about domestic affairs. And that doomed him far more than his having broken his no-new-taxes pledge.

The Bush campaign even tried to see if voters turned off simply to the sight of George Bush. They hadn't, the research showed. They liked him personally. They were just tired of him politically.

The Bush team tested about twenty-five script proposals. Basically nothing worked as conceived. "We were drawing blanks," one of the Bush inner circle admitted. The political admen were so pessimistic they were also being pushed to the side in favor of Madison Avenue people. The New Yorkers were given virtual carte blanche to come up with a message. The men around the President of the United States had no clearly focused argument for his reelection to give them.

The Madison Avenue team aired two ads in early August to boost what they called Bush's "likability." But the ads weren't about anything. Virtually everyone hated them.

When James Baker took charge of the campaign, his new team held a long meeting after Labor Day to get a grip on the advertising campaign—and implicitly to plan strategy in general. The memo in preparation for the meeting explaining the ad campaign showed the weakness in Bush's strategy. The advertising plan had two phases, the memo said. The first would roll out Bush's "plan for America's future," starting with an overall introduction and followed by ads detailing specific elements, taxes, spending, health care, and term limits. Phase two, the attack phase, would compare Bush's plan to Clinton's. Beyond this general discussion of phases, though, there was nothing to Bush's strategy. "We have no restrictions on how we deliver these messages." The meeting that followed was a disaster. Those supposedly in charge were demoted and Baker announced that former Reagan-Bush aide Mitch Daniels would run the ad team. But it turned out Daniels had commitments in Japan that he wouldn't or couldn't sacrifice.

Bush had no ads ready. No one was in charge. There were nine weeks to election day.

Bill Clinton's task was far easier, and his advertising campaign far more competently organized. Mandy Grunwald, the woman who had pushed for Clinton to embrace the popular-culture programs, was put in charge of the advertising effort in June, replacing Frank Greer, her partner in a Washington media consulting firm. Fittingly, Grunwald quickly organized a team based on the model set four years earlier for Bush by Republican Roger Ailes. A small group would decide ad strategy, in this case Grunwald in coordination with pollster Stan Greenberg, strategist James Carville, and communications director George Stephanopoulos. David Wilhelm, who ran the field organization, would help coordinate where the ads would run. Then Grunwald would assign specific ads to the Madison Avenue and political advertising executives she had hired. Clinton's message, in other words, would flow from his top political aides down. It would not be dreamed up on Madison Avenue and then sold to the candidate. What it lacked in creativity would be made up for in coherence. That alone made it unusual for the Democratic party. Grunwald's team was also made up of only true believers. At the time she had assembled her team, Clinton was in third place and a lot of people had refused to work for him.

By August, the team had twenty scripts, approved by Clinton and his close advisers during a long meeting in Little Rock. By the time the election was over, almost all of those scripts were on the air in one form or another and testing successfully. It was another sign of how much easier Clinton's task was.

Grunwald, Greenberg, and Carville had agreed on some basics. The first was always to run one attack message track in front of voters at all times, reminding them of Bush's job performance. Greenberg knew that if they could keep the majority of Americans disapproving of Bush's overall performance they would probably win. A politician's vote, Greenberg believed, can rarely exceed his job performance rating. The other track was to remind voters that Clinton had a plan for change, and a record and biography to suggest he was effective.

Clinton's advertising campaign also had one enormous advantage. By September, Clinton was ahead in so many states, his campaign team gambled that they could skip advertising in most of them. This would prove a critical factor.

Democratic National Committee strategist Paul Tully had done enormous amounts of research to plot how the Democrats could target just the right voters. His goal was to overcome the Democratic party's disadvantage in the electoral map caused by the Republican lock on the South. Tully had reconstructed George Bush's advertising purchases from 1988 and discovered some remarkable statistics. Bush had spent 76 percent of his advertising money in the key battleground states—those that on election day he won by less than four percentage points.

In contrast, Bush had spent only 2 percent of his money in states he would not win, and only 1 percent of his money in states he would win by ten points or more. The rest, 21 percent of Bush's ad money, went in states where he was ahead by between five and ten points.

In short, the Republicans had put their money just where it was needed.

The Democratic strategy had been so disorganized it had taken Tully more than a year to reconstruct it. What he found was that Dukakis had spent almost all his money on network television, which meant that it had been spread out over states he could not possibly win and states he was going to win no matter what.

Now, because he could skip advertising in states where he had large leads, Clinton also could begin advertising in his target states much earlier, even before Labor Day. This, too, was pivotal. The Republicans would probably have to wait to begin advertising. Since Bush was behind virtually everywhere, he would have to advertise everywhere—probably by buying network time. And even the $35 million an efficiently run presidential campaign can afford to spend on TV commercials cannot cover two months of nationwide television. The Democrats, in other words, could be on the air for two or three weeks without the Republicans answering back.

Tully, a hulking, passionate, former Yale football player, had helped the Democrats immeasurably in one other way. For years, he had painstakingly developed a system to measure the voter profile of the United States. It was broken down by the most modern political map of all—not by congressional district like the Republicans'—but by television market. Tully's maps became the basis of an intricate Democratic targeting plan. Each media market in the country was ranked by the number of "persuadable" voters they contained. "Persuadables" were registered Democrats who in the past had voted Republican or who voted Democratic in some races and Republican for president.

Grunwald, Wilhelm, and Greenberg took these maps and began adding other factors—including the cost of buying time in each media market. Then they ranked states into three categories. The first were called Top End states, those where the Democrats led by so much they hoped to never advertise there—California, New York, Hawaii, Rhode Island, Massachusetts. Next were the Play Hard states, where the Democratic lead ranged closer to 15 points—Pennsylvania, New Jersey, Illinois. They could wait in those. Finally were the Play Very Hard States, those where the leads ranged from one point to closer to 10, the toughest and most important states to win—Colorado, Michigan, Ohio, Georgia, Louisiana, North Carolina, Connecticut, New Mexico, Kentucky, Tennessee. Of these, Clinton in the end would lose only one, North Carolina.

By the time they were done, the Democrats would have spent $35 million of their $55 million in federal matching funds on buying TV ads, another $3 million on producing them, and $13 million more from the Democratic National Committee funds on generic party ads, a total in nine weeks of more than $51 million on TV commercials.

How to start was a subject of intense argument, but Clinton's high command finally settled on a positive 60-second ad that contained a taste of several ads to come. Two members of the ad team, Frank Greer and Carter Eskew, had made the case for starting with an expensive 60-second ad. Voters had become so suspicious of advertising, Eskew argued, that he had not produced a single thirty-second ad with a positive message all year that voters believed. The only 30-second spots that worked were attacks. The spot had to be a 60 to be credible. "Something's happening," a narrator began over pictures of Clinton's July bus trip. "People are ready because they've had enough. . . . They're ready for change . . . and changing people's lives, that's the work of his life." Then came Clinton's picture, followed by a statistic-laden account of his record with footnotes on the screen to document them. Change, changing, change, the economy and Clinton's plan. It was the same message as on the stump. It was the same message he had all year. The message was self-evident. They needed simply to have the discipline not to forget it. "Discipline and repetition are your friends," Carville liked to say.

The ad was launched on August 31, a week before Labor Day, three weeks before the Republicans had gone on the air in 1988, and three weeks before Bush would go on the air now.

Nine days later, the second ad came. This one focused on Clinton's plans to reform welfare. Stan Greenberg loved this issue. Clinton had been a pioneer in welfare reform—even Republicans had embraced his ideas—so his record was unassailable. More important, welfare was the perfect symbol. Blacks liked it because they despised the dependence of welfare. Middle-class voters (so-called Reagan Democrats) liked it because it suggested their taxes would not be used to help the poor at their expense. Liberals liked it because it inoculated Clinton from the assault they feared most from Republicans, an appeal to racism. The subtext beneath welfare reform, the idea that echoed after the ad was off the air, was the one dearest to the Clinton strategy of all: that Clinton was a different kind of Democrat.

The ad also contained a statistic Clinton's team would repeat in half a dozen ads: that 17,000 Arkansans moved from welfare to work. The number was misleading. It failed to count how many people had moved the other way—from work to welfare. Since Clinton's reforms began, Arkansas's welfare caseload actually increased by 12.5 percent, but that was still lower than the national average of 34 percent. Through repetition, however, Clinton's campaign so succeeded in driving home the number 17,000 above all that voters kept repeating it back to them in their focus groups. And if Clinton's team could have picked one thing for people to remember, this was it.

September 13, a week later, Clinton aired his third and fourth ads—the two tracks, positive and negative. The positive was a quick reminder that Clinton had an economic plan, and, just as Clinton had done in New Hampshire, it invited people to call an 800 number for a copy of the plan. Clinton's focus group testing suggested that the 800 number was a magic bullet. If Clinton was willing to spend money to send people his plan, he must be serious, people said.

The other ad may have been more important: it was a pure attack on Bush, and it carried its charge by showing film clips of the President dismissing the weakness in the economy intercut with a stream of worsening economic statistics. This technique, of using familiar TV clips of Bush against him, would prove crucial. To the press and to the voters both it made Clinton's attacks seem fair. In truth it wasn't. The clips were intercut out of order. The ad reported economic statistics from March and then showed a clip of Bush from October reacting to something else—an outright distortion. CNN and several newspapers caught it (the networks did not critique the ad) but the Clinton campaign did not change it.

That same day, the Bush campaign finally launched its first ad. The Republicans were more focused now under Baker. Bush had gone to Detroit three days before to launch his economic Agenda and been on television that night for five minutes to talk about it. He even flashed an 800 number for viewers to call for a copy of the plan. Now, three days later, the Bush campaign was ready with its first regular commercial. But getting it on the air revealed the extent of the Bush campaign's lingering problems. The Republicans had spent thousands to film Bush's Detroit speech with 35-millimeter movie cameras. When the film was developed, however, Bush's team found the camera platforms hadn't been secured properly and the footage was jiggly and unusable. The critical campaign event of the fall and they had no pictures. The campaign resorted to using footage of Bush's convention acceptance speech instead. For that, however, there was no film, only the TV video feed, which looked crude and shabby, and Bush's delivery was shrill and unkind. To make it work, the campaign had to hire a special Madison Avenue editor and stylize the ad into something futuristic and high tech.

When the Clinton command saw the Bush spot, it was delighted. The Democrats had expected something powerful that could begin to neturalize Clinton's great advantage—the candidate with an economic plan. Bush's speech in Detroit had been excellent, and the Democrats' focus groups suggested Bush's five-minute broadcast about it had been effective too. Clinton's team worried this new ad would capitalize by detailing points in the Agenda and reprising the 800 number. But the spot had none of that. It was vague, and, at sixty seconds on network TV, it was too expensive to run often. Bush bought 612 gross rating points over two weeks, only enough for the average TV viewer to see it three times in a week. When the Democrats tested their response ad to Bush's Agenda, it only raised more questions than it answered. "Bush has a plan?" people said in the focus groups. Carville, Grunwald, and Greenberg decided they needn't respond. "Nothing is more exhilarating than to be fired upon by the enemy and missed," Carville said. It was September 13 and Bush's pivotal maneuver to get back in the race had failed to register with the electorate.

The Republicans saw their failure, too. The same day the ad began, chief of staff Jim Baker called Sig Rogich, one of Bush's advertising executives from 1988. Rogich had produced Ronald Reagan's famous "Morning in America" film in 1984. He had been a special assistant to Bush.

No one was in charge of the President's advertising campaign, Baker said. He had just gotten off the phone with the President. And they wanted Rogich to come back. Not long afterward, Bush called Rogich himself.

When he arrived, Rogich discovered there were just two commercials produced and no other usable footage. There were six and a half weeks to election day and the President's campaign was starting from scratch. Rogich would supervise in that time the production of thirty commercials. The best of them, Rogich believed, should have run in July and August.

Rogich hardly solved all the problems. Among his first tasks was supervision of the shooting of several ads at Camp David. Perhaps because the well-known French-born Madison Avenue director handling the shooting was unaccustomed to 16 millimeter, the director's footage was also nearly useless. In footage of the Bushes, the filtering and lighting was so bad that Barbara Bush's hair seemed on fire. In the ads with Bush talking directly to camera, the President looked like he had been made up by a mortician, his face waxy and shiny. The ads never aired. Almost another week gone. Still no decent footage.

A few days later, September 23, the Bush campaign managed to release its second ad of the campaign. With the ads shot that weekend in trouble, James Baker and Bob Teeter had decided to abandon promoting the President's economic agenda—for now—and begin attacking Clinton instead. That choice would prove to be one of the most important tactical decisions of the fall campaign. It would be another month until the incumbent President attempted to buy time on television to say anything strictly positive about why he should be reelected.

The Bush command was also debating internally over how to attack. Blast Clinton as a traditional liberal, based on his record in Arkansas and the tax and spend proposals in his economic plan?

Or skewer him over his character and his tendency to waver in his positions. For the moment, the ideological attack prevailed.

In August, the Bush campaign had sent photographers to Arkansas, and a still photographer had come back with pictures of poor children. But the kids were mostly black, and the campaign's high command was fearful of being accused of introducing race into the campaign. The next crew shot with a small video camera, much of it shot from a car. Rogich decided to speed the film up, to make it funny, and add hillbilly music, while talking about how many times Clinton raised taxes. The numbers in the ad were deceptive, but technically accurate. They showed the ad to Bush. He laughed, and the ad went up in ten battleground states, and, in some of them, numbers did move toward Bush.

At the same time, the debate over whether to attack Clinton over character was not settled, and Baker and Teeter decided to follow the hillbilly ad with two more commercials, attacking Clinton on both issues.

One of the few ads that had tested well in storyboard featured two pictures of Bill Clinton with a gray dot over the faces. An announcer would explain the candidate on the left took one position and the candidate on the right another. Then the gray dots disappeared and both candidates were Clinton. The ad attacked one of Clinton's weakest traits, his tendency to take positions on all sides of an issue.

But the committee in charge of ad strategy—adman Rogich, chairman Teeter, cochairman Fred Malek, chief of staff Baker, and Baker's four key aides—started making changes. Some thought the ad was too mean. Others didn't like the dot. Before they were done, Rogich had produced six versions of this ad—none of them satisfactory. They chose one, ran it for six days, and pulled it. "It didn't do us any harm," Rogich would rationalize later.

The Bush campaign also had another more effective ad ready. The commercial resembled one the British Conservative party had aired months earlier in its successful come-from-behind victory over Labor. To pay for his promises, Bill Clinton would have to

raise taxes on the middle class—contrary to his claims. Thus
Clinton was lying (bad character), the ad implied, and a tax and
spend liberal, to boot (bad ideology). If it worked, the spot might
weaken Clinton's strongest point, the economy.

To bolster their charge, Bush's team decided to borrow more
powder from the Brits and say exactly how much Clinton's plan
would cost individual taxpayers. It had a team from Commerce
and the White House add up all of Clinton's programs, make
various judgments about how much they would cost, and then
figure out how much the young Southern governor would need to
raise in taxes to compensate. Their formula was based on several
hypothetical assumptions. The key one was that Clinton's health
care reform package would fail to cut health care costs at all. So
Clinton would need to raise $197 billion in new taxes. (Clinton
contended his plan would balance out and cost taxpayers nothing.)
Next, the Bush camp assumed Clinton's plan to enforce tax collec-
tion on foreign corporations would raise only $1 billion over four
years, not the $44 billion Clinton predicted. On top of that, the
Bush team assumed that another $58 billion in Clinton spending
cuts were "totally fake" and should be ignored. The Republicans
were so enamored of their analysis that Budget Director Richard
Darman proposed they flash an 800 number in the ad that people
could call to find out what their specific tax bill would be under
Clinton. Bush's high command loved the idea, but it was too
expensive.

The problem was that the Republicans' numbers were so
hypothetical they left Bush open to retaliation from a strong opponent. And Clinton was certainly that.

To track Bush's ads as they went on the air, the Democrats had
hired a television satellite tracking company to monitor TV broadcasts in key cities. Anytime a new Bush ad aired, the firm captured
the ad and within minutes alerted Grunwald and beamed the ad by
satellite to the campaign. The night Bush's new tax ad first aired,

Grunwald, Carville, Clinton, and Greenberg knew within five minutes. When they called Clinton on his campaign plane, the candidate already knew, too. He had just called his daughter, Chelsea,
and she had seen the ad while watching TV. Clinton was livid.

In many ways the Clinton campaign had already prepared for
this ad. Clinton's team had strategized for the fall by plotting how
they could campaign if they were the Republicans. "If people
believed this, it would undercut everything we were saying about
the economy and the fairness of Clinton's plan," Grunwald explained. They had to destroy the ad's credibility. And in the
process, they would damage Bush's use of statistics in general, and
the credibility of his advertising in the future. And to do all that,
the Clinton command decided to manipulate the press.

That night, Clinton's economic team began trying to decon-
struct how the Republicans had arrived at their analysis. The next
morning, James Carville, Frank Greer, and George Stephanopoulos began calling journalists around the country—like
Greenfield. On Clinton's campaign plane, Carville's partner Paul
Begala worked on the traveling press.

They had two objectives: to convince the reporters the ad was
untrue and to make sure reporters wrote stories—in language as
harsh as possible—challenging the ad that day. By seizing the
initiative—complaining loudly and first—the Clinton campaign
also made the press question the Bush team more aggressively.

Grunwald, meanwhile, was already at work cutting a response
ad. By 6 P.M., the Clinton campaign was testing Bush's ad and its
response to it in focus groups outside Philadelphia. The Bush ad
was powerful, Frank Greer told Grunwald when he phoned her
from Pennsylvania. It could hurt them even more than Grunwald
had thought. And Clinton's response to it was okay, but people
were skeptical. Clinton's response ad showed part of the Bush
commercial and then froze the frame and stamped UNTRUE across
it. People weren't sure they believed this was really untrue. It was
just Clinton saying so. This is where the plan by Carville and
Stephanopoulos to use the press proved valuable. In effect, the

Clinton campaign had helped ensure the press provided them with what Carville called "outside validation" for their response ad.

As it turned out, the networks didn't do anything that night. Reacting that quickly was difficult on television, and the broadcasts were full of Perot's reentering the race. All three wound up doing critiques a day later.

So Clinton's team had to find out what would be in the next morning's papers. As Grunwald sat waiting in an editing room in Washington, aides in the War Room in Little Rock began calling friends at the Washington *Post, New York Times,* Los Angeles *Times* and *Wall Street Journal* trying to get advance word about what their stories would say. "The War Room was wired," one Clinton aide said. It even knew that the *Wall Street Journal* story would almost certainly be the toughest on Bush.

The Clinton campaign's plan had worked flawlessly. The *Wall Street Journal* did not even critique campaign ads. But after the call that morning from Clinton's campaign, the paper critiqued this ad, the only one of the campaign, and its language was so well suited to Clinton's purposes Grunwald quoted the *Journal* in her response ad. By the next morning, TV stations and reporters had a Clinton response ad to Bush that quoted that morning's papers.

What role press criticism played in blunting Bush's ad campaign generally is impossible to know. Polls by Times Mirror suggested voters tended to disbelieve Bush's commercials and believe Clinton's. But voters were already disposed to disbelieve Bush on the economy. That was why he was behind. It is easy to overrate the influence of tactics and technique on voters. But the episode amounted to the swiftest and most elaborate use by a politician yet of the press's new role as policeman for political advertising.

Was this manipulation of the press by Clinton? Shouldn't the press have done these critiques anyway?

The answer is that the press should have been doing these critiques systematically, but in fact they weren't. ABC did only three stories on ads in the general election campaign. The *Wall Street Journal* did only one. NBC did a few more. CBS critiqued only this one Bush television ad. Clinton's spin effort that day succeeded in getting the press to rightfully denounce a flagrant and irresponsible Bush ad. But Clinton was guilty of distortion and misrepresentation in his ads, too, and generally television and to some extent print was not as aggressive about his.

Nor did the press fully convey how much of Clinton's advertising was attack oriented. Taken together Clinton ran about twenty-four commercials, of which eleven were attack ads. Even Stan Greenberg would remark later that he was surprised at the extent to which the press did not highlight how much negative advertising the campaign did.

There were several reasons for that. One is that Bush's advertising was more negative than Clinton's in aggregate. Bush ran fifteen ads. Twelve were attacks. Another reason is that all but three of the Clinton attack ads employed mostly news footage of Bush to carry the attacks. Clinton's attacks, too, concerned policy, while nine of Bush's twelve attack ads were about character. The press and public also was disposed to be wary of Bush going negative because of the inflated perception that unfair attacks had won Bush the presidency in the first place. Finally, Bush was less competent at attacking in 1992. He didn't use statistics that were clearly documented. His campaign was desperate. And it showed.

The print press took its role as ad policeman more seriously. The Washington *Post* and *New York Times* were scrutinizing every ad, though they sometimes blunted the value of their critiques. Rather than sticking to the accuracy of the message, they larded their truth boxes up with analysis of the strategy behind the ads. The Los Angeles *Times* was more focused in its approach, but it was late with some critiques and skipped some ads altogether because of a lack of space and commitment to the effort.

But television did not live up to its intentions in critiquing ads, and it was the television critiques that the campaigns knew reached voters. ABC at one time had big plans. Dick Wald, the executive vice president of news, had even explored assembling voters at shopping centers to view ads and offer their responses for stories. The plan never went anywhere, apparently because of expense. Jeff Greenfield, who was responsible for the ad watches, had a good deal else to do. The ads weren't that special, he told Friedman, and they weren't driving the race. All that is true. But for the same reason that ads offer the clearest view on a campaign's strategy, they also deserve more systematic attention. If nothing else, Greenfield could have done them on *Nightline*.

CBS and NBC were also less aggressive than expected. NBC's Lisa Myers was dispatched to the Perot campaign. She did only a handful of truth boxes, but Myers for one felt that the Clinton campaign was often as guilty of distortion as Bush's. They just complained more loudly about the other guy. "They were terribly aggressive. It became excessive."

At CBS, Eric Engberg did the best job at the three commercial networks of policing the campaigns. Engberg produced only two stories critiquing TV ads, one about Bush's federal taxes ad, another about Perot's ads. But he also produced pieces catching Clinton and Bush both telling even worse lies in their radio spots than in their TV ads. Engberg also critiqued the candidates' stump speeches, too.

But the critiques that stood out above all others, print and broadcast, were those by Brooks Jackson at CNN. With the luxury of time, and money from a special foundation, Jackson critiqued everything—the ads, the stump speeches, the charges and counter charges, the finances. As a result, he served as an important check on the candidates. Little got by him. Unfortunately, Jackson's work also ranked as one of CNN's few contributions to this campaign.

Cable News Network enjoyed a wildly inflated reputation. After years of derision from the press, CNN founder Ted Turner was finally getting belated credit for his vision in 1980 about the power of cable. *Time* had made him Man of the Year in 1991 following CNN's role during the Gulf War, and surveys conducted by the Times Mirror Co. consistently found the public thought CNN's reporting was more credible than the other networks'. CNN had also become a cash cow for Turner Broadcasting Co.

But CNN's reputation for quality and journalistic influence was greatly exaggerated. For all of CNN's publicity during the Gulf War, it had actually lost every rating point it had gained. By the time the 1992 campaign began, only 50,000 television sets were tuned to CNN's highest rated newscast. That was only two-thirds the number that watched ABC's overnight news show at 3 A.M. (CNN's ratings would rise to 830,000 by the end of the campaign.)

One of the most rueful examples of CNN's bloated reputation was a story the *Wall Street Journal* had run at the beginning of the campaign that discussed CNN's daily half-hour election program, *Inside Politics*. The decision to have *Inside Politics* air each day at 4:30 eastern time—not 6:30 as it had in 1988—was an ingenious stroke, the story suggested. Producers at the commercial networks would watch *Inside Politics* and change their coverage in reaction. Even inside CNN the story was something of a joke. At 5 P.M., the network news shows were all but set. On the Rim at ABC, hardly anyone even watched CNN's show. The truth was that CNN's show ran at 4:30 because Ted Turner had issued a rare edict that viewers didn't give a damn about politics. So he wanted that political show buried outside the prime news hours.

Journalistically, CNN squandered its most important advantage—time. Its stories were not significantly longer than network stories, and what aired showed the lack of off-camera support staff. CNN was at its best when it carried political events live—when it functioned like C-Span, a camera trained on a podium. "Because we were on so early, we took most of our cues from the morning papers," said one of *Inside Politics'* top correspondents. And because it was cheap and easy, CNN filled time by having its anchors interview print reporters. With the exception of Ken Bode's candidate profiles, some of Bill Schneider's analysis and Jackson's work policing the veracity of candidates' stump speeches and advertising, most of what CNN produced with the

$3.5 million given it by the Markle Foundation went for disappointingly tedious, pedantic, and old-fashioned documentaries. The future of political news was not from cable after all.

Against this, Jackson's work stood out because he was systematic and original. By critiquing everything, Jackson wasn't susceptible to being spun by one side the way the press was in the case of the federal taxes ad.

All together, the ads in 1992 weren't as distorted as they had been four years earlier. The misrepresentations were more subtle, and given the nature of politics, less egregious. For that, the press deserves credit. It had raised the potential risk of lying.

Within a few days, Clinton's campaign felt it had so destroyed the credibility of that Bush ad that it withdrew its response commercial. The Democrats had been fired upon again, and while the attack had not missed, they had turned it to their advantage. Now they were again on the offense. Clinton's campaign put up two new spots, one flogging Clinton's "steady progress" as he "battled the odds in one of America's poorest states," and the other using more film clips of Bush to bash the President on his record—in this instance it was Bush breaking his "read my lips" pledge against raising taxes. Clinton's team made sure to use modest language to describe Clinton's past. It wanted to inoculate the Democratic ticket from attack. Grunwald and her team also discovered in testing ads that the only attack commercials voters believed were those that used actual news footage against Bush. The conventional attack spots, using humor or a narrator to carry the charge, were no longer credible. Yet that was what the Bush camp was still using.

Since the Democrats were running ads in no more than twenty states, they bought high numbers in each, enough for the average TV viewer to see the ad ten times in a week or more. The next week they rotated in two more ads, again a positive and negative. The latter, a generic attack against Republicans, was paid for by the party but produced by Clinton's campaign. Clinton was beginning to slip in states like California and New York where he had been ahead by more than 20 points. This spot ran in those states, a generic Democratic spot that would help everyone. A week later, Clinton rotated in yet two new ads, a biographical spot about Clinton's modest roots and another attack spot using clips of Bush. Bush's tactics from four years ago were haunting him, his claim to be a kinder and gentler president, an environmentalist, an education president, and Clinton's use of videotape in the ad helped people remember.

In the Bush campaign, meanwhile, several ads produced or planned were being shelved. One had Bush advocating his check-off plan introduced in his convention speech to reduce the federal debt. Another showed Clinton as a child making excuses for why he hadn't done his homework—an analogy to his various accounts about the draft. Still another featured various world leaders offering testimonials about Bush. Perhaps the most vicious, opened at the Vietnam Memorial in Washington, wondered if anyone of those on the wall had died because Bill Clinton had avoided the draft and ended with footage of Bush, the World War II hero, being fished from the sea.

The Madison Avenue team had run through money like water trying to salvage unworkable ideas through superior production. And the chaos of the campaign had worn people out. "Everyone was trying to find out who they could sleep with to get off this campaign," one of the team said.

Now the Republicans struck with two new plans. Since Clinton was killing them with his quick response to every Republican attack, Bush's team figured it would bedevil him on the hardest medium of all to track. The Bush campaign would produce radio ads that attacked Clinton in the harshest possible way on local issues for all the key states. It will be a stealth attack, campaign chairman Teeter argued. Clinton will panic. Before long, a list of eighty-odd local issues was developed. In time, the campaign would produce roughly seventy radio commercials that would run in some twenty battleground states that theoretically were close enough that Bush could win them and be reelected. The idea struck some as a metaphor for what was wrong with Bush's campaign. It was a clever tactical move. But local issues will only help marginally in a presidential election. This was no alternative for a national strategy. Others thought the plan could help. And Bush needed every advantage he could get. The campaign went ahead with it.

The second approach, which it also followed through on, was to turn the ad campaign into a discussion among the people rather than a referendum on Bush—for now. The campaign embarked on a series of "Man on the Street" ads, in which everyday people talked about the candidates, whom they liked, whom they trusted. If voters were having trouble listening to Bush, let them listen to each other.

By now Sig Rogich was firmly in charge of the ad campaign and, along with political media consultant Alex Castellanos, he began shooting all over the country.

"I don't believe him," says one man. "I don't believe him one bit."

"I don't believe him," says a woman.

"Trust," says another woman.

"I don't know much about Clinton except promises," says a second man.

"He tells everybody what they want to hear," says a third.

Getting the spots on the air was a battle. To make them interesting, Rogich and Castellanos used a hand-held camera that moved and jerked in the way popular now on Madison Avenue. But they lacked the style and grace of a $150,000 Madison Avenue shoot. Teeter in particular thought the style too radical. More moderate versions were cut and sent out.

The Bush team had one other ad ready, too, one attacking Clinton and featuring a *Time* cover from the primaries that had the title line "Why People Don't Trust Bill Clinton." The *Time* cover had been irresponsible in the primaries, and now the magazine tried to repair its reputation by suing the Bush campaign. The White House had already prepared two legal opinions. Citing the press in ads was so standard now that it was one of the reasons truth-squadding ads worked. The *Time* suit should have been laughed away by the rest of the press as a joke.

Ross Perot, meanwhile, had launched his own ad campaign. His first was a thirty-minute "infomercial" in which Perot laid out what he perceived as the problems with the American economy. It was a version of the popular speech he often gave before he was a candidate with the addition of charts. People were astonished at the ratings. No one picked up for days some of the lies—such as Perot's claim that 70 percent of the microchips used in the United States were made overseas. Almost the reverse was true. Thirty- and sixty-second ads were easier to police.

That led to speculation that Perot's infomercials were also a political breakthrough and that candidates trying to be substantive would eschew thirty seconds in favor of these apparently more-substantive thirty-minute programs. The truth about this is the same as it always had been. Thirty-minute political TV shows were nothing new at all. And whether they would be effective for a candidate depended on the candidate. Ronald Reagan delivered a lot of prime time national TV speeches because he was good at it. George Bush did impromptu press conferences with the White House press corps because it suited him. Bill Clinton was good at town hall meetings. In politics, the messenger is the message—and always has been. In the case of Perot's infomercials, Perot was the message. His charts and his infomercials were the props. The subtext was that Perot was different, a nonpolitician.

One of Bush's admen put it well. "If Bill Clinton did thirty minutes with charts, first they would be real charts, not those Perot-fun-with-statistics mockups. And it would be boring and no one would watch."

Ironically, Perot's later commercials undid him in just the

same way. He had promised his last commercials would feature his solutions to the economy. Those solutions never came. Perot resorted to testimonials from family members about what a fine fellow he was instead. Perot had no solutions. He offered just himself, like other politicians. The title of Perot's last ad captured the essence of what he was peddling. "Deep Voodoo, Chicken Features, and the American Dream."

"It sounds like a Woody Allen movie," Mort Dean said incredulously when he called from Dallas.

"An old one," Friedman said. "One of the good ones."

In the final ten days, Clinton's team began to worry about Perot nonetheless. He had attacked Clinton in one of his later ads. Bush's position in the race was stable. He could not get more than 40 percent, probably closer to 37 percent. If Perot did well enough, however, Clinton's aides reasoned that their man theoretically could lose. To counter that, Clinton's team felt it had to do something to reassure wavering Democrats and independents that he was the safe choice. The result was a classic endorsement commercial to close the sale. It showed Clinton at his desk on the left of the screen while on the right scrolled the names of economists who had endorsed him.

At the same time, Perot began to self destruct—Clinton's team felt the race began to stabilize again. And they could end as they always wanted to, with a final reminder of Bush's weaknesses and their strengths.

The day after the last debate, the President aired only his second strictly positive commercial arguing for his reelection. The ad reprised Bush's Agenda for Economic Renewal, and this time the tone was gentler, like Bush, but the ad was only nominally more specific.

For a candidate behind, though, most people in politics are convinced negative messages are more effective. A negative message brings down the other guy at the same time, doubling the ad's ability to move numbers. The campaign felt it had to complement this Agenda ad with an attack.

Rogich wanted to run a version of the most classic attack ad of the Cold War era: it talked about the world being a dangerous place and ended with a shot of the president's empty chair in the Oval Office. "Who do you trust to be sitting in this chair," it concluded. Politicians had been running some version of this since Lyndon Johnson began the era of attack ads against Barry Goldwater in 1964.

Teeter preferred more man-on-the-street ads. The empty chair was pulled. Then came the endgame.

Presidential candidates traditionally conclude their campaigns on election eve with a thirty-minute appeal about what wonderful characters they have. Rogich was convinced such an ad would serve no purpose. Here was a president who had been on stage for twelve years and president for four. What more could he say in thirty minutes on election eve? The only people who watch were voting for him anyway.

As an alternative, Rogich suggested they run a two minute ad for a week, Bush talking to ordinary Americans. He could make all his important points in two minutes as easily as thirty, Rogich reasoned, and people who would never watch the half hour would see it. His team worked for thirty straight hours cutting the spot in time to get it on the air a week before the election. There was no time to test whether the ad was any good.

The Bush campaign's last act was to run one other spot. The Bush team had conceived the ad attacking Clinton's record in Arkansas months earlier, but the idea hadn't tested well in previous versions so it was tabled. Now Rogich went all out. He used stock Hollywood footage of a desolate land in a storm. He called it "the night of the living dead ad." He ended it with a vulture in a tree.

With just days to go, they were introducing a new theme into the campaign—Clinton's Arkansas record—a theme that a month earlier had been dropped in favor of character. "That was a death rattle," one of Bush's admen said. "There was no strategy at the end. There was no plan. The difference is there was calm and no plan at the beginning. There was panic and no plan at the end."

Bill Clinton's last three ads were the ones his creative team had liked best from the beginning. One, made in both a thirty- and fifteen-second version, laid out the case against the Republicans:

It began with the most famous piece of videotape of George Bush's political life. "Read my lips," the President said at his convention speech in 1988.

"Remember?" an announcer asked rhetorically.

Then it cut to another clip of Bush. "You will be better off four years from now than you are today."

"Well, it's four years later," said the announcer. "How're you doing."

If anything, the fifteen-second version was the more powerful.

Finally, there were two positive spots about Clinton, both from the Democrat's strongest moment of the campaign, the July bus tour. The better of the two never mentioned Clinton's name.

From the window of a bus one saw the countryside passing by. The music tugged at the heart. "Something is happening out there," said a voice. "A feeling. Call it hope. That a country can move in a new direction. That the future is something to look forward to. Not fear. If that's what you're feeling, you may have noticed something else. You are not alone."

The picture froze on two men emerging from a crowd: Bill Clinton and Al Gore.

Inside ABC, most of the details behind the campaign advertising strategies were unknown, but the people working the campaign understood the underlying dynamics well enough. A few
days before election day, Friedman asked people in the morning
meeting at *World News* to start considering who should be the
Person of the Week for the Friday after election day.

When someone suggested Clinton's chief strategists, James
Carville and Paul Begala, political producer Nancy Gabriner registered a small protest about elevating the role of handlers and the
advertising they produced.

She knew that Bill Clinton was not winning because his
advertising was better. Audiences were already receptive to Clinton's message, and his staff was skillful enough to do what was
necessary. Similarly, Bush's advertising was not a chaotic mess
because the people running it were incompetent. They had an
almost impossible task selling this candidate. People did not want
to buy what he had to sell, and Bush's aides had no idea what to
do about it except the one thing they knew best.

"If the Republicans pull it out it won't be because of Jim
Baker," Gabriner said, trying to put the role of handlers in context.

"It will be because of . . . ," foreign editor Linda Mathews
began to say.

Gabriner finished her sentence. "Fear."

★

CHAPTER

11

DEBATES

★

Ten minutes before the second presidential debate of 1992 ended, the Clinton campaign's high command gathered in a holding room beneath the University of Richmond Athletic Center for a conference call.

On one end of the line was Clinton's Little Rock headquarters. On the other, in Virginia, were Clinton's top strategists. Also listening were the chairmen from Clinton's fifty state offices. The Democrats had to get their story straight.

This debate was over the moment that woman in the audience asked George Bush how the deficit had affected him, and Bush said he didn't get the question, campaign manager David Wilhelm explained.

That was a metaphor for the whole election, campaign chairman Mickey Kantor suggested. This President doesn't get it. He doesn't understand what the economy is doing to people.

That would be the main point the Democrats would make about this debate, said Wilhelm. And Bill Clinton does get it. He was in touch—especially when he countered Bush's attack on his character. I want to change the character of the presidency, Clinton had answered. That was just right.

In the looking-glass logic of politics, it didn't matter that the truth was grayer than Wilhelm made it sound. It was irrelevant that the woman confronting Bush had probably meant to ask how the recession had affected Bush rather than the national debt, and that her imprecision, not the economy, was what had stumped the less-than-nimble President. What mattered was the black outline of recollection: A citizen asked Bush about the economy and he didn't understand her question. The moment reinforced exactly what was driving the election—that Bush was out of step. If Clinton's team could get the press to repeat their talking point, and replay the video of that moment over and over in the days after this October 15 debate, they would define what this moment came to mean and trap Bush with his own words.

Within minutes Clinton campaign headquarters in Little Rock had written up the "Talking Points" and faxed them to both the group in Virginia and the fifty state offices to use. The document began, " 'I'm not sure I get it,' said George Bush."

In another holding room in the same building, Bush's command team was engaged in the same exercise. Campaign chairman Bob Teeter, chief of staff James Baker, strategist Charlie Black and communications director James Lake thought Bush had been fine. He might have been more forceful at times. But the format for this debate, a live audience asking questions of the candidates, was supposed to be suited to Clinton's strength as a born politician.

Then White House aide Will Feltis arrived with the preliminary focus group results. The debate was still going on so he didn't have the group's final verdict. But the internal results from the focus group session gave them some reason to declare a Bush victory. The group thought Bush had been strongest when it came to specific issues, especially those the Bush camp thought decisive, trust, character, health care, defense. The voters had registered these reactions by turning the dial on hand-held meters as they watched the debate. Ross Perot's score on issues had been second, Feltis said. Clinton came in third. "Tonight was a clear win, a big win for the president," the Bush campaign Talking Points would begin.

These meetings were invisible to the four ABC correspondents, and the five thousand other media people there to cover the debate. Brit Hume, Mort Dean, and Chris Bury, the beat reporters covering Bush, Perot, and Clinton, were sitting on stools on a camera platform in the gymnasium-turned-press-center upstairs. Jeff Greenfield, Jennings's and Gralnick's designated debate analyst, was stationed next door with a camera in the auditorium where the debate was being staged.

When the debate ended, Jennings would go to Greenfield for his assessment. The other three correspondents were standing by. ABC News had won from its parent company time for a thirty-minute special following the debate.

Most Americans knew by now about how the jaded game called spin control worked. They knew how campaign operatives would rush into the press room where the reporters were working and start repeating their Talking Points in the hope of influencing the media's instant analysis.

But what was mostly unknown—and to the Clinton and Bush campaigns more valuable—was the other use of the Talking Points.

In a converted dance studio elsewhere in the building, the Clinton campaign had set up three makeshift television studios and four more for radio. Those were connected to a satellite truck in the parking lot there in Virginia, then linked to a transmitter company in Washington, D.C., and monitored by the Clinton campaign's telecommunications department in Arkansas.

Over the next two hours, with ABC and the other networks long off the air and the newspapers past deadline, the Democrats would conduct more than one hundred interviews with local TV and radio stations around the country praising Clinton's debate performance. In interview after interview, prominent Democrats like Mario Cuomo and former chairman of the Joint Chiefs Admiral William Crowe, would recite the Talking Points the Clinton campaign had given them. And their message wouldn't be filtered through suspicious reporters like Hume and Greenfield. It would go out directly to voters.

The Republican effort was similar though less ambitious. The Bush command had two cameras, the Democrats five. The Republicans set up their gear in a corner of the press filing center, a picture that reinforced the idea that these were political handlers spinning in a press center. The Democrats had made up their studios to look like living rooms, creating the impression that the Democrats speaking may have been at home watching the debate like anyone else. Still, the Bush campaign had booked three hours of interviews on local TV and produced a special interview with George and Barbara Bush, which it sent up on the satellite and fed free to any local station that wanted it—a satellite press release.

In the dance studio one flight below, the Clinton satellite operation was a picture of efficiency, an assembly line of a new kind of spin control. "Hi Paul, how are you," Admiral Crowe was telling anchorman Paul Braun of WBSG-TV in Jacksonville, Florida, an important battleground state for the Democrats.

The pictures of Crowe were beamed from the rented satellite truck in the parking lot into outer space and with the turn of a dial down to the appropriate station around the country. This technological miracle was so common now that Americans watched the procedure's results dozens of times a day on television without thinking about it.

A young man in his twenties, his blond hair greased into spikes, was monitoring each of the makeshift TV studios. David Anderson was one of the Clinton campaign's child volunteers, a satellite whiz kid who had not yet graduated from Oberlin College in Ohio. He was standing at a console of televisions with a headset on and a phone in one hand.

The makeshift TV studios he monitored were just spaces divided by blue curtains and filled with rented furniture. In one, labeled by magic marker and gaffers tape as TV-2, Senator Joseph Biden of Delaware was talking to anchorman Mark Howard of WPVI-TV in Philadelphia, another critical state for Clinton. Admiral Crowe was next to him in TV-3. Mario Cuomo, the governor of New York, was doing interviews from another studio in Albany, N.Y. In Carthage, Tennessee, vice presidential nominee Al Gore was doing his own studio tour for dozens more stations.

Next door, in the utility room turned for the night by the Democrats into radio studios, former Michigan governor James Blanchard was blanketing stations all over Michigan, Maine governor Joe Brennan was hitting stations in New England, former San Antonio mayor Henry Cisneros was doing Spanish language stations in the Southwest. Arkansas senator David Pryor was hammering away in the South. All together, they would do fifty-seven radio interviews that night and sixty-eight television interviews. Most of them were right on script.

"Those questions the audience asked were very excellent questions, particularly the young lady who asked George Bush how the recession had affected him," Colorado governor Romer told Jack Maher from KUSA-TV in Denver. "The President couldn't relate to that question."

Next door Biden was uttering virtually the same sentence. "And George Bush said I don't get the question," Biden was telling anchorman Mark Howard from WPVI-TV in Philadelphia during the late local news there.

"That's the problem," Admiral Crowe was telling June Thompson of KTSP-TV in Phoenix two studios away. "He doesn't get it."

"He doesn't get it," Clinton campaign chairman Mickey

Kantor was telling Roland Smith of WWOR-TV in New York. Kantor had replaced Biden in TV-2.

One man did not use the script. After the first debate New York governor Mario Cuomo took four pages of notes of his own to interpret the debate. Clinton's staff was too intimidated to send him the Talking Points.

There was a crisis in Carthage. Gore had gotten up out of the chair during a live interview to take a call from Clinton. Jeff Eller, Clinton's deputy press secretary, had arrived, and called Tennessee. Get him back in the frigging chair. They did. Gore always did what he was supposed to.

Crowe had emerged as a particular star. He was one of the easiest for the Clinton campaign to book with stations, a patriot, not just a politician. This night, though, popularity had its costs.

"He has to go to the men's room," a young volunteer designated to follow Crowe all night and keep him on schedule rushed up to tell Anderson.

"Can he finish the live shot?" Anderson asked into his headset. It was ten minutes to the men's room and back, Anderson explained to the technicians in TV-3 with Crowe. The next live shot was in five minutes.

The Admiral persevered, and KTSP-TV in Phoenix, the next in line, got its interview.

Campaigns had used satellite warfare in 1988, especially to spin their tales after debates. But what was occurring in 1992 reached a scale unlike anything presidential politics had seen before. In the four years since Bush's election, the cost of satellite time had dropped markedly, and the number of stations capable of receiving these satellite transmissions had soared. So had their interest in generating their own coverage rather than relying on the networks for national news packages. The campaigns had turned to the satellites for one other reason. The old method of controlling the press—the black art of spin control—wasn't working anymore.

Spin was a uniquely American political practice whereby,

after a political event had ended, campaign operatives emerged to try to massage how reporters interpreted the meaning of the event. Spinning gave political handlers a chance to explain away and thus repair the damage a candidate had done to himself, or to inflict damage on the opponent that their candidate might not have. Like a surgeon who could save a patient in trouble, the practitioners of the art were dubbed spin doctors. And in their operating room, it was not the event that counted, but the perception.

Campaign operatives had been spinning in earnest since 1976, when Jimmy Carter and Gerald Ford agreed to televised debates, reviving the exercise from its 1960 debut. Debates in particular were suited to spin because they were difficult to analyze. Audiences lacked the information to make concrete judgments, and they were inclined to consider the opinions of postdebate experts before they made up their minds. As the press corps grew in size and came to include more reporters inexperienced at covering politics, a growing number of journalists were open to suggestion, too.

Veterans of an era when the political press corps consisted of a handful of political specialists saw spin as part of the decline of political journalism. "Nobody has any faith in their own opinions anymore," Washington columnist and TV pontificator Robert Novak mused after a debate in 1988. "Can you imagine H.L. Mencken asking a political functionary, 'What do you think?'"

Spin also thrived because newspapers increasingly felt they had to bring something more to the events they covered than simply telling people what happened. Television had already done that. So analyzing the strategy behind the debate became part of the morning story.

It was part of a syndrome in which information traveled faster than audiences could process it. Before most people knew about the event, the press had moved onto secondary analysis of it.

With each campaign the doctors of spin grew bolder. In 1980 and 1984, campaign operatives stayed outside the press room.

They hovered instead out in the hallways to do their spinning, and reporters seeking help would come find them. In 1988, the doctors began wandering inside. By the first debate of 1992, held at Washington University in St. Louis, the press room became part of the handler's formal itinerary. The printed White House schedule of the President's trip included a diagram of the press filing center with areas designated where the campaign wanted "senior spinners" to operate and another for younger staff like Torie Clark and Judy Smith, designated simply as "spinners." Young aides followed the senior spinners around with walkie talkies so that their whereabouts might be centrally monitored.

Spin had become institutionalized. And that transformation certified it had also survived past its usefulness.

Mark Halperin, the young off-air producer from ABC traveling with Clinton, thought he had arranged a coup for correspondent Chris Bury at the first debate in St. Louis. Halperin convinced Clinton communications director George Stephanopoulos to come to the press room and spin Bury even before the debate was finished, thus enabling Bury to know the Clinton campaign line before ABC went into its post-debate analysis program. Stephanopoulos and the rest of the Clinton team, in turn, reasoned that they would impress reporters with their confidence if they burst into the room early—an example of the Clinton campaign's tendency to be overly clever.

When Stephanopoulos set foot in the pressroom, a sea of cameras, their soundmen umbilically attached by wires, surged toward him, klieg lights on. As Stephanopoulos reached Bury to whisper the campaign's analysis, thirty camera crews shot the two of them conferring.

"It's all over," Stephanopoulos tried to persuade Bury. "Clinton will be the next president."

Sitting on either side of Bury, Morton Dean and Brit Hume broke out laughing.

Nonplussed by Stephanopoulos's ardent spin and appalled

by the orgasm of cameras around him, Bury tried to fight his embarrassment.

Others at the first debate in St. Louis had similar experiences. Ellen Warren, the veteran correspondent from Knight-Ridder, laughed so hard while listening to Bush spokeswoman Torie Clark spin that she failed to write anything down. Tom Oliphant of the Boston *Globe* told everyone that the press should set up new rules for spin doctoring, since the pressroom that day in St. Louis was a basketball gym. "In the lane, three seconds out," he said, applying the rules of basketball. "If someone can't get off their line in three seconds, it's a foul."

A sea change had become grinningly obvious.

Spin was dead.

Hume, Fred Barnes of the *New Republic*, and columnist Novak began talking about it as they watched the spectacle around them. Is there any point to this? Hume asked. No, Novak barked. People simply had been lied to too often. He remembered too well the time in 1976 that Republicans argued President Gerald Ford had scored a major rhetorical coup by contending the people of Poland were not suffering Soviet domination. Barnes vividly recalled a Democratic operative arguing that Michael Dukakis had "humanized himself" in 1988 by not flinching when asked how he would feel if his wife were raped and murdered. The only statement a spin doctor could make now that a reporter might believe, Hume thought, is if he said his candidate had failed.

The point seemed painfully clear to Greenfield in Richmond the night of the second debate. When he reached the pressroom after the debate and the post-debate analysis show had ended, Bush campaign executive Fred Malek found him and tried to declare the night a Bush victory. By then, however, the public polls had already come out, showing the night a victory for Clinton and Perot, or at least a clear loss for Bush. "That's not what our poll shows," Malek said. He opened his briefcase, as if he were going to pull out the poll and then stopped. "No, I'm not going to show you our numbers, but . . ." How lame, Greenfield thought. The technology of instant polling had simply overrun the spin doctors.

The campaign tried new variations on spin. During the debates, both Clinton's and Bush's teams started dropping written documents called backgrounders on reporters' desks in the filing center—facts with documented citations to buttress their points and contradict the other guy's: "Bill Clinton's first clear lie tonight was his claim that his tax increase would 'trigger in at family incomes of $200,000.' . . . Clinton has waffled in defining the war aims he proposes for American military in the Balkans." From the standpoint of the national press, it was a step in the right direction from pure spin, which as often as not was mostly bull.

This year, the Bush campaign also tried a new trick to massage public perceptions of the debates. The morning after each debate, adman Sig Rogich did people-on-the-street interviews with faithful Republicans proclaiming their man the winner. With satellite technology, the footage shot at 6 A.M. was cut by noon and shipped to the three networks by 3 P.M. and on the air before dinner—an amazing feat of technology. The spot played for just a day or two while the consensus over the debates hardened. Just another bit of information to add to the mix.

"I saw the debate last night and I just got one conclusion. It's all George Bush," a man in a diner said into a hand-held camera. "I still have a lot of confidence in my president," said a woman. "I don't trust Clinton."

The biggest change in 1992, however, was the use of the satellite tours. If they couldn't spin reporters, they would take their arguments directly to voters through local television and radio. Local news was often easier to control than national press. Best of all, it was usually live, which gave the campaigns nearly total control. It was the same point Jennings had worried about at the beginning of the year. On live, a skilled politician owned the air.

The people who ran the satellite tours for the two campaigns saw another benefit, too, one that spoke to a powerful change in American culture. Leslie Goodman, the Bush campaign's deputy communications director, believed that local news now had more credibility than network.

The Clinton campaign agreed. "You get a more local association because you are on with the local anchor," said Jeff Eller, who ran Clinton's satellite operation. "You are tying it back home, to people's community." By contrast, Eller said, "I'm not sure the network stuff sticks."

The Republicans had been watching this evolution for years. The Democrats, many of them young, some of them volunteers, learned about it through the course of the campaign.

After a Texas TV station approached the campaign in June about doing an electronic town hall with Clinton, the campaign abandoned plans to buy time to do these and began offering the candidate to stations for free. In June, WSB-TV in Atlanta, known for its ambitious political coverage, did a town hall with audiences in several locations around Georgia. The week after the Democratic convention, when the country was hearing about Clinton's bus tour, the Democrats arranged another town hall with WHAS in Louisville. The "Kentuckyana Town Hall" broadcast Clinton and Gore into Kentucky and southern Indiana on WHAS's money.

By mid-summer, the town hall phenomenon was taking off. Around the first of August, Eller booked Clinton on a joint town hall with KOMO-TV in Seattle and its sister KATU-TV in Portland, stations that already did a crude local town hall broadcast every afternoon. Clinton loved it. Jim Wooten's favorite question of the campaign, the one that crystallized the year, was asked here. A man stood up in Portland and asked Clinton via satellite, "I am a pagan witch, and I would like to know how you feel about atheism and pagan witchcraft."

The week after the Republican convention the Clinton campaign enjoyed what it saw as a breakthrough in the town hall circuit. A group of local television stations owned by Times Mirror Co. in Los Angeles sponsored a town hall linking its stations in St. Louis, Birmingham, Austin, and Dallas. Jeff Rosser, the station manager in Dallas, contacted colleagues about coming in too—he hoped the campaign didn't mind. Rosser's list now reached twenty-two markets, across the south and midwest. In Dallas, the local station promoted the town hall for three weeks. The program in that city finished second in the ratings to Roseanne, the No. 1 rated TV show in the country.

Now they were rolling. After the hurricane in Florida, Clinton did five stations there. In Jacksonville, the town hall had a 20 rating and a 30 share, better than most prime time entertainment shows.

When Bush declined the first debate invitation arranged for by the commission on presidential debates Sept. 22, in East Lansing, Michigan, the Clinton campaign arranged another electronic town hall hosted by stations in Detroit, Flint, Lansing, and Grand Rapids. In Detroit, the program again got a 20 point rating and a 32 share, coming in ahead of *Wheel of Fortune.* Eller couldn't believe it. "We beat the Wheel," he kept muttering through a grin.

This had gone far beyond the satellite interviews the campaign had always anticipated, the sort of thing candidates were known for in 1988. They did those too, though not with Clinton. To do local satellite interviews you had to run on time. Clinton never did. Through the entire campaign, he did cumulatively only five hours total of satellite interviews. The bypass that Friedman had anticipated back in January didn't suit Clinton, so it never materialized.

For his surrogates, it was another story. After joining the ticket in July, Gore averaged three or four hours a week. The campaign used him especially to trail Bush, booking him into the same markets where Bush was campaigning each day. The Republicans had used the trick first by having Quayle track Clinton's bus tour in July. But the Bush campaign didn't sustain it. The Clinton campaign did.

Tipper Gore and Hillary Clinton averaged another two or three hours each. But the secret story of the Clinton satellite campaign was actually New York governor Mario Cuomo. He let the campaign know after the Democratic convention he would do an hour a week. By November Cuomo had done one hundred stations around the country, most of the nation.

The Clinton campaign's field operation also revealed the growing importance of local media. The traditional role of field operations involves tracking potential voters and getting out the vote. But those are also operations that can be piggybacked on the efforts of other Democratic campaigns. Under field director David Wilhelm, Clinton's field operations aimed equally at getting the campaign on local television. State organizations staged events, sent surrogate Democrats out, trailed the Republicans and retaliated with counter statements.

All told, the Clinton campaign's goal was to get on television in seventy-five separate markets every day—in addition to the networks.

Then there was radio.

Republicans had innovated the use of radio in the Reagan years. The effort seemed to reach its zenith in 1984. The party that year taped Reagan's and Bush's daily events, then used volunteers to call radio stations around the country offering the highlights, called "actualities."

The Clinton campaign's efforts evolved almost by accident. Richard Strauss was in his senior year at UCLA when the campaign began. In January, he decided to withdraw from school to volunteer for Clinton's campaign in New Hampshire. Strauss had worked for the college radio station and summers in the medium.

Soon he was using his tape recorder to make actualities of Clinton's events and offer them to local stations around the state. By the Michigan primary a month later, Strauss was feeding fifty stations in the state every morning.

Over the summer, when Jeff Eller and George Stephanopoulos arranged the Clinton campaign's local media strategy for the general election, it took the use of political radio further than it had ever been taken before.

Eller set up an 800 number through a telephone company vendor that had 1,100 incoming phone lines and a computerized voice mail menu. Each day, the campaign recorded new campaign events as they occurred and placed them on the system. The 7,500 radio stations nationwide could call the campaign's radio 800 number to record these audio feeds, or actualities, for themselves. The system was a computerized voice mail menu like many businesses now employed. Radio news directors could push one for soundbites from Clinton; two for quotes from Gore, and three for quotes from some Clinton surrogate like Admiral Crowe or Mario Cuomo. Hispanic radio stations could push four for something in Spanish. Push five for a message aimed at African-American radio stations. Push six for quotes aimed at young voters, a service directed especially for college radio stations, those hungry for material.

In the general election period from Labor Day on, the campaign averaged two hundred to five hundred calls a day, delivering their message without any filter.

The campaign also had radio equipment in 45 state offices. That meant they could have local personalities adding their comments to the ones from the national campaigns and packaging those to local stations. Those 45 states averaged another 40 feeds each, more than 1,600 a day. The Clinton campaign thus was delivering its own messages directly to roughly 2,200 stations daily, or about 30 percent of the radio stations nationwide. That was outside the realm of the national radio networks controlled by Mutual Radio, ABC, CBS, or the Associated Press.

To make the actualities more appealing to stations, the campaign fed Clinton's events to its radio department in Little Rock off a satellite so the candidate's events on the 800 voice mail system had studio-quality sound.

Most of this was invisible to Friedman at ABC. He had expected the campaigns would bypass the networks for local. As far as he knew, it wasn't happening.

Actually, what was happening was more subtle. The campaigns didn't know what would work and what wouldn't. So they did everything—network, local, popular culture, radio, talk shows, and entertainment shows. The ability to control the agenda had simply become more difficult than they could ever imagine. And everyone had a role.

The debates were a clear example. What decided how the public viewed the debates now was a complex mix. The instant analysis of the networks and newspapers were still a part of it, with whatever massaging the campaigns could manage. So were the sound-bite wars, that choice of moments from the debates that producers and correspondents around the country picked out to replay in their stories. For many Americans those moments from the debate that echoed in the news for the next two days became the debate. Yet the decisive factor, most in politics believed, were the instant polls the press conducted in the moments after the debate.

As the first debate ended, Jennings decided to lie back. He hoped the program would be helpful, but he wanted voters to decide for themselves which candidate had done well. He particularly did not want to declare winners.

But you fly by the seat of your pants on live television. There is no time for a meeting after the debate, no precise game plan. The thing ends, you go to commercials and start. At the top of the post-debate special Greenfield waxed so enthusiastic about Perot that Jennings thought it close to the edge. "This was the Ross Perot who attracted so much interest last spring before driving off the main highways of politics." When he got to Cokie Roberts, a third of the way into the special, she did exactly what Jennings wanted to avoid. "Let's call a spade a spade. Perot won this debate," Roberts said. Jennings cringed but said nothing.

Jennings was interviewing undecided voters from *World News* focus groups when producer Nancy Gabriner slipped him a note that ABC's instant poll had come in. He maneuvered into a commercial to confer with Jeff Gralnick in the control room, and when they came back on the air, twenty minutes after the debate had ended, he announced to the public what it thought of the event just ended. It thought Clinton the winner, though within the margin of error—28 percent for Clinton, 24 percent for Perot, 18 percent for Bush, and 26 percent declaring it a tie.

By the next morning, Mike Schneider on *Good Morning America* was leading with all the polls—including CBS, *Newsweek*, CNN-*USA-Today*-Gallup, the balance of which showed Perot the victor. And by that evening, Jeff Alderman in ABC's polling unit was doing a second debate survey that reflected the day's press coverage—this time with a sample that included people who had heard about the debate only secondhand—and by now the consensus had hardened. Clinton's narrow edge had turned into Perot's clear victory. Thirty-seven percent said Perot had won; 24 percent thought Clinton and only 11 percent Bush, with 26 percent still calling it a tie.

The press coverage, in other words, had played its classic role of widening margins of victory. The polls also focused coverage around the horse race. On ABC, there was almost no discussion of the substance of what the candidates had said. What little there was Jim Wooten had provided. "There were no glaring errors and no outrageous lies," he said on the air.

Interestingly, the print press's analysis was less generous to Perot and had less impact. The *New York Times* and Washington *Post* declared Clinton the political victor. He had accomplished what he needed, while Bush had not. Perot was amusing but irrelevant. Except to voters.

Two nights later, Gralnick and Jennings did not do a post-debate analysis show. (The show would have interrupted the schedule for *Roseanne*, then the No. 1 rated TV program in the country, and the network would not relinquish the time.) But as he went off the air at the end of the debate, Jennings did his best to squeeze in what he could. He began by offering viewers a warning. Through each of the debates, Jennings and Gralnick had Friedman's American Agenda team gathered around the Rim on the second floor to watch for factual accuracy. The vice presidential debate was a holocaust for the truth, they called to tell Gabriner, especially Quayle's side.

"Some of the charges made this evening are not accurate. So perhaps our best recommendation to you at home is to take a look at your newspaper tomorrow morning or watch the television or listen to the radio," Jennings said signing off. Afterwards Roone Arledge called. Don't tell these people to read the morning papers, he said. Have them watch *Good Morning America*.

Jennings also had Greenfield deliver a brief analysis. "One of the best public performances Quayle has had. Al Gore seemed very programmed." Some around *World News* squirmed. They thought Quayle was a disgrace—a man out of control. That was the problem. Politics was in the eye of the beholder. But Greenfield had the microphone, and in the age of opinion journalism, the era of shows like the *McLaughlin Group*, these guys were in the business of offering their opinions.

On NBC, Tim Russert was delivering the opposite verdict. "The consensus here in the pressroom is Al Gore had a much better night than Dan Quayle."

Then something weird happened. NBC's poll the next day bore out Russert. ABC's bore out Greenfield.

NBC's poll was taken of random voters that night. But ABC's reinterviewed people who had agreed in advance to be surveyed after the debate by ABC. That raises the strong likelihood that

Greenfield's gut reaction influenced if not defined the poll. The issue is largely academic. The vice presidential debate, by all measures, had no consequence on the election.

But it raises a red flag for the future. In the era of instant polls, which use the methodology of reinterviewing the same panel of people, there is a new danger of the networks' instant analyses becoming self-fulfilling prophecies.

The campaigns' own research suggested neither poll was really correct. The Bush campaign's dial group preferred Gore, but only slightly. The Democrats' didn't measure the debate.

Actually, Quayle's performance was as highly calculated as Greenfield had imagined. The Friday before, the Vice President had staged a rehearsal debate with Warren Rudman playing Gore in which he was every bit as subdued and presidential as the press might have wanted. "Flawless," one aide said. But on reflection Quayle's team thought it politically misguided. They were too far behind—which had been Bush's problem. Quayle needed to throw fire bombs, and turn every question into an attack on Clinton on two issues, taxes and character. If it sounded shrill, so what. He was the Vice President. That was his role.

At the second presidential debate in Richmond two nights later, no polling was necessary. Clinton had certainly fared better than Bush in the town hall format. Perhaps it was just as well, some at ABC thought. The ABC poll had been erratic. On the eve of the second debate they had Clinton's lead down to seven points, a result confirmed by no other poll, including Bush's internal surveys. Jennings and Friedman had been burying the poll at the end of the political report, and they soft-pedaled this one as much as they could. "Governor Clinton is down to a seven-point lead over President Bush. The margin of error is plus or minus four percentage points," Jennings said on the air. "But as Brit alluded, some polls show the gap wider. And during the week, with three debates, the numbers in a lot of polls can be quite different."

As he watched the Richmond debate in the ABC truck outside the hall, White House field producer Terry Ray watched the
President he and Hume had covered for four years and began to
think it was over. Ray sympathized with the Republican anger
about press bias against Bush. He thought ABC had been unfair—
in the subtle shadings of the lead-ins, in the skepticism of the
economic reporting. But as he watched this debate he saw Bush
overmatched by a Clinton who seemed more impressive than he
had recognized before.

"I'm not interested in his character," Clinton said of Bush.
"I want to change the character of the presidency."

"That was really strong," Ray said. "He turned that issue
exactly right on Bush."

In time, Ray began asking questions like any other voter.
What would this guy Clinton really be like as president?

Afterward, Jennings again had trouble keeping his analysts
from calling it. Greenfield thought Clinton "extremely effective"
and "commanding the atmospherics." Bush, on the other hand,
kept looking at his watch "as though he had someplace more
important to go."

It was not that the Clinton crew had successfully sold their
spin so carefully agreed upon in the conference call. The authors
of the post-debate analysis stories actually did not even listen to
the spin doctors. They were too busy writing. Greenfield did his
post-debate analysis from the hall, where no spin doctors could
talk to him.

The Bush camp, meanwhile, was deluding itself into thinking
Bush had fared well enough—one of its failures throughout the
campaign. His team saw the president and the campaign through
Republican eyes, which forgave the president his weaknesses. It
never managed to find the perspective of the undecided voter, that
element of the public essential to a Republican victory.

When the full results from the focus group arrived that night in Richmond, Bush had not won. He had come in last. But Bush's men had not waited for that information before deciding to argue that Bush had prevailed.

When they came into the spin room, Bob Teeter and James Lake were shocked that everyone seemed to agree Bush had committed the worst of all debate sins—he had demonstrated on camera the very failures that people perceived in his presidency. He had misunderstood voter questions. He had seemed impatient, even uninterested, with the squalid necessity of actually having to wade out into the audience and seduce voters. In short, he had lost this debate even more than others had won it, which in the context of what this race was about was the most damaging thing he could have done.

Again, the print press tended to discount Perot, even though the public polls and the Bush dial group suggested the billionaire had won the debate. "For Perot tonight was the night the novelty began to wear off," the Washington *Post* wrote. "The audience . . . seemed less interested in colorful maxims and sweeping promises," said the *New York Times*.

The next day, Bush had trouble hiding his disappointment, in contrast with the glee he showed after the vice presidential debate two days earlier. "On the stump in New Jersey this afternoon, the President barely mentioned last night's debate," Hume began his piece the next night.

In the days after, ABC's pollster saw Clinton's lead surge. So did the other public polls. Jennings mentioned the range on the air—from ABC's 19 points to Newsweek's 15. He even named the rival polls. If ABC's numbers were to be believed, the race had shifted 12 points in four nights.

At the final debate on October 19 in East Lansing, Michigan, the press again played a key role in the outcome, this time by helping Bush beyond what even some of the Republican's key aides thought he deserved. The Bush dial group showed that for the third time in a row voters thought Perot had prevailed. The press polls varied, with Clinton prevailing in two polls, Perot in one, and Clinton and Perot tying in another. The best Bush did was second.

But the press the next day judged the debate a victory for Bush. Only ABC of the three commercial networks even did a post-debate program (along with PBS and CNN), and on all three Bush won marks for improvement. The print press was even more generous. The *New York Times* declared Bush had "changed his ways for the better." The Washington *Post* said Bush "made the most of it." The next day, Hume and producer Terry Ray saw Bush campaigning in Georgia buoyed by the debate and the press's reaction. With two weeks left, the man suddenly had more energy. The attacks on Clinton were focused and spirited. Bush spent the day imitating the Atlanta Braves baseball team's famous tomahawk chop to symbolize what he would do to Clinton. He kept citing his support of the Braves over the Toronto Blue Jays in the World Series as sign of his decisiveness. "I'm for the Braves, courageously." In his endearingly goofy way, Bush was enjoying himself.

But most evidence suggested that instant polls, not the press's analysis, mattered most now. Looking at the same evidence that was causing this surge in confidence and focus in his President, Bush's pollster Fred Steeper that day back in Washington arrived at an ironic conclusion, the same one Hume had come to weeks earlier. There was no way now Bush could win.

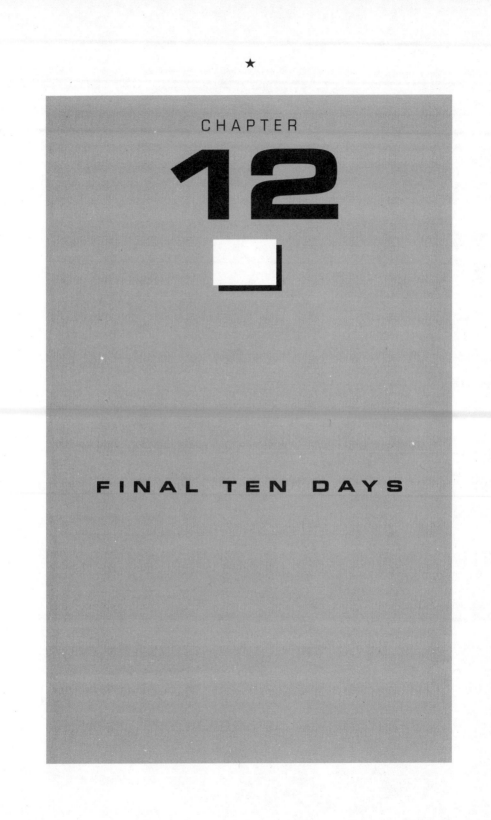

★

CHAPTER

12

FINAL TEN DAYS

On Thursday, October 22, when the early returns of a poll arrived at CBS and the *New York Times*, the numbers showed Bush leading. It couldn't be right.

Bush had largely blown the debates that had ended four days before. Since then, news had leaked that the Republicans had not only investigated Clinton's passport file but his mother's, too. Bush simply couldn't have turned the election around suddenly.

CBS and the *New York Times* continued polling. When the final numbers came in, Clinton was up by 5.

That Monday, three days later, the same thing happened to Jeff Alderman's daily tracking poll at ABC. On Sunday Clinton was up by 15 points. Monday Bush was up by 3. What should they do?

Daily tracking polls are different from traditional polls. And they are dangerous tools for the press. Rather than taking a snapshot in time—by sampling a large number of people all at once the way a traditional poll does—tracking polls measure changes in public opinion over time. They do that by surveying small groups of people each night and then adding two or three nights together to get a rough idea of trend lines, such as whether a candidate is moving up or down. The technique was developed to track the effect of coffee commercials in the 1960s, and when it was brought to politics by Reagan in 1976, tracking samples were thought to be fine for sensing a candidate's direction, but too small to reliably pinpoint a candidate's exact standing. So when the ABC-Washington *Post* consortium began using tracking polls for public consumption in 1984 anyway, many pollsters, such as NBC's pollster Mary Klette and CBS's Kathy Frankovic, saw great risk. The results were too imprecise. The general public would not distinguish between the precision of a conventional poll and the rough trend lines of a tracking poll. Neither would most journalists. Jeff Alderman at ABC disagreed. He had used tracking polls in 1984 to catch the rise of Gary Hart. And he started his tracking poll this year around the first of October.

When the strange Bush number arrived, Alderman decided there was only one thing he should do. ABC was adding two nights together to arrive at its figure each day. That meant Clinton was still up by 7 points. The night before, the two-day sample put Clinton up by 11. Yet it might sound odd to tell viewers he had dropped four points overnight. But at least the four-point drop since Monday was within the margin of error. They would just use it, and see what happened the next night. Maybe Bush really was ahead.

ABC's poll had jumped around a lot already—especially early in the fall when it was conducted jointly with the Washington *Post*. One week in late September, it had Clinton up by 21 points. The next week, 9. Alderman's ABC tracking poll had been more stable, but not completely. Friedman and Jennings felt trapped into running all these polls, since they couldn't know which numbers were wrong. But they had remained adamant most of the year about how to treat them. If you led the broadcast with a poll, they felt, viewers saw everything you said in the context of those new numbers. They had managed to lead with polls only three times all year. Mostly they had buried the tracking poll at the end of the political report. The other ABC programs were not so careful. Since each ABC News program operated independently, and no one laid down division-wide edicts about these things, the morning news led with the polls virtually every day. So did the weekend news. If he had wanted, Arledge could have stopped that.

As it turned out, ABC's tracking poll problem that last week resolved itself without viewers ever finding out. The day after Bush was ahead by three, Clinton was up again by 15 points. Averaged together, it meant that Clinton was still up by 7 points. No change. Viewers had no idea that one of those nights Bush had led. But the numbers in the days that followed "raised your hair a little," pollster Alderman said. If he defined the electorate narrowly enough, Bush was actually leading, he told Friedman and others around the Rim. Polling is a craft, a difficult one, and it is amazing the polls are as accurate as they are.

The problem is the sheer number of them—more than two hundred media polls between July and election day. Polls had become the press's biggest bias, not liberalism or malice or recklessness. Polls were the lens by which the press viewed everything. If Perot had reentered this race with 35 percent of the vote instead of 7 percent he wouldn't have been demonized. If Bush were leading and Clinton losing, Jim Baker and even Bush would have been considered uncanny battlers. Clinton's caution would have been considered a character flaw.

But polls were pervasive because they were good business, not always good journalism. If a news organization had a poll, other news organizations would quote it. It was a predictable way of creating exclusive news that got one's name out in the press—a marriage of journalism and advertising. Polls were out of control, distorting journalism, and for all the wrong reasons.

The most glaring example of poll mania came that last Wednesday, the day after ABC's tracking poll showed Bush ahead. Now, the CNN-*USA Today*-Gallup poll showed the race at 2 points, and CNN was out flogging the numbers hard. Gallup got those numbers by assuming the electorate would be the same as four years earlier, an assumption that most evidence suggested was wrong.

Polls had dominated CNN's coverage already. "We spent a

zillion dollars on them and we reported the shit out of them," one of CNN's most senior journalists said. Though CNN had talented poll analyst William Schneider to talk about them, the network had committed most of the mistakes with polls—from using one-night tracking samples on the air to leading its broadcast many nights with the daily polling numbers—that the commercial networks had learned to avoid.

When the CNN-Gallup poll came out, Bush campaign pollster Fred Steeper knew it was almost certainly wrong. His own polls had the spread between Bush and Clinton closer to seven or eight points, not one. Stan Greenberg's numbers for the Clinton campaign were also seven.

On the Rim, Friedman's deputies had fretted the numbers all day. Alderman had Bush ahead that Monday night two days before. And Bush seemed so energized. Maybe the CNN numbers were picking up something. But how did that square with the state-by-state analysis Hal Bruno did each week, which showed Clinton winning decisively in the electoral college? Off the record, the White House had even confirmed Bruno's analysis.

By 5:30 P.M., they had to make a decision. To be fair, maybe they should mention CNN's numbers. Mike Stein, the head writer, could weave it into the script when Jennings mentioned ABC's tracking poll, someone said.

Then Friedman seemed to snap. These frigging polls. This was crazy. "That poll is probably aberrational," he said slowly, like an exasperated professor. "Bush's own pollster said today [on TV] that the spread was probably more like five or six, which means it is probably seven or nine. I don't think we should put something on the air that we think is wrong." It was typical of Friedman. He didn't believe they had to account for everything viewers might hear somewhere else—not if it was bullshit.

Jennings made no mention of it. CBS led with the poll, counterbalanced with ABC's shaky 7-point tracking poll. NBC also led with the polls and described the race as tight, even though the CNN poll was the only one that was close. By Friday, NBC was calling it very tight, a race "that has everyone on the edge of its seat." CNN's poll by then had it at one point. Clinton's private polls still showed it at seven, unchanged.

There is no precise explanation of why the race narrowed that last week. Races always tighten. Ambivalent Republicans were coming home. Bush was campaigning better. For the most part, Bush wasn't really gaining much. Perot was, bringing Clinton down. Bush pollster Fred Steeper also thought the press had boosted Bush by praising his final debate performance—an ironic twist given Bush's berating of the media.

Steeper also believed that the release on Tuesday, a week before the election, of a new government economic index, the Gross Domestic Product (GDP), helped as well. "The numbers gave some people a slightly more positive feeling about the country," Steeper said his polls suggested. "And any slightly better feeling about the country always went straight to Bush."

The press, including ABC, treated the GDP numbers skeptically, and the next day Bush hammered away at the media for not being more upbeat about them. But the press in this case mostly reflected the prevailing economic view. ABC quoted Allan Sinai, a Republican who had advised Bush. Other economists went so far as to suggest the Bush administration had cooked the books. For all of the press's many sins in 1992, skeptical reporting of the GDP figures a week before the election wasn't one of them. The fact that a month later it became clear that the economy was actually stronger than even the GDP figures suggested reveals only that the economists were wrong.

With only a week to go, Friedman was no longer sticking as closely to the plan. The candidates' campaign days were stories by themselves, no matter what they said. Bury recited Clinton's day faithfully.

By Thursday, Hume thought Bush was veering out of control from the strain. At a community college in Macomb County outside Detroit, movie star Bruce Willis introduced the President by announcing that he was "pissed off" that Clinton could say he was qualified to be commander-in-chief. When Bush came on, he called Clinton and Gore "two bozos" who knew less about foreign policy than his dog Millie. And Gore was "Ozone Man," as he had been for several days running. "This guy is so far off in the environmental extreme, we'll be up to our neck in owls and out of work for every American. This guy's crazy. He is way out. Far out. Far out, man."

It was classic Bush—at once human, frenetic, endearing, and then all of a sudden spastic. Hume had long ago given up thinking Bush could win. But the Michigan performance demonstrated the President's inability to sustain his balance for long. Then Gerald Ford gave the day's weirdness a perfect accent. As Ford walked off a plane with Bush in Grand Rapids, a reporter asked, "Is he [Bush] going to win Michigan?" Ford looked at the reporter and shook his head in an emphatic no. "Forget it. Forget it." When producer Terry Ray saw the footage later at the filing center, he fell out of his chair laughing. It was a meaningless gaffe by gaffe-prone Gerry Ford, but he and Hume found the picture was irresistible. On balance, it was unfair but probably harmless. Something else, however, was also clear. The last week, when ABC and the rest of the networks returned to doing a daily story about the candidate's stump appearances, pretty pictures, gaffes, and goofs again tended to dominate.

The irony of Friedman's 1992 approach is it often lacked the sense of the roar of the grease paint and the smell of the crowd. This piece had it. Friedman called it the single best campaign-day piece of the year.

The following day, Friday, Bush's surge had ended. When he called into the Rim, Hume said Bush seemed flat all day, almost solemn. Mrs. Bush had made it clear she disapproved of his calling his opponents bozos yesterday. His crowds were small. The energy of the last week that had spasmed the day before now seemed to have left him spent.

That afternoon, the special prosecutor in the IranContra case released his new indictment of former Reagan defense secretary Caspar Weinberger and included in the press announcement a Weinberger memo that seemed to suggest that George Bush, too, may have not been forthcoming about his role in the scandal. Afterwards, Bush and his advisers blamed the special prosecutor and the press coverage for stalling the President's surge. They had a point that the coverage was exaggerated—predictably. Did it influence the election? The overwhelming course of the election—and even Bush's own internal polls—make it clear the answer is no.

Bush was never within range of winning. If the IranContra reindictment had not come down, Fred Steeper argued that the trend line in Bush's campaign poll showed Bush and Clinton tying in popular vote on election day. But even Steeper acknowledged, "We were never close in the state-by-state polls." On election day, Steeper was actually surprised at how close Bush came. Clinton pollster Greenberg said the same thing. Publicly, starting on Monday that last week, Alderman's two-day average showed Clinton ahead by 11, then 7, 7, 9, and finally on Friday it dipped to 4 points and on Saturday's newscast 3. Alderman stopped airing his poll on Sunday, but on Monday it would have showed Bush trailing by 5.

Was there bias in the press? Yes—though there are more conservatives at ABC News and elsewhere in the media than many people think.

But the liberalism of the media is more complicated than the ideologues like to admit. The media's ideological slant is not a manifest conspiracy to harm Republicans, but a failure to understand some of their arguments. That's why journalists counter the charge of bias by noting how much they strive to be fair. The press weakness is not the absence of good intentions. Its bigger failure is a lack of intellectual rigor. Parsing the logic of a candidate's arguments is harder than making judgments about the strategic motive behind them. And examining a candidate's ideas opens reporters more easily to charges of bias. So the press tends to avoid ideas and stick to facts, to be more aggressive—and often more unfair—about such indiscretions as whether Gary Hart was too weird to be president, whether Bill Clinton was hiding something about his past sex life or draft status or financial records, or whether George Bush had failed to come clean on IranContra. As the 1992 election demonstrated, ironically, these ideologically neutral issues are often less useful to voters than journalists rationalize them to be.

Where the press's bias hurt Bush was that reporters failed to take the President's arguments seriously. Reporters who cover Washington are more vested in a government engaged in great works than in a government intent on getting out of the way. While they were trying to be fair, journalists simply did not give Bush's laissez-faire proposals as serious consideration as Clinton's activist proposals. And since reporters spend more effort covering political technique than ideas, they never challenged their own core cultural and philosophical assumptions and thus remained vulnerable to intellectually lazy and reflexively liberal descriptions of Republican policy. This kind of bias didn't stop the press from conveying Bush's arguments. It merely colored the tone of their stories in ways subtle enough that these journalists didn't see it. More skillful Republicans than Bush have had no trouble conveying their message through this filter—especially on television, where politicians arrange and control the words and pictures. All Bush had to do was to make his economic plan a priority, to flog it night after night, and demonstrate to reporters and the public alike that he believed in it.

Rather than being a victim of bias, Bush's problem was that he lacked a strategy for reelection. And then his losing campaign began to collapse in on itself. His lack of skill as a campaigner, his failures as a communicator, his inattention to domestic affairs, his wavering philosophical core, his consequent failure to sustain a message, the public's loss of faith in him, the tyranny of the polls—these all fed on each other through the magnifying power of a news media that now played twenty-four hours.

Yes, the press made Bush's job harder. It usually does. But more dangerous than ideological bias in the media is hysteria. The press has become so large, conducts so many polls, examines so many trivial details, that to audiences on the other end context and nuance are lost. And television compounds the problem by compressing everything into the grammar of two minutes.

If the press had a victim it was Perot, not Bush. Over the years, the Texas magnate had created so much inflated mythology about his life that he had reason to be fearful. The press could unmask the parts of the myth that were false.

Early on, Perot had correctly seen how the press had become an obstacle between the voter and the process, and he challenged that—for which he deserved enormous credit. He reconnected millions of people to the election, by exciting people directly, and by forcing the other candidates to face issues they would have otherwise ignored. But Perot's challenge to the press went too far. He came to believe that because the press was unpopular it was also illegitimate—that because people were angry with the press they rejected the larger role the press was trying to play. There Perot was sadly naive and probably dangerous. When the election was over, the academics would begin having seminars to analyze it. One was entitled "Are the Traditional Press Irrelevant?" Perot's candidacy had raised the question, but it also had answered it. Misguided, yes. Irrelevant? Not close. So it was fitting, perhaps, that Perot's final significant moment in the campaign was standing alone at a microphone furiously, pathetically, denouncing the press for doing what it was supposed to.

He had emerged from the debates with his reputation mostly restored. Jeff Alderman's poll and others showed Perot's support had climbed back to 21 percent, up from 7 percent before the debates began. Although people didn't remember it this way, that was roughly where Perot's support had been before he had dropped out of the race in July—and before he had been labeled as a quitter.

But within minutes of being declared the winner of the third debate in the media's polls, Perot blew up at reporters. "You guys hate that I'm in the race," he told them. "What a bunch of jerks. . . . You guys have less respect in this country than Congress."

Inside the Bush campaign Fred Steeper could see Perot surging. Steeper's internal polls showed Perot poised to pass 20 percent in the polls. Steeper expected the Texan to hit 25 percent.

Three days later Mort Dean's story aired challenging whether any assassins tried to kill Perot and his family as the candidate claimed. Dean never heard from Perot after it ran. In fact he never spoke with Perot again.

Then *60 Minutes* pursued a story Perot had been peddling privately about having dropped out of the race in July because he feared someone might have phony pictures of his daughter. On camera, Perot confirmed the tale to CBS.

The next day, the press grilled Perot's son for a half hour about all the various contradictions in his accounts of his past. Perot watched from an office nearby until he could stand the spectacle no longer. He appeared from behind a curtain and took over the podium. "Let's get a few things straight," he began. "Is anybody here from ABC? Is Morton Dean here?"

Dean was watching on CNN from his office in New York.

Perot was still bristling about Dean's story about the assassins. "I told [ABC] that story happened," Perot snapped. So did two of his friends, Murphy Martin, a former ABC news correspondent, who now worked with Perot, and Tom Muir, another Perot associate. "And when that story was run, neither Murphy Martin's confirmation nor Tom Muir's confirmation was ever aired."

Dean marveled at Perot's persistence, but he thought the man was wrong. Dean had talked to Martin and Muir. And neither could confirm the story. They knew only what Perot had told them. If he had used them on the air, Dean thought, the case that Perot made it up only would have been stronger.

But Perot wasn't done. He could only conclude, he said, that ABC had a "death wish to inaccurately report a story."

Later, someone would pop into Dean's office and ask if he was worried about that. A death wish?

Is that how Perot meant it? Dean wondered. As a threat?

Perot then lost control completely. "It happened in the middle of the night," he stormed at the reporters. "There was one man and a dog. I'm not going to get into that with you because it's none of your business. . . . I don't have to prove anything to you people to start with. Number two, I have given you proof that would satisfy any reasonable group in the country on an issue that is not related to the president's race. Was I making up stories or not? No. I wasn't. That's all you needed to know."

The moment perfectly captured Perot's attitude about the media. When confronted that a major part of his biography was contradicted by proven facts, he challenged the press's right to ask.

Perot's performance led the nightly news that night, the day after he had appeared on *60 Minutes*. His surge ended. Remarkably, it did not drop. He would end the race exactly at that point—19 percent.

On election eve, ABC made one last possible contribution to the outcome. It was the second of two lavish fifty-state surveys ABC had conducted to find out the electoral college picture—and get ABC some publicity in the process.

Friedman hated it.

Four years earlier, ABC had done a fifty-state poll just like it, which had run the day of the final debate between Michael Dukakis and George Bush. The night was Dukakis's last chance to revive his candidacy and the poll had intruded on the race.

Friedman and Jennings had devoted thirteen of their twenty-two minutes to the survey. Their intent, they claimed, was to get beyond the devastating headline—that Bush's lead was insurmountable. The effect, however, was a hype of their poll. Worse, much of what Jennings had said about it was grossly misleading.

He had said they had "just conducted" it when in fact some parts of the poll were three weeks old—old enough to be unreliable. He had said, too, that ten thousand people were being interviewed, but, broken down, the sample in each state ranged from as few as one hundred to as many as five hundred—sample sizes that were too small to be reliable. To the press corps, the one-of-a-kind poll substantially raised the bar Dukakis had to jump, unnerving Dukakis and buoying Bush only hours before a debate. Lee Atwater, Bush's campaign manager, later called it "the most devastating thing of the whole campaign," and Hal Bruno had to go on *Nightline* that night and defend it—even though he thought the poll was garbage. History was no less kind. Jack Germond and Jules Witcover in their book about the campaign called it "out of bounds" and "bizarre."

Now, four years later, ABC management wanted to do the poll again—this time twice—once ten days before the election and the second time election eve. Friedman was absolutely opposed. Jennings thought perhaps doing it once, ten days out, was safe if they handled it right, but he opposed the election eve poll.

In the Tuesday editorial meeting two weeks before election day, everyone in the room knew Friedman was against the poll. Weiswasser seemed ambivalent. Roone was clearly for it. It told them something meaningful, he thought, and it was ABC's alone: it would get the network attention.

Over the two hours, the meeting turned into a classic Arledge ritual dance, the subtle and in many ways ingenious art of getting his way without imposing his will. How did the poll work? Arledge asked. Was it reliable? What was the margin of error? Arledge was stalling. Of course the poll was reliable. He was wearing down resistance. It went on for more than an hour. Finally, after this dissertation on the poll's credibility, the group got around to the question of whether to use the thing. By stalling, Arledge had shown how much he wanted it. Weiswasser wasn't opposed. Finally, Friedman simply said no. The poll was fine. It was a valuable tool, and they should use it internally to guide them about how to cover the race and interpret other polls. But let's not use the thing on the air. Let's not declare the race over with ten days to go. The very fact that it was so huge—eleven thousand voters—was the problem. The poll would sound too conclusive. They would get hammered for it.

Then Jennings weighed in and Friedman had lost. As long as we are careful about how we describe it, the anchor said, they could use it tonight, but he was opposed to using it election eve. The weight of the anchor and the president of the news division settled it. The rest of the meeting concerned what language they would use.

Friedman waged one last battle against the poll. He refused to lead with it. Arledge tried to argue with him, but he never ordered him to change. It was Friedman's show.

"We have just completed a survey of more than eleven thousand likely voters in fifty states," Jennings explained after the first commercial. "And it certainly makes clear what the challenge is for President Bush." Clinton was clearly leading in eighteen states worth 261 electoral votes, nine short of being elected. And he could get those probably from the nine other states in which he led.

Bush was clearly ahead in no states and leading in only three, Jennings said. He had just 18 electoral votes.

Actually, the poll also forced ABC to do one more positive piece about Bush. Hume and producer Terry Ray had not prepared a story for that day. Bury had a piece ready about the huge crowds Clinton was getting. They couldn't leave Bush out without a story that night, not with this poll running. Friedman called Hume and they rigged up a story that cobbled together several days of campaign footage and featured Bush dumping on the pollsters. Hume ended it with footage of Bush wandering back into the White House late the night before with his dogs. "He must be glad to get home at the end of these long days. But he'll be out there again every day and night until the end. It may look grim, but he's been counted out before and ended up here in the White House anyway."

On election eve, Friedman again lost the argument over the poll, this time even with Jennings on his side. Friedman again refused to lead with it, and Arledge again declined to force him. This time the poll may have helped Bush slightly. Jennings introduced it by saying the race was getting somewhat tighter. It showed Bush now leading in states with 81 electoral votes, up from 18 ten days before. And Clinton was down, the number of electoral votes he controlled by overwhelming leads had shrunken to 104 from 261 a week before.

Actually, this was mostly silliness. A closer look showed nothing had really changed much. Clinton still led in states with about 300 electoral votes. Only the size of his lead in some states had narrowed.

For as long as networks have existed, part of the prime election night competition was who called the race first. Whose computers were better. Whose analysts were better. An entire discipline of public opinion survey research was developed inside the networks—measuring the American electorate on election day. The network polling units, accountable to no one, worked largely in secret, their precise methods not fully examined by the academic journals, their periodic problems hidden and even lied about. The pollsters were like Mandarins, jealous of their results, secretive in their techniques, disparaging of their competitors, but wielding enormous power and over the years developing methods to study the American voter that have had profound influence over the practice of American politics.

In the early years, the network Mandarins competed to count the actual vote. They hired Boy Scouts and veterans and members of the League of Women Voters and anyone else they could find to call in results from every precinct in the country. The network with the best system of counting and telephones would be first to flash the number on the screen. The effort eventually became so expensive—the California primary alone in 1964 cost nearly $2 million—that after 1964 the networks surrendered and formed a consortium to count the numbers jointly. No reform movement or law passed did more to finally end ballot box corruption in this country than the resulting News Election Service formed to serve the networks.

By the mid-1960s the Mandarins were learning a new way of competing to project who would win the election first. They did so by identifying what they called "pure" or "key" precincts, areas of the country that were dominated entirely by one demographic group, Italians, Poles, white collar professionals, etc. If they counted the votes in these "keys" quickly, the Mandarins found that based on demographic models of the electorate they could accurately extrapolate how the rest of the country could vote—even before it had happened.

The stakes now were enormous. The almighty networks not only could bring the world into people's living rooms. They could predict the future. The day after each election, the network whose analysis was fastest to call the election took out full page ads in the papers to boast about it.

Then the country changed and the network Mandarins had to change again. As American culture shifted in the 1970s, becoming less ghettoized, the key precincts began to be less predictive. Italians no longer all lived with Italians, Irish with Irish. Only blacks remained in their own districts. So in the late 1970s NBC and CBS began inventing another revolutionary technique—exit polling. As people left the voting booths, network researchers would query them and in the course of twenty questions classify voters by income, ethnicity, ideology, find out who they voted for and why. These were fed into the network computers and even more precise extrapolations about the race were possible. In 1980,

Ronald Reagan's forces used network exit polling results from the primaries to discover a surge in working people crossing over to the Republican camp. The search for these blue collar Reagan Democrats became a key focus of their general election strategy. For years, the Mandarins denied they were using exit polls to project the elections. They insisted instead that they were using actual votes and key precincts. "It was a lie," one of the Mandarins now admits. "And we all knew it." But the exit polls had become so quick and accurate that in 1980 Jimmy Carter conceded his loss based on their predictions hours before people stopped voting in California. Western voters became incensed and claimed the networks were influencing turnout for local races, in effect persuading people not to vote by telling them it wouldn't make any difference. The research never proved conclusively the outcome of local races were influenced, but the networks agreed to a compromise anyway. They promised they would not project the outcome in any state until after the polls had closed in that state—even though they had the capability to do it much sooner than that.

By the mid-1980s the competition was mostly between ABC and CBS. NBC no longer felt it could afford to play. And CBS pollster Warren Mitofsky was always cautious anyway. Despite the enormous pressure, he often resisted being first to project to avoid making mistakes. So after the 1988 election, the grand election day competitions between the Mandarins finally died altogether. Just as the huge election units the networks once commanded to study the campaign had disappeared, the networks no longer felt it was worthwhile to spend millions to beat the competition with their election projections.

So this year the networks would share one exit poll, one computer, one analysis. (Though each network could pay extra to add proprietary questions to the exit poll if they wanted.) CBS's Mitofsky would run it, using the field organization that had belonged to ABC. Now there was one Mandarin left, one method, just as jealously guarded by Mitofsky as it had always been. The other networks would continue to do traditional telephone polling through the course of the election, but election night was now done cooperatively.

What the Mandarins did not admit was that there were problems in their mysterious methods of predicting the future. Unlike telephone polling, exit polling is difficult to control. The researchers do not know what their surveyors dress like, how they sound, whether some kinds of voters might be disposed to answer and others not. In 1988, the exit poll data on election day overstated Democrat Michael Dukakis's vote. With only one exit poll, the chances of problems could increase. They were saving money. But they were also taking a greater risk.

Viewers never saw it, but the exit poll data leaned Democratic again in 1992. Mitofsky called Georgia at 7 P.M., for Clinton and at some point during the evening pulled it back.

He also called New Jersey early, and then the state closed up so much that Clinton only won it by one percentage point.

For all that, Mitofsky, in general, was conservative. He waited to call Wisconsin, and he didn't call Ohio, giving Clinton the election, until 10:48. The three networks were in commercial, having just won assurances from their polling units that Ohio was going to wait. When Carolyn Smith called Gralnick in the control room, he decided to break out of the commercials. Neither of the other two executive producers, Bill Wheatley at NBC and Lane Vernardos at CBS chose to tamper with the commercials, so Gralnick had a small coup, a scoop of a minute or two.

When they came off the air election night after 1 A.M., Jennings admitted he had favored George Bush four years earlier. He had high hopes for Bush. And he felt betrayed. He sounded like someone who thought he knew George Bush, knew how Bush was raised, had been raised like that himself. It sounded as if he thought Bush had failed who he really was, or was supposed to be.

"I'm Anglican," Jennings said. "An Anglican betrayed is a dangerous thing." But Jennings thought he had kept his feelings out of his broadcasts.

Clinton was harder to read. For all the hours, all the tape, the press had never revealed him all that well. The country did not yet know what it had bought. The papers the next day would talk about whether Clinton had a mandate. Some talked about the American people reembracing the idea that government could solve problems, that citizens had to take responsibility for each other, accepting higher taxes and greater sacrifice. The mythologizing had already begun. Clinton had won because he represented change, a change from George Bush. But he had defined change in terms that were deliberately general and generally painless. As Ted Koppel would have put it, Clinton had Vanna-tized his campaign, he had kept things sufficiently general and open-ended to avoid being punished for his positions. He was also, it was clear, a young man, surrounded by an even younger staff. They would make mistakes. They would reach too far. Clinton's agenda would be defined by his presidency, not by his campaign. And there was little that the press could have done to change that.

In the exit survey data about character, however, was something potentially important. For the two decades since Watergate, Americans had wanted to know more about a candidate's private conduct so they could make inferences about his public character. They wanted to protect the nation from Watergate-style abuses. This year there was a break in that chain. The public had doubts about the private character of Bill Clinton. But they had more doubts about the public character of George Bush. They were about to elect a presumed adulterer president. They would choose a man who had avoided the draft and then been evasive about it over a war hero. They would do that because there were special circumstances this year, a change in generation, the end of an era of cold war, the beginning of an era of economic war, the end of an era of opulence, the beginning of an era of need. But it at least left open the possibility that if Clinton's presidency was successful the country might step back from the faulty syllogism that a candidate's private behavior reveals something deeper about his public character and deserves greater attention than his public record.

When the overnight ratings came in the next morning, the mood at ABC was triumphant. ABC had not only won the ratings, they had blown the doors off the competition. From 7 P.M. until 2 A.M., a quarter of all homes watching television watched ABC. Their ratings were up 20 percent over four years earlier. Overall, network ratings had grown almost 25 percent from 1988. And ABC dominated.

A month later, Gralnick got a call from a friend in finance. ABC had turned an operating profit on its political broadcasts this year, from the first primary night in New Hampshire, the conventions, through to election night. It may have been the first time in history a network had ever taken in more advertising revenue than it had spent in news and production costs on those occasions. And four years from now Gralnick was certain of one thing. ABC would have to cut costs even further. Everyone would. Though this may have been the last year they had not been cut too much. That was why they had all been gambling, and worrying.

"Ah, I remember the day when Roone said we would all cover politics at our own peril," Friedman said that next morning after the election.

"He won't remember he said that," Gralnick said.

"A selective memory is a valuable thing in this business," Friedman said.

From a distance, journalism may seem an elaborate form of pandering, of providing people with what interests them, of drawing a crowd. It should be more.

For a year, the American press had taken responsibility for its coverage, even if it did so grudgingly. It had conceded that what it published and broadcast had consequences, that the act of observation altered the event—a step toward intellectual honesty. And it was shocked, by a public it had underestimated, into taking the words and ideas of politics seriously again, a little.

The business now stands at a point in between, especially television. The obvious path is to soften its coverage, to move toward entertainment values, adding dollops of news like sneaking medicine to children. But that is a false choice.

Newspapers once before went through a passage like this in the 1960s, as their industry matured from a vibrant dynamic business into a series of local municipal monopolies. The ones that survived spent the money on covering news—not by being clever and cheap. The same will be true now in a new period of crisis. Those in the press who fail to take the public seriously, who appeal to a lower common denominator, or who pander to cynicism and fear, ultimately will suffer. So will those who provide essays where they should news, or who become too fascinated with their popularity or their machismo. People have too little time and too many other choices for entertainment.

Journalism in the end is about providing people with information that will help them live their lives. It is about lifting people, offering signposts to what is important, binding the culture, and appealing to our better nature. If the traditional press does not provide that, a new press will rise in its place, probably through a new television delivery system.

Thirty years ago, the management at CBS gathered to find a way to win the dominance in TV news over NBC's Huntley and Brinkley. Network news of the day was eleven minutes around four minutes of commercials, wrapped into another fifteen minutes of local news. CBS decided to expand to a half hour, over the objections of their local affiliates. Within a year, television had become the dominant source of news in America. Afternoon papers began dying. A sea change in the culture had begun. Only a similar act of initiative and commitment will survive into the next era, an era already arriving.

★

EPILOGUE

JEFF GREENFIELD DIDN'T like the speech. As he stood on the camera scaffolding above the west side of the Capitol building on that bristling cold and squinting clear day on January 20, 1993, he thought William Jefferson Clinton's inaugural address was too self-conscious, too clever, too inauthentic. On the air, Greenfield only hinted at this, in a way most viewers probably missed.

"This was a very self-conscious attempt to say 'I am the inheritor of John Kennedy,' in many ways word for word," Greenfield said off the cuff into the red light of the camera minutes after the speech. "Kennedy said, 'Let us begin.' Clinton said, 'Let us begin anew.' Kennedy said, 'The trumpet summons us again.' Clinton said, 'We have heard the trumpet.'

"With one glaring exception. He said at one point in the speech, in a very marked departure from the Kennedyesque rhetoric, 'This capital like all capitals is a place of intrigue, where everyone worries about who's in and who's out, who is up and who is down.' That's very nontraditional presidential rhetoric, yet I have to say instinctively I think that is more central to what Bill Clinton believes about the culture of Washington than anything else in the speech.

"All Democratic presidents are prisoners of that Sorensen-

Kennedy-Goodwin rhetoric, that Romanesque, 'Let us do this. Let us not do A but let us do B. Our time has come.' But in that one paragraph I thought I heard the real quintessential Bill Clinton with a very modern kind of rhetoric breaking through."

As Jennings watched Greenfield on the monitor, he wondered if he had found someone who might sit beside him when David Brinkley retired. Greenfield's ability to deliver substance on television was rare. And the former Bobby Kennedy speechwriter's ability to cite lines from thirty-two-year-old speeches from memory was ferocious.

There would be many changes coming, long before Brinkley's retirement, which was not scheduled any time soon.

Greenfield that March came close to leaving. CBS offered him a pot of money, a chance to do regular analysis on the evening news, and other incentives. ABC got him to stay by matching the offer.

The network had battled over who would cover the White House, too. Roone Arledge had wanted to lure Brit Hume to a new Sunday magazine program called *Day One* that was starting in March 1993. The future of television news was magazine programs, not covering the news. Magazine programs could make big money in prime time because they were cheap to produce. Covering the daily news was expensive and ratings were declining. Jennings had pleaded against it, even writing a letter of protest, with Friedman's help.

If Bill Clinton is elected president, Jennings's draft memo said, it would be a fateful mistake to "damage the most important program at the division and the most important beat at the program at a moment when it will be as critical as it was during Ronald Reagan's first days in 1981."

Hume finally chose to remain in news. "Do I want to look back and say I took a hidden camera into a supermarket or that I was present at the summit to end the Cold War," he said.

Cokie Roberts's star continued to rise. She would be a senior Washington correspondent, not given a specific beat, and became a permanent member of *This Week with David Brinkley* and a semiregular replacement for Ted Koppel on *Nightline.*

Chris Bury would move to Washington as a *Nightline* correspondent. Jack McWethy would stay at the State Department.

Wooten's future was less certain. His contract was up on election day and he had worked for the next several months without any contract. In twelve years of television, he had worked at everything from essays for Brinkley's show to covering Congress to covering politics. He wanted to become ABC's Washington bureau chief, but was only a dark-horse candidate. He had offers from other networks, and from elsewhere, and he was waiting to see what happened. For now, he was being used to float above and do essays about politics and culture around the country. Not long after inauguration day, he wrote as good a television piece as anyone could. It was an account of the late Supreme Court Justice Thurgood Marshall's memorial service at the National Cathedral. Wooten wrote only three lines for himself, one of them his name. For the rest he let the eulogies and the pictures speak for themselves. He wondered how long the network would have room for him.

ABC had also wooed NBC White House correspondent John Cochran to cover Clinton's economic plan for *World News,* but NBC News refused to let him out of his contract.

Then there were the budget cuts. Nearly 10 percent of ABC News's 1,300 staff accepted buyouts in February, nearly half of whom were under forty. In his time at ABC News, Weiswasser had cut $25 million from ABC News's $360 million budget. That should have been enough. Every program at ABC News was now profitable. And the most profitable, in terms of its sheer size, was *World News,* which by virtue of being No. 1 could charge roughly $15,000 more for every thirty seconds of commercial time than its competitors, a difference in revenues of more than $30 million a year.

On inauguration day, Friedman watched not from inside the control room anymore but sitting in the *World News* Washington office. There would be many changes indeed. He was leaving *World News*. On February 1, he moved to the executive fifth floor, replacing Weiswasser as executive vice president of news. Arledge remained. Friedman, however, was now sitting in the office next door, charged, as Weiswasser was, with overseeing management of the division. Friedman quickly set in motion a subtle but crucial reorganization. From now on everything at ABC News flowed through him, and he, in turn, reported to Arledge.

Friedman, Jennings, and Arledge would have to choose a successor for him at *World News*. The choice would drag on for months, and in the meantime Bob Roy ran the broadcast, with Jennings increasingly infuriating people as he exerted more control. "It is never good to have the broadcaster worrying about more than his own role," said one ABC executive.

The election had not left Friedman more optimistic. He thought, for instance, that CBS had made a mistake following his lead on the election. It might have passed him in the ratings if it had skipped politics and pursued its own down-market strategy. In time, he suspected, it might, but it had to be careful not to resemble local news too closely.

As for politics, ABC had failed through the primaries, Friedman acknowledged. "I still don't know how to do it. Maybe we should just do it the way we always did, covering it day by day."

Television had still failed to accomplish the task it might have been best at—biography. It had never devoted an hour to profile each man who might be president. It assumed voters already knew everything, an assumption that was mistaken.

To the extent that they had done some things right, though, Friedman thought the irony was the larger trend. People thought the mainstream press and the networks were becoming irrelevant. They were not. *World News* remained the most profitable part of ABC News, by far and away. The more pressing worry was that television might never again have the resources and the commitment to cover a campaign properly. In early March, Friedman, still settling into his new executive role, expressed confidence that

ABC News, at least, would uphold that commitment.

That day, Michael Gartner resigned as president of NBC News tainted by the scandal of its magazine program, *NBC Dateline*, having faked an explosion of a General Motors pickup and using mislabeled footage of dead fish for a story on the nightly news.

"We are going to be even more substantive, more serious and upscale," Friedman said reassuringly of ABC.

He was feeling optimistic that afternoon. He was finding, as he dealt more closely with Cap Cities, that his bosses were more interested in quality than he had thought. Some of them still recognized Arledge's talents. And Friedman had more power himself. The future, this day, as the first warm wisps of spring swept across Manhattan, looked bright.

★

BIBLIOGRAPHY

Auletta, Ken. *Three Blind Mice: How the TV Networks Lost Their Way.* New York: Random House, 1991.

Bagdikian, Ben H. *The Information Machines: Their Impact on Men and the Media.* New York: Harper & Row, 1971.

Bliss, Edward, Jr. *Now the News: The Story of Broadcast Journalism.* New York: Columbia University Press, 1991.

Boorstin, Daniel J. *The Image, or What Happened to the American Dream.* New York: Atheneum, 1961.

Broder, David. *Behind the Front Page: A Candid Look at How the News Is Made.* New York: Simon & Schuster, 1987.

Cronkite, Walter. The Theodore H. White Lecture, Joan Shorenstein Barone Center. Cambridge: Harvard University Press, 1990.

Crouse, Timothy. *The Boys on the Bus: Riding with the Campaign Press Corps.* New York: Random House, 1973.

Diamond, Edwin. *The Media Show: The Changing Face of News, 1985–1990.* Cambridge: MIT Press, 1991.

Dionne, E.J., Jr. *Why Americans Hate Politics.* New York: Simon & Schuster, 1991.

Donovan, Robert J., and Ray Scherer. *Unsilent Revolution: Television News and American Public Life.* New York: Cambridge University Press, 1992.

Efron, Edith. *The News Twisters*. New York: Nash Publishing, 1971.

Epstein, Edward Jay. *News from Nowhere: Television and the News*. New York: Random House, 1973.

Frank, Reuven. *Out of Thin Air: The Brief Wonderful Life of Network News*. New York: Simon & Schuster, 1991.

Germond, Jack W., and Jules Witcover. *Whose Broad Stripes and Bright Stars?* New York: Warner Books, 1989.

Goldberg, Robert, and Gerald Jay Goldberg. *Anchors: Brokaw, Jennings, Rather, and the Evening News*. New York: Birch Lane Press, 1990.

Graber, Doris A. *Processing the News: How People Tame the Information Tide*. New York and London: Longman, 1988.

Greenfield, Jeff. *The Real Campaign: How the Media Missed the Story of the 1980 Campaign*. New York: Summit Books, 1982.

Greider, William B. *Who Will Tell the People: The Breakdown of American Democracy*. New York: Simon & Schuster, 1992.

Hallin, Daniel. "Sound Bite News: Television Coverage of Elections 1968–1988." Essay, Woodrow Wilson Media Studies Project. Washington, D.C., 1990.

Henry, William A., III. *Visions of America: How We Saw the 1984 Election*. New York: Atlantic Monthly Press, 1985.

Hertsgaard, Mark. *On Bended Knee: The Press and the Reagan Presidency*. New York: Farrar Straus & Giroux, 1988.

Hume, Brit. *Inside Story: Tales of Washington Scandals by the Young Reporter who Helped Jack Anderson Dig Them Out*. New York: Doubleday, 1974.

Iyengar, Shanto, and Donald B. Kinder. *News That Matters: Television and American Opinion*. Chicago: University of Chicago Press, 1987.

Jamieson, Kathleen Hall. *Eloquence in an Electronic Age: The Transformation of Political Speechmaking*. New York: Oxford University Press, 1988.

———. *Dirty Politics: Deception, Distraction and Democracy*. New York: Oxford University Press, 1992.

Kusnet, David. *Speaking American: How the Democrats Can Win the Nineties*. New York: Thunder Mouth Press, 1992.

Lichty. Lawrence W. "Watergate, the Evening News and the 1972 Election," in *American History, American Television, Interpreting the Video Past*, edited by John E. O'Connor. New York: Frederick Ungar, 1983.

Lichty, Lawrence, W. and George A. Bailey. "Reading the Wind: Reflections on Content Analysis of Broadcast News." Essay. Television Network News, Issues in Content Research. Washington: School of Public and International Affairs, George Washington University, 1978.

Murray, Levin. *Talk Radio and the American Dream*. Lexington, Mass.: Lexington Books, 1986.

Noonan, Peggy. *What I Saw at the Revolution: A Political Life in the Reagan Era*. New York: Random House, 1990.

MacNeil, Robert. *The People Machine: The Influence of Television on American Politics*. New York: Harper & Row, 1968.

Matusow, Barbara. *The Evening Stars: The Making of the Network News Anchor*. Boston: Houghton Mifflin Company, 1983.

Mickelson, Sig. *From Whistlestop to Soundbite: Four Decades of Politics and Television*. New York: Praeger, 1989.

———. *The Electric Mirror. Politics in the Age of Television*. New York: Dodd, Mead, 1972.

Minow, Newton N., John Bartlow Martin, and Lee M. Mitchell. *Presidential Television*. New York: Basic Books, 1973.

Moore, David W. *The Super Pollsters: How They Measure and Manipulate Public Opinion in America*. New York: Four Walls Eight Windows, 1992.

Napolitan, Joseph. *The Election Game and How to Win It*. New York: Doubleday, 1972.

Patterson, Thomas E., and Robert D. McClure. *The Unseeing Eye: The Myth of Television Power in National Politics*. New York: G.P. Putnam's Sons, 1975.

Robinson, Michael J., and Margaret A. Sheehan. *Over the Wire and on TV: CBS and UPI in Campaign 1980.* New York: Russell Sage Foundation, 1983.

Schram, Martin. *The Great American Video Game: Presidential Politics in the Television Age.* New York: William Morrow, 1987.

Schwartz, Tony. *The Responsive Chord.* New York: Anchor Press/Doubleday, 1973.

Weaver, Paul H. "Is Television News Biased?" *The Public Interest* 26 (Winter 1972).

White, Theodore H. *America in Search of Itself: The Making of the President 1956–1980.* New York: Harper & Row, 1982.

———. *The Making of the President 1960.* New York: Atheneum, 1961.

Wooten, James. *Dasher: The Roots and the Rising of Jimmy Carter.* New York: Summit Books, 1978.

INDEX